D1114477

fear for the authors' safety. But the publication of the *New Nobility* in English is welcome; it should be essential reading for those who hold naïve hopes about Russia's development or who pooh-pooh the fears of its neighbors."

—*The Wall Street Journal*

"A relentless investigation that demonstrates how, with Putin's rise, the KSB has taken its place 'at the head table of power and prestige in Russia.'"   —*Kirkus Reviews*

"The authors bring hard-digging, fact-based journalism to an aspect of Russia that has been hard to document and understand. . . . [S]ober and probing."

—*Foreign Policy Online*

"This compelling book is a distillation of [Soldavov & Borogan's] work on the website. Drawing on considerable research it describes how the KGB, for decades at the violent vanguard of the communist dictatorship, switched effortlessly after the fall of the Soviet Union, preserving the stability of the new ultra-capitalist Kremlin; same people, many of the same methods, different name and economic system."

—*Sunday Times* (UK)

"[*The New Nobility*] is the product of two profoundly courageous Russian journalists who are meticulous about their reporting. . . . It is because they are Russian and superbly professional journalists that this book offers dozens of insights that no outsider could provide."   —*The Guardian*

"[A]n inside look at the KGB by a pair of fearless Russian journalists, Andrei Soldatov and Irina Borogan. Charting the organisation's heyday, decline and creeping return to power, it promises to raise the hairs on your neck as effectively as Ackroyd's ghost stories."   —*The Guardian*

"Drawing on extensive investigations, the two journalists have written a gripping account of how veterans of the KGB seized control of the Russian state. . . . This book paints a chilling picture of a country dominated by a power-hungry clique. Anyone who wants to understand Putin's brave new Russia should read it."   —*New Statesman*

"A non-fiction book that reads like a spy thriller. . . . *The New Nobility* is an important book, well written and meticulously researched by two journalists with the right sources, both inside and outside the FSB."   —*Basil and Spice*

"Impressively detailed and unsettling. . . . Soldatov and Borogan have done an excellent job in shining a light in some of Russia's darkest corners."   —*Irish Times*

"Fortunately there are inquisitive and intrepid journalists like Andrei Soldatov and Irina Borogan to bring nuance, analysis and old-fashioned shoe-leather reporting to the subject of the revival of Russia's security services. . . . The authors pull no punches in their criticism of endemic corruption and incompetence in the country's security forces. But they do so with a refreshing lack of hysteria, drawing conclusions from facts they were able to document and refusing to indulge in conspiracy theory."   —*Moscow Times*

"*The New Nobility* is an unnerving look at the real power behind the new Russia."   —*Mother Jones*

"For those looking for yet more evidence that the security services are pulling the strings in modern Russia, look no further than this extraordinary new book from the fearless journalists at agentura.ru. Soldatov (who has written for Russian Life) and Borogan have compiled a history of FSB activities and operations over the past decade that paint a very vivid picture

of a security service that has become Russia's new ruling class. . . . With amazing accounts of some of the most significant security crises and counter-terrorist activities of the past decade, Soldatov and Borogan offer insights into FSB operations that have not been offered anywhere to date. . . . A must read."
—*Russian Life*

"This important monograph, written by a brave and talented team, is a history of the KGB (now called the FSB) over the last fifteen years."
—*Literary Review*

"A thorough and very brave examination of an organization that has a tight political, commercial and economic grip on Russia."
—*Financial World*

THE
NEW
NOBILITY

THE
NEW
NOBILITY

THE RESTORATION
OF RUSSIA'S
SECURITY STATE
AND THE
ENDURING LEGACY
OF THE KGB

**ANDREI SOLDATOV
AND
IRINA BOROGAN**

*PublicAffairs
New York*

Hardcover edition first published in 2010 in the United States by
PublicAffairs™, a member of the Perseus Books Group.
Paperback edition first published in 2011 by PublicAffairs™.

PublicAffairs books are available at special discounts for bulk pur-
chases in the United States by corporations, institutions, and other
organizations. For more information, please contact the Special Markets Department at the Perseus Books Group, 2300 Chestnut Street,
Suite 200, Philadelphia, PA 19103, call (800) 810-4145, ext. 5000, or
email special.markets@perseusbooks.com.

Designed by Pauline Brown
Text set in 11 point Palatino LT Std Light

Library of Congress Cataloging-in-Publication Data

Soldatov, Andrei.
  The new nobility : the rebirth of the Russian security state / Andrei
Soldatov and Irina Borogan. — 1st ed.
    p. cm.
  Includes bibliographical references and index.
  ISBN 978-1-58648-802-4 (alk. paper)
  1. Federal-naya sluzhba bezopasnosti Rossii. 2. Intelligence
service—Russia (Federation) 3. Internal security—Russia (Federation) 4. National security—Russia (Federation) 5. Federal-naya
sluzhba bezopasnosti Rossii—Officials and employees. 6. Social
classes—Russia (Federation) 7. Russia (Federation)—Politics and
government. 8. Political culture—Russia (Federation) I. Borogan, I.
(Irina) II. Title.
  JN6529.I6S67 2010
  363.28'30947—dc22

                                                          2010013623

Paperback ISBN 978-1-61039-055-2
Ebook ISBN 978-1-58648-923-6

10 9 8 7 6 5 4 3 2 1

CONTENTS

FOREWORD
BY NICK FIELDING

FOR MORE THAN a decade the Web site Agentura.ru, with content written and edited by the authors of this book, has consistently covered one of the most difficult and dangerous beats in world journalism: the Russian intelligence services. Difficult because the Russian services in all their multifarious forms are notoriously secretive and jealously protect their activities. Dangerous because they have little tolerance for criticism.

In February 2010, for example, the Web site revealed that the same FSB press office that issues official accreditation to journalists in Moscow was now officially authorized to monitor and surveil them. As Andrei Soldatov revealed in *Index on Censorship*, Order no. 343, signed by FSB director Alexander Bortnikov on July 15, 2009, expanded the list of FSB generals allowed to "initiate a petition to conduct counterintelligence measures that restrict the constitutional rights of citizens." The list now includes the FSB's Directorate for Assistance Programs, the same one that is in charge of relations with journalists and which includes the Center for Public Communications—the FSB's press office.

Intrusive surveillance, however, has not stopped physical attacks on journalists: Seventeen Russian journalists have been murdered in mysterious circumstances since 2000. In only one case has there been a successful prosecution.

In a comment that appeared on the Agentura.ru Web site recently, Soldatov summed up the present state of affairs: "Russian news media are pulling back on investigations, cutting budgets, and trimming staff. In the course of the past decade, experienced investigative reporters have been dismissed and investigation desks shut down. The situation has been worsened by a gradual closing of the public domain—even the doors of agency press offices have been slammed shut. By the mid-2000s the Federal Protective Service allowed only photo ops inside the Kremlin; the military intelligence directorate, Russia's largest intelligence agency, has no press office at all; the Foreign Intelligence Service has refused to comment on any of its activities after 1961; and the Center for Public Communications at the FSB does not answer media requests."

Both Soldatov and co-author Irina Borogan have themselves been the focus of FSB interest on many occasions during the past decade as they sought to tread the precarious path between revelation and retribution. They covered with distinction the school siege at Beslan and the Moscow theater siege, revealing major shortcomings in the way both tragedies were dealt with by the Russian intelligence services.

But more important, they have continued to shine a light into some of the deepest recesses of the Russian state. The obsession with Kremlin watching that characterized Western intelligence activity during the Cold War all but disappeared with the collapse of the Soviet Union, with the emphasis shifting to the so-called "war on terrorism" and the West's preoccupation with radical Islam. Russia itself was in chaos in the immediate aftermath of the collapse. No one could predict where things would go and whether or not the former Eastern bloc would move toward democracy or despotism.

For four years—between the 1991 dissolution of the KGB and 1995, when the FSB was created—there was an interregnum. But as the Russian state came to terms with a post-Communist existence, it consolidated itself and its security apparatus. President Boris Yeltsin's appointment of Vladimir Putin, a former KGB officer, to head up the FSB in 1998 marks the beginning of a new era. By 2000, as soon as he became president, Putin began to rebuild the intelligence services and to concentrate power in their hands. While the FSB's predecessor had been a "state within a state," subservient to the Communist Party, the FSB has in many ways become the state itself—its officers now directly responsible to the president, and its former members owning and controlling the commanding heights of the economy.

During Putin's decade in power the FSB was strengthened immeasurably. It took back powers that had been removed, and it expanded into new areas. The FSB developed an ethos of guardianship toward the state that more than echoes the attitude of the old Tsarist bureaucracy. The title of this book, *The New Nobility*, spells out just how far things have reverted. Most important, the intelligence bureaucracy now considers itself above criticism, impervious to the demands of democracy. There are few signs now of the short-lived efforts to build a civil society that briefly flourished under the stewardship of President Yeltsin.

Little of note has been published on the Russian intelligence services in the past decade. And never before has anything like this been written by Russian journalists for publication in English. For anyone who wants to know the ins and outs of Russia's secret service, explained by two people with an encyclopedic knowledge of the subject, this book is highly recommended.

PART I

THE FSB REGAINS POWER

INTRODUCTION

OVER THE LAST decade in Russia, the Federal Security Service (FSB), the modern successor of the Soviet secret police (KGB), has been granted the role of the new elite, enjoying expanded responsibilities and immunity from public oversight or parliamentary control. For eight years, a veteran of its own ranks, Vladimir Putin, held power in the Kremlin as the Russian president, and in the years following, his influence was felt as prime minister. The FSB's budget is not published; the total number of officers is undisclosed. But according to even cautious estimates, FSB personnel total more than 200,000. Putin made the FSB the main security service in Russia, permitting it to absorb many of the former parts of the KGB and granting it the right to operate abroad, collect information, and carry out special operations. Under Putin, former and current security service agents permeated the ranks of business and government structures, and the FSB resurrected as models old KGB idols: the founder of the early Soviet secret police, the CheKa, Felix Dzerzhinsky; and the most prominent of the KGB bosses, Yuri Andropov.[1]

When Putin was elected president in 2000, the Russian secret services were in an extremely difficult situation. They had been left behind in the pell-mell rush toward market reforms and democracy of the 1990s. Their ranks had been thinned by the lure of big

3

money that the best of them could make in Russia's turbulent and often violent new capitalism. For those who remained, there were daunting new challenges on fronts they had never faced before: the festering war in Chechnya, the increased frequency of hostage taking, and the rise of terrorism spawned by the war in Moscow and other cities far from the Chechen battlefield. The FSB faced pressures of corruption that far exceeded what could have been imagined in Soviet times. It suffered, too, from deep public distrust, a legacy of both the Soviet KGB's activity and the chaotic first decade of Russia's post-Soviet experience. It struggled with turf wars and open rivalry for power and resources with former KGB colleagues, now in other, separate organizations, all vying for power and limited resources from the state. On top of all this, Putin gave the FSB a new, even riskier role. The FSB was charged with protecting the stability of the political regime—Putin's own rule—and the country.

These changes must not be mistaken for a revival of the Soviet KGB, although many former dissidents, journalists, and even the security services themselves have characterized it as such. The Soviet KGB was all-powerful, but it was also under the control of the political structure: The Communist Party presided over every KGB section, department, and division. It was no coincidence that the KGB was officially described as an "advance regiment" of the party.

In contrast, the FSB is a remarkably independent entity, free of party control and parliamentary oversight. If the FSB has an ideology, it is the goal of stability and order. FSB officers now regard themselves as heirs not only to the KGB but also to the secret police that the Tsars deployed to battle political terrorism.

At the end of 2000, Nikolai Patrushev, who succeeded Putin as FSB director, gave his traditional interview to mark the holiday celebrating the founding of the CheKa, the Bolshevik secret police. Patrushev described the FSB's personnel as follows:

> I don't want to give a fancy speech, but our best colleagues, the honor and pride of the FSB, don't do their work for the money. When I give government awards to our people, I scrutinize their faces. There are the highbrow intellectual analysts, the broad-shouldered, weatherbeaten special forces men, the taciturn explosives specialists, exacting investigators, and the discreet counter-espionage operational officers. . . . They all look different, but there is one very special characteristic that unites all these people, and it is a very important quality: It is their sense of service. They are, if you like, our new "nobility."[2]

The goal of this book is to reveal the ways this "new nobility" has grown and performed in the last decade. The security services see themselves as the only forces capable of saving the country from internal and external enemies, the saviors of a nation sundered by the upheaval and chaos of the 1990s. Perhaps it is a legacy of old Soviet propaganda films, in which KGB officers were portrayed as the intellectual elite, that FSB officers today refer to themselves as the best and the brightest. The reality is far more complex. The security services have been given a high pedestal in Russia, but faced with the challenges of terrorism and corruption they have become something very different from either the Soviet secret services or the intelligence community in Western countries. In some ways the FSB most closely resembles the ruthless *mukhabarat*, the secret police of the Arab world: devoted to protection of authoritarian regimes, answering only to those in power, impenetrable, thoroughly corrupted, and unopposed to employing brutal methods against individuals and groups suspected of terrorism or dissent. The FSB has failed to become a paragon of the rule of law, and Russia is still a long way from true democracy.

One particularly notable development under Putin was the expansion of the FSB's reach into foreign territory. While the effectiveness of foreign operations remains open to question, Russia's security services have clearly extended their range, with the full support of the state.

For many years, the green uniforms of the FSB closely resembled those of the army. In fact, the two institutions were distinctly separate, the idea being that supervisor and supervised should not mix. In 2006, Putin went a step further and signed a decree changing the Russian security services' uniform from green to black. The color of the night has never been popular with the Russian special services, but Putin's decision was driven by historical symbolism—a nod to a moment during the civil war of the 1920s when the White Army, losing its fight against the Bolsheviks, found inspiration by creating units peopled with officers dressed in black uniforms. They wore black tunics as a symbol of their scorn for earthly goods and were strictly religious. The regiment of Lieutenant General Sergey Markov called itself a "brotherhood of monastic knights who sacrificed their liberty, their blood, and their lives for Russia." This chapter of history continues to shape the thinking of those individuals serving in the FSB today.[3]

THE SEARCH FOR the truth about the FSB is hampered by the agency's extreme secrecy, as well as the uncertainty and danger involved in expressing opinions openly in a time of political authoritarianism in Russia. Our investigation was made almost entirely from the outside looking in, scouring every available resource for evidence of the services' actions but without the aid of official archives or internal documents. We did, however, benefit from many sources in the security services who spoke to us.

This book is largely based on our experience as journalists. We have spent over a decade reporting on and writing about the Russian security services. In 2000, we founded Agentura.ru—a journalism-based Web site for monitoring the Russian services. In recent years we were forced to leave four Russian newspapers, and we have been interrogated more than once by the FSB. In 2005, *Moskovskie Novosti*, one of the most popular liberal weeklies in the late 1980s and early '90s, changed hands, emerging barely recognizable from the shake-up. Once upon a time, we had both worked there. In November of that year, we were looking for the next step. Yevgenia Albats, a prominent Russian political journalist and the author of *KGB: State Within a State*, suggested we write a series of stories about the revival of the security services for the online *Ezhednevny Journal* (one of the few remaining sites where it was possible to publish independent political commentary). By then the FSB had already assumed responsibility for electronic intelligence and border control, gained the right to conduct intelligence operations abroad, resurrected a section of political surveillance, and restored a plaque honoring Yuri Andropov, the longest-serving KGB chairman, at FSB headquarters. To us, the idea of comparing the FSB with the KGB was attractive. Many considered the KGB unique in terms of its ruthlessness and ubiquity, given its legacy of Stalinist repression, total surveillance inside the country, and spectacular killings abroad—including the poisoning of Bulgarian dissident Georgi Markov in London in 1978. The monstrosity of the Soviet secret police was such that it inspired some dissidents to argue that Putin himself was but a small part, a puppet in a larger KGB plan to retain power after the fall of the Soviet Union. In this light, the strengthening of the FSB was seen as another step toward resurrecting the KGB. But what we found out was quite different.[4]

We were in Beslan during the 2004 hostage crisis in which 334 people were killed as the FSB special forces stormed a school captured by Chechen terrorists. We witnessed the process by which the FSB built a new system for managing espionage, under which several Russian scientists were accused of spying and sentenced to many years in prison. And we followed and reported on the offensive tactics adopted by the Russian secret services abroad: the 2004 assassination of former Chechen vice president Zelimhan Yandarbiyev in Qatar and several mysterious killings of Chechens in Azerbaijan and Abkhazia during 2006–2007. We hope this book might help the reader understand the process by which the FSB evolved into the organization it is today.

THE DAWN OF A NEW ERA
THE BIRTH OF THE FSB

THE KGB, KNOWN formally as the Committee of State Security, was an omnipresent force in the Soviet Union. Established in 1954, the agency was an outgrowth of several Soviet security organizations. It combined dozens of different functions: gathering foreign intelligence, guarding national borders, protecting Soviet leaders, obtaining counterintelligence, silencing dissent, and closely monitoring all aspects of Soviet life, from the church to the national military. In order to carry out its myriad tasks, the KGB was afforded a generous budget by the Soviet leadership, one that provided for the KGB's own armed forces team and elite special operations groups.[1]

The KGB's headquarters were in Moscow, but—as with the Stalin-era secret police—its structure was replicated within every Russian region. Any foreigner fortunate enough to travel through Russia was inevitably followed by local KGB agents.

Within each Soviet university, plant, or research center was a security department known as the "first section." These sections were ostensibly created to prevent spies from infiltrating the Soviet system. When agents in the first section found no spies, they turned their attention to monitoring the "moral climate of the collective," recording conversations and making note of rumors. Occasionally members of the first section interfered in family affairs. In a time when divorce and adultery were grounds for state mistrust, reporting such transgressions to leadership could both ruin a person's career and ultimately prevent a Soviet citizen from being allowed to leave the country.

Despite its sprawling and intrusive structure, the KGB was restrained in one very significant way: The Communist Party was keeping watch. Each division, department, and office of the KGB had a party cell, a peephole by which the state could monitor its agents. The Guidelines of the KGB, approved in 1959, established as much: "The party organizations . . . provide the development of real criticism and self-criticism. Party organizations and every communist have the right . . . to report about shortcomings in the work of the organs of state security to the respective party organs."[2] The Politburo, deeply traumatized by Stalin-era purges, was determined to keep the secret police in check.

Embedded as it was in Soviet life, the KGB suffered the same inefficiencies that defined Soviet bureaucracy. Intelligence officers sent abroad on espionage missions compiled reports from Western newspapers and presented them as sensitive information provided by "sources." And those agents who were sent abroad to spy were not necessarily the best or the brightest. The KGB worked on a thinly veiled system of nepotism. Those with the best connections were promoted. The sons of the Soviet elite, realizing the advantages of being stationed in the West, supplanted trained agents. KGB agents in the Soviet army, put in place to ferret out corruption among high-ranking military officers, were often themselves corrupt.

The KGB organization was rife with internal rivalries. The foreign intelligence directorate, or First Chief Directorate, a powerful agency arm, looked down upon counterintelligence officers. The directorate felt it was more enlightened because of its exposure to the outside world, and it felt the counterintelligence agents were narrow-minded and inward looking. The KGB was not a monolith, but deeply divided by internal factions, jealousies, and conflict.

The internecine rivalries within the KGB were well hidden in this extremely secretive atmosphere. When the failures of the Soviet system became clear during Brezhnev's reign, the KGB chairman, Yuri Andropov, deliberately promulgated a myth that the KGB was the only uncorrupted body capable of saving the state. Andropov, the longest-serving chairman of the KGB, was infamous for the brutal repression of both the Hungarian revolt in 1956 and the Prague Spring of 1968. In November 1982, when he assumed leadership of the Soviet Union, he carefully nurtured the notion that the KGB was made up of intelligent people, not brutal secret police. He was keenly interested in broadening the KGB's functions in economics, an area traditionally distant from the secret services, in an ambitious plan to build his own team to steer the country. Andropov sought to fight the Soviet Union's stagnation with an emphasis on workplace discipline and measures to combat corruption, but his methods proved largely ineffective during his short reign. (He was in power for less than two years.) Yet when the Soviet Union disintegrated in 1991, the myth of the KGB's greatness survived.

AMONG THE PLOTTERS involved in the 1991 coup attempt against Mikhail Gorbachev prior to the Soviet Union's collapse was

Vladimir Kryuchkov, the head of the KGB. Boris Yeltsin, the silver-maned icon of the democratic movement who had been elected president of the Russian republic earlier in the year, stood up to the coup plotters. In its aftermath, Yeltsin approached the KGB warily. His goal was to weaken the agency by splitting it into smaller independent agencies. The general feeling was that the only way to control the secret services was by strictly delineating areas of responsibility and not allowing intelligence to operate inside the country or counterintelligence outside it.

With so much uncertainty in the wake of the Soviet collapse, Yeltsin was unwilling to disband the KGB entirely.[3]

With the fear of the disintegration of the organization was acutely felt in the KGB's hulking headquarters on Lubyanka Square in central Moscow. On August 23, 1991, KGB leaders watched apprehensively as crowds of Muscovites overturned the monument to Felix Dzerzhinsky, Lenin's first security chief.

In the year that followed, the KGB initiated an unprecedented era of openness. KGB officers welcomed human rights activists searching for files on those who had been repressed during the Stalin years. KGB generals became guests on TV shows, and the leadership of the secret service invited dissidents to visit the Lubyanka headquarters.[4]

The KGB opened its doors to many who had never dreamed they would be allowed to view the secret archives of decades of repression. Nikita Petrov, a historian with the human rights organization Memorial, recalled the first time he was invited to the small town of Kuchino, outside Moscow, for his initial look at documents in the agency's storage site. The KGB archivists were dumbstruck to see him. "They were shocked at seeing me wearing shirt and jeans in the place where even the visitors from the KGB headquarters were very rare," Petrov said.[5] The KGB even suggested that some of the activists take part in the sweeping changes. Sergei Grigoriants, a famous Soviet dissident who spent nine years in jail, was invited to join the KGB's supervisory committee, but he refused, fearing that his name might be exploited.[6]

With the collapse of the Soviet Union in late 1991, the KGB was restructured. The largest department—initially called the Ministry of Security, then the Federal Service of Counter-Intelligence (FSK), and finally the Federal Security Service (FSB)—would be responsible for counterespionage and counterterrorism.[7] The KGB's former foreign intelligence directorate was transformed into a new espionage agency called the Foreign Intelligence Service, or SVR.[8] The division of the KGB responsible for electronic eavesdropping and cryptography became the Committee of Government Communication, later called the Federal Agency for Government Communications and Information, or FAPSI.[9] A relatively obscure directorate of the KGB that guarded secret underground facilities continued its functions under a new name: the Main Directorate of Special Programs of the President, or GUSP. The KGB branch that had been responsible for protecting Soviet leaders was renamed the Federal Protective Service, and the Soviet border guards were transformed into an independent Federal Border Service.

The changes meant that the new counterintelligence agency, the FSK, after 1995 known as the FSB for its Russian name, *Federalnaya Sluzhba Bezopasnosti*, was stripped of the overseas intelligence functions of the KGB. The agency no longer protected Russian leaders and was deprived of its secret bunkers, which fell under the president's direct authority. It maintained a nominal presence in the army. In its new incarnation, the agency was pruned to something resembling Britain's MI5.

Meanwhile, party control over the KGB dissipated. Yeltsin's response was to encourage rivalry in the splintered intelligence community, providing a precarious system of checks and balances. Under Yeltsin, the foreign intelligence agency remained in direct competition with military intelligence; the FSB struggled with the communications agency, which kept a close eye on the social and political situation in Russia. After obtaining a report from the FSB director, Yeltsin could compare it with the report from the communications director. The communications agency was particularly crucial, as it controlled the central electronic vote-counting system, which offered a sneak preview of voting outcomes in real time for the Kremlin.[10]

In 1993 a new agency, the tax police, was created to address catastrophically low Russian tax receipts, and inter-service rivalry intensified. The new tax police engaged in bitter competition with the department of economic safety within the FSK and later FSB. Meanwhile, the new service charged with protecting the president was transformed by its chief, Alexander Korzhakov, a former Yeltsin bodyguard, into what many described as an updated Praetorian Guard. The agency employed parapsychologists and clairvoyants to prepare prognoses and analytical reports for Yeltsin, independent of the communications agency and the FSB.[11]

❧❧❧

UNDER HIS REIGN, Mikhail Gorbachev had been roundly criticized for the use of force to quell independence movements and nationalist revolts in the Baltics, Azerbaijan, and Georgia. Ultimately, the crackdowns failed to bring the regions to heel and served only to hasten the collapse of the Soviet Union. Yeltsin, by contrast, had urged the restless regions to take all the power they wanted from the center, when that center was the Soviet Union. But once he became the Russian president, he confronted the same centrifugal forces.

In 1992, Yeltsin faced a crisis in the Ingush-Ossetian conflict in the North Caucasus. The ethnic Ingush attacked Ossetians, triggering a reprisal. Yeltsin used the Russian army to support the Ossetians. This move led to the first major ethnic cleansing on Russian soil, when Ingush families were expelled from the disputed Prigorodny district. According to a 1996 Human Rights Watch report, "Russian officials disbursed large numbers of weapons to North Ossetian authorities, who then handed them out to both North Ossetian security officers and to paramilitary groups and militias. . . . Russian forces either aided in the evacuation of Ingush civilians—'polite' forced evacuation—or spearheaded attacks against villages held by Ingush militants, forcing out both civilians and fighters."[12]

Leaders of the Russian security services and Yeltsin interpreted the outcome of this conflict as a sign that force could be used effectively to quell ethnic tensions in the North Caucasus.

But this approach resulted in disaster in November 1994, when leaders of the breakaway republic of Chechnya intensified their demands for independence from Russia. In an operation planned in secrecy, the security service (then the FSK) organized an attack on the Chechen capital, Grozny, that was disguised to look like a march of opposition forces. The men carrying out the attack had been recruited from the Russian armed forces. Among others the

FSK paid off to join the operation were members of Russian tank crews. According to eyewitness accounts by Captain Andrei Rusakov, Lieutenant Alexei Rastopka, and Captain Alexander Shihalev, the men were summoned by the FSK officer attached to their regiment, who introduced them to two counterintelligence officers from Moscow. The counterintelligence officers presented the tank officers with a contract to join the operation, the only copy of which was retained by the FSK officer "for secrecy reasons." The recruited officers and soldiers were then transferred to the town of Mozdok in North Ossetia, where they were deployed in unmarked tanks. The three columns of tanks disguised as opposition militants were dispatched to Grozny in late November to serve as a demonstration of force to the separatist Chechen leader, Dzhokar Dudaev, a former general in the Soviet army who was posing an increasingly strident challenge to Yeltsin with his demands for Chechen independence.[13]

Sergei Kozlov, a short, fit soldier with a mustache and a former officer in special forces military intelligence with a straightforward style, recalled that he was approached in late 1994 to join the operation. He told the authors he was urged by the FSK to lead a group of forty former military officers for a reconnaissance and diversion mission to Grozny in exchange for one thousand dollars. "In these circumstances I thought the sum would be just enough to pay for my funeral," said Kozlov.[14] Assuming the operation would be nothing more than a show of force, the armored columns headed toward the Chechen capital with no reconnaissance or cover. The tanks were supplied with additional fuel tanks—a measure that ensured them long-distance range but which would never have been made if a battle had been anticipated. On November 26, the disguised "opposition forces" were ambushed by Chechens and burnt in the streets of Grozny. The few officers left alive were captured by Chechen militias and were dismissed by the authorities as "mercenaries" or "volunteers" hired by unknown forces. The incident caused grave doubts in the Kremlin about the abilities of the FSK.

After the FSK was renamed the FSB in 1995, it met with another failure in the war against Russian organized crime. In 1996, a secret branch was established in the FSB to prosecute mafia-style groups. The crime unit was infamous as the most ruthless, brutal, and corrupt section of the intelligence services.[15] (Purportedly, the unit had been given license to adopt vicious methods in fighting criminal activity.)[16] In 1998, after officers claimed at a November 17 press conference in Moscow that they had been ordered to kill prominent Russian oligarch Boris Berezovsky, the unit was disbanded.[17] In the aftermath, Nikolai Kovalev, then FSB director, lost his position.

Also in the mid-1990s, a storm arose in the rivalry between two powerful security services: the FSB and the communications agency. An Investigative Directorate of the FSB accused Major General Valery Monastyretsky, the chief of the communications agency's financial department, of corruption. The FSB Investigative Directorate opened a criminal inquiry into charges that Monastyretsky received 1.5 million DM from Siemens-Nixdorf Corporation in exchange for a profitable contract.[18] However, the authors were told by reliable sources that the investigation was aimed not at Monastyretsky but rather at his boss at the communications agency, Alexander Starovoitov. News of the accusation was leaked to the Russian news media.[19] But Yeltsin preferred to stay on the good side of the communications agency, ensuring his access to the electronic vote-counting system (which the agency controlled) on the eve of the 1996 presidential election. Furthermore, Yeltsin believed that inciting a healthy rivalry between the two agencies would keep them under control.

This volatile, imperfect system hobbled along through the twilight of Yeltsin's years. On July 25, 1998, Yeltsin appointed Vladimir Putin, a little-known Kremlin official and KGB veteran from St. Petersburg, to serve as the new director of the FSB. Putin was viewed at the time as a big question mark, in part because he had never risen above the rank of lieutenant colonel in his sixteen-year KGB career, and during the chaotic years of perestroika and glasnost, he had been on duty in Germany.

These years were times of upheaval in Russia. In 1998, Russia defaulted on its debts and devalued the ruble in a financial crisis that bankrupted millions of people and cast doubt on the Western capitalist model. Russians wanted to find simple answers, and many looked for a strongman to replace Yeltsin's perceived vacillating, weak character. This desire for decisive leadership came to a head in September 1999, when 216 people were killed in bombings in two Moscow apartment buildings. Putin, by then prime minister, pointed the finger at the Chechens, vowing to "rub them out in the outhouse." His tough talk vaulted him to immediate popularity as he launched a new military offensive in Chechnya.

When Yeltsin resigned on New Year's Eve of 1999, Putin, a man whose outlook had been formally shaped by nearly two decades in the KGB, became acting president. Now the stage was set for an Act Two in which the methods of the security services would be adopted to govern Russia.

꙰꙰꙰

WITH PUTIN'S RISE, it was rumored that the Kremlin was preparing to recombine all parts of the former KGB into one special service.[20] This seemed confirmed when the founders of the Russian secret services under Yeltsin—independents accustomed to aggressively defending the interests of their structures—lost their posts one after the other. In December 1998, Alexander Starovoitov, founder of the communications agency, was forced out. In February 1999, Sergei Almazov, creator of the tax police, resigned under pressure. And in April 2000, Vyacheslav Trubnikov, the director of Foreign Intelligence, was forced to step down.[21]

These moves were followed in 2003 by a major reorganization. In March Putin abolished the tax police, the communications agency, and the border guards as independent agencies.[22] The border guards were merely absorbed by the FSB. The tax police had been more active than other services in the 1990s. They created their own corporate culture and ideology and became the first Russian security service to fund a TV series promoting their image— *Maroseyka 12* (for the address of its headquarters), with famous Russian film actors cast as tax police officers. It became quite popular despite the dubious reputation of the service.

In 2003 all officers of the tax police were redeployed to fill the ranks of a new agency combatting the narcotics trade, led by Viktor Cherkhesov, a former KGB operative and close friend of Putin. (Cherkhesov had earned a reputation at the KGB as the officer who had initiated the last prosecution of dissidents in the Soviet Union.)[23] Neither the tax police nor Cherkhessov had any experience in fighting drug dealers. Not surprisingly, the new agency started with the prosecution of veterinarians for dealing in keta-mine, an anesthetic used only for animals, and Moscovites for cultivating opium poppies at their dachas.[24]

Once the most powerful rival of the FSB, the communications agency was divided up between the FSB and the Federal Protective Service, which guarded Kremlin leaders. Over the course of twelve years, the communications agency had created an industrial empire engaged in information security. In the 1990s the agency was in charge of licensing information security software—firewalls, cryptography, and so on—and used this privilege to grant licenses and government contracts to its own companies. (It even tried, albeit unsuccessfully, to obtain control of the Russian stock exchange, SWIFT codes, and the Russian part of the Internet.)[25] The agency justified its efforts with its claim that the Internet—an American-born invention—required their control within Russia. In 1996, General Vladimir Markomenko, then deputy director of the agency, testified before the State Duma that "the Internet is a threat to National Security."[26]

In 2003, the communications agency's empire fell, and the FSB absorbed the most crucial part of its former adversary: overseas electronic intelligence.

The second benefactor—the Federal Protective Service—meanwhile was assigned to handle lines of government communications and analytical structures with "sociological" services.[27]

Under Putin's jurisdiction, the FSB also got the upper hand over the Ministry of Internal Affairs, an agency combining the functions of national police and an investigations department similar to the FBI. The FSB placed counterintelligence officers in key posts in the ministry, ranging from the position of deputy minister to chief of administration for internal security (which oversaw internal misconduct). Purportedly established to strengthen discipline and morale inside the corrupted ministry, the larger purpose of the FSB officers' presence was to broaden the agency's control. Finally, in 2003, Rashid Nurgaliev, an FSB general and close friend of Nikolai Patrushev (then head of the FSB), was appointed minister of internal affairs.

The Kremlin, now with Putin at the helm, reinstated the FSB as warden of army morale, charging the agency to watch for potential mutiny. In February 2000 Putin signed into law new "Regulations About FSB Directorates in the Armed Forces," which expanded the agency's functions of military counterintelligence and gave it the right to fight organized crime. Putin's decree further broadened the role of FSB officers in the army to include detecting possible threats to the regime. Added to their professional responsibilities was the fight against "illegal armed formations, criminal groups, and individuals and public associations which have set as their goal a violent change of the political system of the Russian Federation and the violent seizure or violent retention of power."[28] The FSB had gained considerable ground.

The agency's advancement was not always one of absorption. When the FSB could not subsume the rival foreign intelligence service, it created its own department with regional branches for gathering foreign intelligence. It was officially called "organs of external intelligence" and was established within the main analytical structure of the FSB department devoted to analysis, forecasting, and strategic planning.[29] In this way, the FSB entered the field previously dominated by the foreign intelligence service and military intelligence.

The architects of the overhaul were all friends who once served in the FSB's regional departments in St. Petersburg and neighboring Karelia, a group including Putin, Patrushev, Nurgaliev, and Cherkhesov. Others involved were Victor Ivanov, deputy chief of the Kremlin administration and the main personnel director, and Igor Sechin, another deputy chief of the Kremlin administration in charge of the secret services in 2000–2008. They all helped each other and their junior colleagues, who were to fill the ranks of the FSB's central apparatus. As a group, they were known as *piterci* (people from St. Petersburg).

The FSB gained power and scope even when Yeltsin sought to use checks and balances to keep the security services under control. Later, under Putin, the FSB managed to outstrip the other security services. After a few years of his reign, the FSB had no parliamentary oversight and no competitors.[30] Rather than a revival of the Soviet KGB, the FSB had evolved into something more powerful and more frightening, an agency whose scope, under the aegis of a veteran KGB officer, extended well beyond the bounds of its predecessor.

FRIENDS IN HIGH PLACES
CULTIVATING THE SECURITY SERVICES

THE FALL OF the Soviet Union was, for the tens of thousands of people in the KGB, a personal disaster. The overwhelming majority of officers had joined the ranks of the KGB not because they were inspired by Communist ideals or the allure of the omnipotent Soviet secret police, but for the guarantee of stable, well-paying jobs with lifetime tenure, pensions, health care, and housing. For many the KGB was a family business that spanned generations. In the inner circles of the KGB, officers lived in a world of acquaintances, became accustomed to hierarchical structures, and fell out of touch with life beyond the walls of the Lubyanka headquarters. Contact with the outside world was limited by the culture of the secret police. While in 1991, many former KGB officers lamented the collapse of the Soviet Union, most did not know what to do in the new circumstances. Their biggest fear was that they would lose the apartments, salaries, health care, and pensions that had long been assured by the state. In the dawn of a new era, former KGB officers faced the rise of a market economy with trepidation.

Some KGB veterans found they had skills and knowledge useful in the wild capitalism of the early years after the collapse. Those most in demand were for private security agencies at a time when business disputes were often being settled violently in the streets. This included the fighters of the Alpha elite special operations unit because of their indisputable expertise in personal protection and martial skills. Specialists in surveillance and interception who could help businesses spy on competition and defend against espionage were also sought-after. The former generals and colonels of the KGB were prize hires for these security agencies, which were structured in such a way as to literally duplicate the shape of the old KGB, with the same "lines" and directorates but on a smaller scale.[1]

Those who remained in the security services were motivated by patriotism, or feared the risks of starting over in chaotic times, or a little of both. But soon they, too, were beckoned by the new capitalism. KGB officers trained to protect the Russian state were now lured to protect Russia's tycoons—the oligarchs. For their part, oligarchs realized it was cheaper to exploit the security services than to pay for their own private secret services. Those who hired former KGB officers were often as interested in their contacts, files, and access to the security structures as they were in meaningful protection.[2]

A wave of lawlessness engulfed everyone—businessmen, the new security agencies, even the government officials and agents who represented the state. For some businessmen, it was more economical to pay the FSB or the Interior Ministry to intercept phone calls by a competitor than to carry out the job themselves.

For the officers who did not leave the state, jealousies were often sparked at the sight of a former colleague parking a luxury car outside of headquarters. As honest officers were forced to comply with the orders of corrupted generals, the FSB's morale was corroded. The rank and file often seemed to be sleepwalking through their jobs. (It is known that some officers who were supposed to recruit agents simply asked the teenage children of friends to fill out the required paperwork, perhaps in exchange for such valued privileges as taking a good course in English.)[3] With morale declining, the leadership of the FSB struggled to regain its Investigative Directorate, which had been disbanded in 1993, and by 1995 succeeded in having it restored.[4] Now the FSB combined the functions of a secret service and a law enforcement agency with the right to investigate the crimes of businessmen. In effect, more opportunities were provided for corrupt officers who could be used not only to conduct investigations but also to help businessmen fight their competitors.[5]

For people inside the security services, strict and repressive state control seemed the only possible answer to the FSB's internal corruption. Disenchanted FSB officers were obsessed by the Chinese approach of freewheeling market capitalism governed by political authoritarianism.[6] By the end of the 1990s, these officers saw in Putin's leadership hope for resurrection of the order that they remembered from Soviet times. A lingering resentment toward the oligarchs, many of whom were Jewish, was keenly felt. (In Yeltsin's time, a common complaint heard in the halls of the Lubyanka headquarters was that "the Jews sold out Russia," reflecting a sense of dismay that rich tycoons had manipulated the president and were at fault for the country's economic woes.)[7]

Those who remained inside the state security structures blamed the corruption of their own generals on the radical democrats of the early 1990s who had subdivided the KGB and weakened the security services and the country. These democrats, many of them connected with Soviet dissidents, were viewed at Lubyanka as the puppets of Western intelligence services, part of the overall Western plan to ruin the mighty Russian state.

The outlook of these officers is decidedly provincial and inward looking, and the reason for this is rooted in the structure of the organization. The FSB is comprised of two unequal parts: its headquarters, which has never had a staff of more than a few thousand personnel, and its regional offices, estimated to employ hundreds of thousands of individuals. Although there have been major changes at headquarters, the structure of the regional directorates has remained largely unchanged for decades. Today this system tends to drag the FSB into a provincial mind-set. These fossilized provincial state security agencies are constantly shaping the special service from within, due to the FSB's system of personnel rotation: Colonels and generals are moved from one regional directorate to another and are eventually offered positions on the central staff at FSB headquarters. The center is crammed full of officers who were promoted from the regions, bringing with them a provincial outlook.

The Russian Orthodox Church has similarly helped foster the FSB's xenophobia. The security service and the Church have been moving closer in recent years. In December 2002, the Cathedral of St. Sophia of God's Wisdom was reopened just off Lubyanka Square, a block away from the FSB headquarters. Patriarch Aleksey II himself blessed the opening of the cathedral in a ceremony attended by then FSB chief Nikolai Patrushev.[8]

Despite having been a target of the KGB in Soviet times, the Russian Orthodox Church has always been closely connected with

the state. The Russian Tsar was the head of the Church;]
brand of orthodoxy is based on the concept that Moscow is "tne
Third Rome" (after ancient Rome and Constantinople) and on a
belief in Russian uniqueness. Being "unique," Russia sees itself as
surrounded by numerous enemies that the FSB must combat. In
this vein, the Russian Orthodox Church is always suspicious of
Catholic expansion. As recently as 2002 five Catholic priests were
expelled by the FSB from Russia, some of them accused of espionage.[9] The FSB helps to protect the Orthodox sphere of influence
against Western proselytizing, and in return the Church blesses the
security service in its struggle with enemies of the state.

IN SOVIET TIMES, the members of the KGB were part of an elite. But
when the Soviet Union collapsed and Russia plunged into the new
capitalism, few KGB officers emerged as business leaders. They
were outflanked by younger, fleeter hustlers: a new breed of oligarchs. Instead, KGB veterans found their calling in second and
third tiers of the new business structures, running the security departments of the tycoons' empires. No longer masters of the uni-
verse, they now served the new rich.

Putin's offer to the generation of security service veterans was
a chance to move to the top echelons of power. Their reach now
extends from television to university faculties, from banks to government ministries, but they are not always visible as men in
epaulets. They go dressed in business suits into a zone of influence
where power flows back and forth—sometimes the agents are the
exploited, and other times they are the infiltrators.

The Russian saying "There is no such thing as a former KGB
officer" has more than a bit of truth in it. Many officers, supposedly

retired, were put in place as active agents in business, media, and the public sector while still subordinated to the FSB. A special euphemism was invented for such agents: a DR officer, where DR means *destvuyushego rezerva*—of the active reserve. The term has a long history, being used from the 1920s until the 1990s. In 1998, DR officers were renamed APS officers, for *apparat prikomandirovannih sotrudnikov* (apparatus of attached officers) but in essence remained the same.

The status of an agent on active reserve is considered a state secret. It is prohibited by law to reveal it. This army of hidden FSB officers does not identify itself to the rest of society, and they often work in organizations entirely undercover—while sending reports to FSB leadership and actively recruiting members. It is hard to know precisely how many officers are working on active reserve, but the total is probably in the thousands.

In one of the more striking known examples, the FSB placed one of its officers in a prominent spot at a major television channel. In June 2002, former FSB spokesperson General Alexander Zdanovich, who had also been an officer in military counterintelligence and the main FSB official historian, was appointed deputy director general of the state-owned Russian Television and Radio Company, known by its initials VGTRK, which owns several television and radio stations including the Second Channel, considered the country's main official station.[10] At first Zdanovich was said to be responsible for company security, but soon afterward it became clear that his powers were much wider.[11]

When hostages were captured by Chechens in the Dubrovka Theater during the musical show *Nord-Ost* in October 2002, Zdanovich essentially told newscasters how to cover the event. At the peak of the crisis, Zdanovich was an official member of the operations staff, with one hand in both the security agency and the other in the news media.[12] In September 2004, when hostages were taken in the school in Beslan, North Ossetia, the authors met Zdanovich on the streets of Beslan just two hours before the school was stormed. Zdanovich was invited to the scene of a crisis by the security agencies—even though he was appointed to the television channel. In December 2004, Zdanovich's role in defining how television would handle hot topics for the Kremlin was confirmed by Vladimir Putin, who signed a decree congratulating Zdanovich on his "active participation in information support of the Presidential elections in Chechnya."[13]

In the years to come, Zdanovich was responsible for supervising the creation of television programs highlighting the FSB's successes. In 2005–2006, the serial *Secret Guards* was broadcast about FSB agents carrying out surveillance on the streets. The show, aired on the Second Channel, was produced with the help of the FSB.

This was a far cry from the period of relative freedom in the early 1990s when a private television channel, NTV, stood up to the authorities and broadcast uncensored news reports on the first Chechen war. Now, with Zdanovich and others, Putin and the security services were directly influencing what millions of Russians saw on their television screens.

Not all the officers on active reserve for the FSB were in such high-profile positions. Many deliberately avoided the limelight but still exercised a certain degree of power. One example is Mikhail. He is in his early fifties, with obvious Asiatic features, simple manners, and modest dress. He looks like anything but an FSB colonel. An ethnic Tatar, he volunteered for the KGB as a young man out of a sense of idealism. Earlier in his career he was responsible for keeping his eye on Islamist movements in Uzbekistan. After the collapse of the Soviet Union he was transferred to Moscow to serve with the Central Apparatus of the FSB, where his specialization proved valuable in the counterterrorism department. (While he bears a Tatar name, he presented himself as Mikhail, a Russian name, after tiring of his xenophobic colleagues.) After he fought in the first Chechen war, he was brought back to Moscow; he became a colonel by the mid-2000s and was sent to Moscow city government as an "officer of active reserve" to supervise the city's policy toward Muslims. By day, he works in the municipal government dealing with such questions as where to build a new mosque in the city and how to address tensions between Tatar and Azeri minorities in the capital. At the same time, he quietly recruits agents in these ethnic communities, monitoring Islamist trends, gathering intelligence, and passing information along to the FSB.

ACCORDING TO FSB rules inherited from the KGB, active reserve officers should receive only one salary. If his salary at the FSB was higher than in the company he infiltrated, the officer was allowed to keep the difference. But if his salary in the FSB was lower, he was ordered to return the difference to the FSB. If he had no such intention (as it turned out in most cases), he had the option of refusing the FSB salary.

The officers on active reserve were caught in an absurd hall of mirrors. It was assumed in the FSB that if they went off to another company to work, they were still loyal to the security agency. However, many who went on active reserve during the explosive growth of Russian capitalism became more loyal to their profitable companies than to the security agency. In some cases they regarded the company as their primary boss and the FSB as "in their pocket"—a source that would provide access to precious data and personnel.

Those officers who were sent to small companies, mostly majors and colonels, largely maintained loyalty to the FSB and never turned down the service salaries, because they wanted to further their careers with the security agency. By contrast, generals on active reserve, who were courted by the biggest corporations and banks and were offered huge profits, often quickly forgot about their comparatively small generals' salaries. They became powerful business representatives within the FSB. Mostly in their late fifties or early sixties, they acted in full knowledge that they probably would never again have a future in the secret services.

This tension between the generations of security officers led to a breach, as younger officers grew increasingly frustrated by the fortunes of the older group. Colonels and majors started to question a policy designed to benefit generals. According to one FSB colonel of the active reserve, who spoke to the authors on condition of anonymity: "The main question is the old point about two salaries. I was sent with elements of disguise, so I was forced to do my official job and then the job for the FSB, having meetings with agents at night, so why am I refused a second salary? [The rule] was established by the secret order of the FSB director, but the order has not been duly registered in the Ministry of Justice, so there is no way to challenge it."

Perhaps no one knew more about the active reserve than Putin. In the final years of the Cold War, Putin served in East Germany for the KGB. When he returned to Russia in 1990, he was transferred to the active reserve and attached to Leningrad University. The following year, he was transferred to the office of prominent democrat Anatoly Sobchak, the mayor of Leningrad. On August 20, 1991, he finally retired from the KGB.[14]

Once Putin became president, the wave of security people moving into business and government went well beyond those who were serving the FSB on active reserve. In many cases, Putin cleared the way for people who had worked in the KGB and elsewhere to gain high-level positions outright. Known as the *silovikii*, their ranks swelled under Putin. For example, Igor Sechin, who had served in military intelligence, became a deputy prime minister and chairman of Rosneft, the huge state-owned oil company. Sergei Ivanov, who had served in the foreign intelligence branch of the KGB, became deputy prime minister. Former KGB agent Viktor Ivanov became deputy chief of administration of the Kremlin when Putin was president and later was named to head the anti-drug agency. Vladimir Shults, a former deputy director of the FSB, is now part of the leadership of the Russian Academy of Science. The telecommunications business of the huge Russian business empire Alfa Group was headed by former deputy director of the Federal Protective Service Anatoly Protsenko. A former Soviet intelligence officer in New York, Vladimir Yakunin, became president of Russian Railways, one of the world's largest railroad networks. Yuri Zaostrovtsev, the former head of the FSB's Economic Security Department, was appointed vice president of Vneshekonombank, the main institution used by the government to manage Russian state debts and pension funds.

General Alexander Perelygin had one of the most mysterious careers in this twilight zone. He began his career in the Soviet

KGB providing technical support for surveillance. In the early 1990s, he was deputy chief of the Moscow department of the FSB. By the end of the decade he had become the security adviser to Moscow mayor Yuri Luzhkov. It is not known when or if he left the FSB, but what is notable is just how many times he appeared to stand at the intersection of power politics and business. After many visits to Latvia, he was accused by the Latvians of interfering in their politics and refused an entry visa in November 2000.[15] He later became a major player in the Moscow real estate market. He was appointed deputy head of the Department of Investment Programs for Construction in Moscow. He became the mediator between the secret services and developers in the most sensitive area—purchasing land previously owned by the secret services.[16] It was a very profitable business because prices for Moscow real estate were comparable with those in New York and London in the early 2000s, and the Russian secret services had been granted huge areas in the heart of the city since the Stalin era. In this and other appointments, Perelygin appeared to move with ease between the state and business. Later in the decade he was appointed deputy director general of Norilsk Nickel, the world's largest nickel and palladium producer, where he was in charge of security. In recent years, his talents were employed in the attempt to save the reputation of Russian biathalon stars after a doping scandal disqualified them from participating in the Olympics.[17]

As THE SECURITY services moved into other jobs in the new Russia, there were stirrings of discontent. They were aired in an open letter published on October 9, 2007, by Viktor Cherkesov, then the head of the anti-drug agency. Cherkesov, a close friend of Putin whose wife co-owned a private news agency and a newspaper in St. Petersburg, was a former KGB officer. His letter (titled "We Can't Let Warriors Turn into Traders") put forth the analysis that Russia had been falling into chaos in the 1990s only to be caught and saved by the "hook" of the security services. "Some wanted the society to be fragmented completely," he said, "but this hook saved the society." Nonetheless, he went on, the security services had suffered their own internal tensions. Many of the best and brightest in the ranks of the KGB went on to make their own fortunes elsewhere. Cherkesov, whose own deputy was caught up and jailed in a bitter, internecine battle among security services, lamented that the agencies were turning on each other in fierce competition. They appeared to have lost the unity of the Soviet days. "Today," he warned, "experts and journalists started to talk about the 'war of groups' inside secret services. In this war there can be no winners. This 'all against all' war can end up with the collapse of the whole corporation. . . . The caste is destroying itself from within, when warriors become traders."[18]

As examples of men like Perelygin made clear, the new order of the FSB extended a degree of protection and stability to its officers through continued high-level placement beyond the agency itself. But the promotion of a selective group, coupled with the fierce rivalry of former colleagues, fueled division.

"THE INTERESTS OF THE STATE DEMAND IT"
SPYMANIA

I N MAY 1999, Putin was the director of the FSB and also head of the Kremlin's security council, a group of high-ranking officials who set national security strategy. It was a time of instability in Russia, just months after the country had suffered a major economic crash. President Boris Yeltsin seemed to be drifting. One day Putin went to the offices of *Komsomolskaya Pravda*, a mass-circulation broadsheet daily. At the newspaper he gave an interview in which he was asked, "There is a concern that you and your friends might organize a military coup d'état?" Putin replied, "And why do we need to organize a coup d'état? We are in power now. And whom would we topple?" Then the newspaper interviewers suggested: perhaps the president?

"The president appointed us," Putin said, with a half-chuckle.

Instead of an internal threat, Putin pointed to foreign espionage as Russia's gravest enemy. He declared, "Unfortunately, foreign intelligence services, besides diplomatic cover, are very active in using in their work various ecological and civil society organizations, the business and charity foundations. That is why these structures, however pressed we are from the media and the public, will be always under our steadfast attention. The interests of the state demand it."[1]

The FSB got the signal. In the years to come, all the institutions Putin had named would become the targets of such investigations. The surge of espionage prosecutions reflected a sea change in Russia's direction. During the 1990s, with the country weak and on the verge of bankruptcy, when Western powers extended a hand, Yeltsin welcomed them. But being the recipient of handouts, combined with a sense of constant upheaval, led to feelings of humiliation and resentment; these only deepened after the economic crisis of 1998 and the renewed war with Chechnya in 1999. A central thrust in Putin's rise to power and popularity was a response to this feeling of defeat—to show that Russia would not be pushed around any longer and that Putin would establish a sense of order and calm. His campaign to ferret out foreign spies was part of his larger reassertion of power and order in Russia.

Human rights organizations and charity organizations were targeted in 2000. In August, the FSB accused Halo Trust, the British mine-clearing charity, of gathering intelligence in Chechnya and teaching Chechen rebels techniques to create explosives.[2] In 2002, the FSB was behind the refusal to renew the visas of thirty Peace Corps volunteers working in Russia who were suspected of "gathering information of social-political and economical character."[3] In 2006 the next target was Russian nongovernmental organizations. Some prominent Russian human rights organizations, including Moscow Helsinki Group, were accused of accepting money from British intelligence. A documentary that aired on public television identified several British diplomats as spies responsible for funding Russian NGOs.[4]

Putin personally backed the allegations. On February 7, 2006, at a meeting with leaders of the FSB, Putin said, "Russia's counter-intelligence has acted professionally. I can only express my regret that this scandal has cast a shadow on nongovernmental organizations. But you have nothing to do with it. Those who accept financial assistance—you must know your partner."[5]

In November of the same year Putin accused the political opposition of "behaving like jackals near foreign embassies."[6]

Scientists were put in a special category. During the Cold War, most Soviet science research centers' contacts with foreign organizations were highly restricted, but in the 1990s they were encouraged to look for overseas financing on their own. This practice prevailed for almost a decade, but in the 2000s the FSB changed the rules of the game, claiming that many state secrets had been leaked as a result of democratic reforms and insisting that a regime of secrecy should be restored. In 2004, the Russian scientific community was horrified when Valentin Danilov, a physicist and a head of the Thermo-Physics Center at Krasnoyarsk's State Technical University, was charged with espionage and sentenced to fourteen years in prison because of his center's contracts with the Chinese.[7]

Environmental groups were singled out for particular attention. The most notorious case was that of the Norwegian group Bellona. Alexander Nikitin, an activist who had called attention to nuclear risks in the Russian submarine fleet, was arrested on February 6, 1996, and accused of espionage. Nikitin was finally acquitted, but not until December 1999.[8]

In November 2002 the premises of the Irkutsk organization Baikalskaya Ecologicheskaya Volna (Baikal Ecological Wave) were searched by the local department of the FSB. The organization's mission was to monitor Lake Baikal, the oldest (25 million years) and deepest (1,700 meters) lake in the world, situated in southeast Siberia. The FSB announced that it had opened a criminal case against the organization for divulging state secrets, and simultaneously provided local newspapers with materials indicating that the environmental group was complicit in espionage. The charges were dropped in a matter of days due to public outcry.[9]

In the business community, Norway's telecommunications corporation, Telenor, became an early target of the FSB's spy campaign. In December 1998, Telenor formed a strategic partnership with VimpelCom, Russia's leading cellular telecommunications operator, and by the mid-2000s Norwegians owned 26.6 percent of VimpelCom's voting stock.[10] In 2005, Telenor was prevented by the FSB from buying additional shares that would have increased their ownership to 45 percent. The security service sent a letter to the Federal Anti-Monopoly Service ruling the stock purchase unacceptable because Vimpelcom was considered a strategic Russian company, and Telenor was suspected of intelligence activities with close ties to Norway's secret services.[11] The Federal Anti-Monopoly Service refused to grant approval for the purchase.

IN 2003, THE FSB appointed Nikolai Oleshko deputy head of the security service's Investigative Directorate, which made him the chief spy hunter. Oleshko had begun his career tracking down spies within the Soviet Army Group in East Germany in the 1980s. In the early 2000s, he became known as an expert in such cases and was put in charge of investigating espionage cases in the directorate. In 2004, when he was elected head of the directorate, he began a restructuring campaign that gave high priority to counterintelligence. The First Section, responsible for investigating spy cases, had a serious staff shortage.[12] According to lawyer Yuri Gervis, who served a decade in the KGB's investigation department before resigning in 1993, "The professional employees are lost. For instance, the First, the so-called 'spy section,' has no investigators except for the chief of the section, who graduated from the FSB Academy. There is nobody to catch real spies, and therefore the FSB is making spies out of people who communicate with foreign organizations in the course of their work." As result, "espionage cases are conjectural, weakly backed by evidence, and all classified top secret in order to conceal errors."[13]

In 2004 Oleshko convinced the FSB's leadership to put his First Section in charge of all regional branches, a move that increased the significance of the section and the importance of the "spy" department overall.

The new system was given its first real test not long after it was established, when Oleshko's officers were asked to intervene in a case that had almost been ruined by the regional office in Kaluga, a city south of Moscow.

In 1999 Igor Sutyagin, a military analyst at the Institute for the Study of the United States and Canada, was accused by the Kaluga Regional FSB Department of giving information to foreign intelligence. The FSB had determined that Sutyagin had contacted Sean Kidd and Nadya Lock, two representatives of Alternative Futures, a mysterious London-based firm that had hired Sutyagin as a part-time consultant on questions related to Russian military technology. Sutyagin met Kidd and Lock in Europe and Britain, and was paid for his consultations.[14] The FSB told journalists that Kidd and Lock were U.S. defense intelligence officers and presented what the FSB described as phone numbers and an address for Alternative Futures in London. But by then the firm had disappeared.

The suspicious character of Alternative Futures appeared to be confirmed by the authors of this book. Soldatov and Borogan went to London in 2004 in search for the third person in the story: Christopher Martin, who was named in the Alternative Future's advertisement leaflet. The authors also wanted to check out the address of Kidd's house in Copthorne, Crawley, West Sussex, mentioned by Sutyagin's lawyers as a place where he met Kidd and Lock. With the help of British journalists, the authors found the phone number of Christopher Martin. Remarkably, what Sutyagin had understood as being Kidd's house turned out to be registered to Christopher Martin. Soldatov called Martin to ask him about his connections with Sutyagin. But Martin was firm in his statement: "Yes, it is my address. But I know nothing about the case. Periodically I hand over the house as I often work abroad. I have nothing to add." A month after the conversation the house was put for sale.

Sutyagin was charged with treason and tried in Kaluga. During the proceedings, the Kaluga FSB failed to present evidence that Sutyagin transferred secrets to Alternative Futures and failed to find anyone who had passed Sutyagin secret information he could sell to the firm. Instead, the FSB made the case that Sutyagin collected information by analyzing publications in the Russian press. That analysis alone, it seemed, was deemed an act of treason.

In 2001, the Kaluga Regional Court ruled that there were insufficient grounds to prosecute Sutyagin, and the case was sent to Moscow for more detailed investigation. Although Kaluga's FSB officers involved in the investigation were promoted, it was generally thought in Moscow that the case had been bungled and might be lost. In 2002 the Sutyagin case was transferred from Kaluga to Moscow, and Sutyagin was placed in Lefortovo prison. Oleshko was personally put in charge of the next trial, this time held in the

Moscow City Court. In response, Sutyagin requested a trial by jury, then a new practice for Russian courts.

A jury trial of the Sutyagin case, chaired by Judge Petr Shtunder, began in November 2003. Three months later Shtunder announced he would not proceed with the case. He gave no explanation. In March 2004 a new trial began, this time chaired by Judge Marina Komarova. In April the new jury found Sutyagin guilty and he was sentenced to fifteen years of hard labor.

After the sentencing, Sutyagin's astonished lawyers declared the jury had been manipulated by the FSB, but to no avail. Soon after the verdict, the defense discovered that one of the jurors had been on a list of candidate jurors for the Moscow District Military Court. It was a mystery how he had ended up at Moscow City Court. The juror appeared to have been specially transferred to the trial. In August Sutyagin's lawyers identified the juror as Grigory Yakimishen.

Who was Yakimishen? The authors attempted to find out more about the mystery juror. The authors learned Yakimishen was a longtime KGB foreign intelligence agent who had served in Poland and had been involved in the biggest spy controversy in that country, when in 1996 the prime minister was accused of spying for Russia and was forced to resign. Yakimishen was identified in the Polish media as the source of information about the prime minister's involvement with Russia. According to Russian law, secret service officers are not permitted to sit on juries. In the case of Sutyagin's trial, jurors were polled about past work experiences and were dismissed if they listed any involvement with law enforcement or secret services. While others admitted they had and were dismissed from jury duty, Yakimishen did not reveal his past, according to Anna Stavitskaya, Sutyagin's defense lawyer.

Irina Borogan called Yakimishen at home, but their conversation was very brief.

"Grigory, we are preparing a publication about the Sutyagin case. Could you tell me, did you serve at the Russian Embassy in Poland in 1994–1996?" asked Borogan.

"I pledged in court not to compromise the secrecy of the investigation, and the court has a copy of my work record book," said Yakimishen.

"But could you say whether you were working in Poland or not?" Borogan insisted.

"Next question, please," was the answer.

"Could you comment on the scandal linked to your name that was widely covered by the Polish media?" asked Borogan again.

Finally Yakimishen lost his patience and said, "I do not intend to answer any more questions. Don't call me ever again."

It appeared that Sutyagin had been convicted of treason by a jury that included an intelligence officer previously involved in a spy scandal. More broadly, the Sutyagin case illustrated the way justice under Putin would be decided: not by rule of law but by arbitrary rule of a few people in power. The state had decided to make a point with Sutyagin by finding him guilty of treason. Despite evidence suggesting a rigged jury, he was sent to prison by all means possible.[15] In July 2010 Sutyagin was exchanged for one of the Russians recently accused of espionage in the United States.

EVERY YEAR THE FSB reports the discovery of something on the order of a hundred traitors and dozens of spies. In 2008, according to the agency, 149 foreign spies were unmasked. In December 2008 FSB director Alexander Bortnikov told journalists, "The activities of forty-eight career officers of foreign intelligence services have been stopped, as have the actions of 101 local assets of foreign special services."[16] Despite the impressive statistics, there is no equivalent number of actual prosecutions and trials on spy allegations in Russia every year.

For example, the FSB considered "career officers" to be those foreigners whose activity was found suspicious and they were prevented from visiting Russia, while "local assets" were deemed to be those Russians who were suspected of the intention to sell state secrets to foreign intelligence services. The local assets cited in the statistics are never identified by name because most of them are so-called initiators—people who were going to contact the foreign embassies on their own initiative but were caught early. In most cases the intended recipients never got wind of them.

Although the Russian secret services have had difficulty making spy charges stick, they have nonetheless reaped generous promotions for their efforts.

In 1997, the secret services tried to prosecute military journalist Grigory Pasko in Vladivostok in the Russian Far East. Pasko had been working with a Japanese TV station on reports about nuclear waste dumping in the oceans. Because he was being paid by foreigners, he was an easy target for the Russian secret services. In the case, supervised by German Ugryumov, then head of the local FSB department, Pasko was accused of espionage. Pasko was acquitted in 1999, but in 2000 the Supreme Court tried him again. In December 2001 he was found guilty and sentenced to four years in jail. He was released in January 2003.

For his part, Ugryumov was promoted to deputy director of the FSB in Moscow. In January 2001 he was put in charge of counterterrorist operations in Chechnya. The same year, Vladimir Putin

conferred Russia's highest award, the Hero of the Russian Federation, on Ugryumov. It was widely rumored that Ugryumov was
slated to become the next director of the FSB when he died in May
2001.[17] Lower-ranking officers on the Pasko case were also promoted. Investigator Alexander Yegorkin, who headed the investigative group on Pasko, was appointed chief of the Investigation
Section of the FSB Pacific Fleet Department. When the court found
out that Yegorkin had violated the Criminal Proceedings Code during the investigation and had forged documents for the criminal
case, he was reprimanded but shortly thereafter promoted to
major.[18] Later, Yegorkin was moved to Moscow, where he headed
the military counterintelligence division at the FSB Investigative
Directorate.

In the late 1990s the city of Vladivostok led the way on the spy
front. In July 1999 the FSB searched the apartment and laboratory
of oceanologist Vladimir Soifer, purportedly because his ecological
research posed a threat to the country's security. In the end, the
case was resolved by a pardon, despite the fact that no crime had
been identified. Soifer appealed the pardon in an attempt to clear
his name, and in May 2001 the case was dismissed. By then, General Sergey Verevkin-Rakhalsky, head of the FSB department in
Primorye, who had initiated the investigation, had moved on to
Moscow. In 2000 Verevkin-Rakhalsky was appointed deputy minister for taxes and duties, and in 2001 he was promoted to the rank
of lieutenant general and senior deputy director of the Federal Service of Tax Police.

The rapid career advancement by the counterintelligence officers from Vladivostok was noted by colleagues in other regions.
Soon, spy hunts were being mounted across the country, even in
the calmest regions. In January 2002 the Penza FSB department

made a name for itself by unmasking a 22-year-old spy who had ostensibly recruited a 16-year-old boy. It later turned out that the supposed spy was an English teacher who had asked a student to bring in his father's photographs of the Baikanur Space Center (the Soviet analogue of Cape Canaveral). The FSB claimed that the teacher was planning to sell the photographs to the U.S. embassy.[19]

IF THERE WAS a single case that led the investigators from the "spy section" of the FSB Investigative Directorate in Moscow to reorient their hunt for spies, it was that of Valentin Moiseev. Moiseev, former deputy director of the First Foreign Ministry Department for Asian countries, was arrested on July 4, 1998, and accused of passing secret documents to the South Korean intelligence service.

Former FSB officer and lawyer Yuri Gervis put it as follows: "What was actually done with Moiseev is called creating a recruitment opportunity. The intelligence service of South Korea could use his friendship with Cho Son Yu—an adviser at the South Korean Embassy in Russia—to recruit him. The FSB was investigating the activity of Cho Son Yu, and the service got to know of Moiseev's acquaintance with the South Korean. Then the FSB acting reserve officer attached to the Foreign Ministry began meeting with Moiseev on a regular basis asking for information. Later, the FSB used the materials provided by Moiseev as evidence against him. This is provocation, from the juridical point of view."[20] As it turned out, the evidence against Moiseev was unsubstantiated. In the list of supposedly secret documents transferred by Moiseev, the FSB included "An agreement on protecting migrant birds."[21] The trial involved a total of five judges, as one judge after another failed to deliver the "right" sentence. Finally, the Supreme Court overruled the Moscow court's sentence of twelve years behind bars—and the term was reduced to four years.

The choice of investigators on the Moiseev case was also peculiar. One turned out to be the son of the director of Lefortovo Prison, where Moiseev was being held. Another, Yuri Plotnikov, had taken part in the investigation of Edmond Pope, an American citizen who was accused of espionage. Yuri's father, Oleg Plotnikov, had been the prosecutor in the same case.[22] Both investigators were promoted after Moiseev's case ended. Senior investigator Vasily Petukhov, who pleaded Moiseev's case, started as a captain and senior investigator and shortly afterward was promoted to lieutenant colonel. A year later he was to head the First Section.

Nikolai Oleshko, then head of the "spy" division in the FSB Investigative Directorate, headed the group investigating the Moiseev case.

The challenges of each spy trial made the FSB look for a different approach. The FSB found it was better to try spies under charges of economic rather than criminal law. Those steamrollered were suspected not of espionage, but of illegal export of technology and of economic crimes. Those accused of involvement were directors of well-funded research institutes with profitable international contracts.

The new approach was attempted with Oscar Kaibyshev, the director of the Institute for Metal Superplasticity Problems, who attracted FSB attention in 2005. Initially, the 65-year-old scientist was charged with disclosing state secrets. His colleagues, the academic community, journalists, and the general public supported him with a vocal campaign. Soon, Kaibyshev's crime was reframed as the export of dual-use technology, and he was painted as a man involved in illegal commercial schemes. In August 2006 Kaibyshev was sentenced to six years probation.[23]

In October 2005 the academic Igor Reshetin, general director of TsNIIMASh-Export,* his CFO, Sergei Tverdokhlebov, and his deputy for security, Alexander Rozhkin, were arrested by the FSB. All three were placed in Lefortovo.

FSB investigators did not accuse them of spying or of divulging state secrets. The men were charged with embezzlement and violations of export rules. Later they were accused of passing dual-use technology to China and also of smuggling.

In December 2007 the three were sentenced to five to eleven years behind bars. A few days later a letter from one of the convicted men was published on Human Rights Web site (www.hro.org), stating: "If our director had agreed to take part in a dialogue with the secret services, there would have been no dire consequences, while both his personal position and that of his firm would have been bolstered in the space technology market. The firm would have been protected by the FSB's economic security service."[24]

The FSB most likely allowed for the letter's publication in hopes that in the future, individuals in similar scenarios would take such advice to heart.

THE SOVIET REGIME used espionage fears to control the population. The KGB believed that dissident movements could not survive without Western support. In supposed efforts to prevent spy infiltration, the KGB actually traced every foreign contact of every Soviet citizen. Each Russian who went abroad in Soviet times was obliged to report all his meetings and conversations.

---

* TsNIIMASh-Export is a state-owned Russian space technology company run by the Central Scientific Research Institute for Machine Building, and located in Korolyov, the center of the Russian space community and home to "Mission Control" for all Russian space flights.

By contrast, the current Russian government displays no intent to exert such universal control.

In the chaotic first years after the Soviet collapse and the rise of the new Russia, the FSB occupied a modest place in society: Oligarchs employed corrupt officers, and the role of the security services in Chechnya was largely ignored. In these transitional times, the FSB looked like a bygone Soviet-era institution. They needed to find a new place in new circumstances. By leading the way in the headline-grabbing hunt for spies in the last decade, the FSB was attempting to reestablish its preeminence in society. It needed budget resources, prestige, and demonstrable success stories to compete with other security institutions and to win the respect and support of businessmen.

While the FSB claimed it was preventing the sellout of Russia and its manipulation by outsiders, the prosecutions offer no evidence that such a threat existed. In the first decade of the twenty-first century, no big fish with access to sensitive information was ever accused of spying. Instead, charges of espionage were aimed at minor figures, evidence was weak, and in some cases the proceedings were rigged. The effect of Putin's strong-arm campaign to ferret out dissenters from within has meanwhile fueled distrust and suspicion.

THE THREAT WITHIN
INFILTRATING COUNTERMOVEMENTS

WHILE THE HUNT for foreign spies operating within Russian organizations was designated one of the FSB's top priorities under Putin's direction, a countermovement, designed to acquire intelligence from informants planted in liberal organizations, was simultaneously put into play.

In February 2008, Andrei Soldatov received a curious phone call from Thomas Buch-Andersen, a journalist at the Danish Broadcasting Corporation in Copenhagen, who told the author that he had a man with him who claimed to have been an FSB plant in the United Civil Front organization, a liberal political group that had been formed to try to preserve democratic electoral procedures in Russia. Soldatov was skeptical, worrying that it would be hard to get information for such a story. But he asked Buch-Andersen to send clips from the interview. After listening to it, Soldatov and Borogan discussed the prospect of investigating the man with their editors at *Novaya Gazeta*, concluding that it would be worthwhile to do so.[1]

At the time, the United Civil Front was one of Russia's main opposition movements, led by world chess legend Garry Kasparov.

Once the youngest world chess champion, in the 1990s Kasparov turned to politics, supporting some marginal parties and political movements. In the 2000s Kasparov tried to establish an opposition movement outside of Putin's Kremlin. Kasparov's movement, "The Other Russia," adopted grassroots organizing methods; in 2006–2009 a series of marches were held in Russian cities, most of them violently suppressed by law enforcement authorities. The Kremlin was terrified the demonstrations could catalyze peaceful protests known as color revolutions, which had successfully toppled the authoritarian regimes in Serbia, Georgia, the Ukraine, and Kyrgyzstan in 2000–2005. The Kremlin believed that the protests were inspired by Western institutions. Kasparov had only a few thousand followers, but he managed to successfully establish himself as an outspoken critic of the Kremlin in the Western media: constantly interviewed, he published columns in the *Wall Street Journal*, the *Financial Times*, and the *New York Times*. For the FSB, such commentary was Kasparov's biggest sin. Kasparov was deemed to be an agent of the West who might be used one day by hostile foreign forces to overthrow the political regime in Moscow.

The FSB plant in question was Alexander Novikov, who had first appeared in Denmark in early 2008. Novikov had apparently traveled from Russia to Finland, where he applied to the Red Cross for help, before making his way to a refugee camp near Copenhagen. A week later he arrived at the office of the Danish Broadcasting Company, where he claimed he was a Russian FSB agent who wanted to cease his activities and obtain political asylum.

Soldatov thought the only way to check this out was to go to Copenhagen. Two days later he met with Novikov in a small conference room at the Danish journalist's office in Copenhagen. Novikov, 36 years old, was a tall, imposing man with thick grey hair. When Soldatov started asking him some questions, Novikov said, "Let's go out on the street for a smoke."

Novikov related to Soldatov that he had been raised in Transnistria, a small breakaway province of the Republic of Moldova. This thin sliver of land has been plagued with strife since Transnistrian authorities proclaimed independence from Moldova in 1990—a move that ultimately resulted in a bloody two-year war. Today, the territory is a kind of gangster state, a crossroads for weapons shipments and smuggling. Even Russia, which supported Transnistria in its war against Moldova, refuses to recognize it.

Novikov, smoking on the street and later speaking for several hours to Soldatov in the conference room, said that he had graduated from medical school and continued his training in Russia at the Tomsk Medical Institute, a military institution. In 2002 he moved to Moscow where he worked as a doctor in several clinics. At the time of his first contact with the FSB, Novikov reported that he'd been working as a representative for Werwag Farma, a German pharmaceutical company. In exchange for a modest salary, he ran from clinic to clinic, trying to sell Werwag Farma products.

But from this point in his narrative, Novikov's story took a strange turn. He claimed that at the beginning of 2006 he was walking down Bolshoi Kiselny Lane in the center of Moscow and spontaneously decided to drop into an FSB building to ask after someone he knew from his Transnistria days, with whom he'd lost touch and had been hoping to find for some time. Soldatov was puzzled; the FSB was decidedly not the kind of place one stopped into on a sunny day to inquire about a long-lost friend.

Once inside the building, Novikov said he had talked with an officer named Alexei Vladimirovich. The officer wrote down Novikov's address and phone number, and later called him to suggest that they meet in order to "discuss an interesting offer."

Novikov recalled that he had met the FSB officer in a small park in a pleasant district of Moscow. The officer brought three sheets of paper to the meeting, saying it was a contract for cooperation with the FSB. The contract had a one-year term, with an opportunity for extension. Novikov was said to be paid a flat rate of 8,000 rubles per month (this would be the equivalent of more than $320, a third of his Werwag Farma salary).

In exchange, the officer asked Novikov to infiltrate the newly formed United Civil Front (UCF) to collect information. Upon accepting the offer, Novikov was given the operational name "Mikhail." With Alexei Vladimirovich, Novikov outlined a cover story that would help him penetrate the organization: He would tell the movement staff he was planning to help form an independent trade union for medical workers.

From the beginning of his interaction with Novikov, Soldatov had doubts about his story. There were many unanswered questions. However, it was possible to verify that Novikov had been an active member of the United Civil Front's Moscow branch. Records, interviews, and photographs showed he had taken part in numerous demonstrations and pickets and had been detained by the police. The last such occasion was in November 2007, when he was detained for holding a lone picket near the Interior Ministry headquarters in Moscow at 38 Petrovka Street. The picket was in support of Kasparov.

Novikov reported that during his collaboration with the FSB, he was assigned a new handler. In May 2007 Alexei Vladimirovich, who had gone on duty to Chechnya, was replaced by Alexei Lvovich, a young man, only about 28 years old. There was one more man working on the scheme, whom Novikov presumed was the handler's supervisor. He introduced himself as Andrei Ivanovich. He met Novikov only once and asked him about his activities in the Moscow branch of the UCF.

Novikov told Soldatov how he had regular meetings with his handlers, mainly on Rozhdestvensky Boulevard, near the Moscow branch office of the FSB. Novikov was regularly asked to give a written account of his activities inside the UCF, as well as receipts for the money he received from his handlers. Novikov always wrote it by hand and signed it "Mikhail." His handlers were interested in any information about the UCF: the dates of planned protest actions, relations inside the movement, and the names of individuals close to Garry Kasparov. Novikov was instructed to open an email account where he would receive email from the UCF, which he would then forward to Alexei Lvovich. The handler also gave Novikov a cell phone number to contact.

During his interview with Soldatov, Novikov shared his email account password with the author, allowing him to read all the messages to and from Alexei Lvovich. Their exchange began in July 2007 and continued until February 2008. Novikov had sent along all the information he had garnered about events in the Kasparov movement. In some messages the handler said he had money to give to Novikov. For example, on February 4, 2008, the FSB man wrote: "Alexander Alexeievich! You disappeared again. What's happened? Call me urgently. Alexei Lvovich."

Novikov suggested that he had personally played an important role in helping the FSB disrupt Kasparov's political activities. Specifically, he said, he had provided information to the FSB about where Kasparov planned to hold meetings to obtain signatures to become a candidate in the 2008 presidential election. On December 10, 2007, the Kasparov initiative group was blocked without explanation from renting a theater hall in Moscow. When Kasparov's supporters tried to find another location, the proprietors of venues large enough for his purposes all flatly refused. Kasparov needed to gather five hundred people, but it became difficult without a hall, and the Central Election Commission forbade dividing the group into parts. According to Novikov, he provided the FSB the information about each venue that Kasparov wanted to rent.

For its part, the FSB seemed intent upon infiltrating Kasparov's movement, but not necessarily in controlling it. Outright control lay in the hands of the Kremlin, which devoted great efforts to suppressing opposition to Putin and to creating friendly youth political movements.

As Novikov described it, his FSB handlers were mostly interested in seeing his role expand within Kasparov's movement. They always gave him instructions about whom to communicate with and how to behave in order to assure promotion. In January 2008, Novikov reported good news: Lolita Tsaria, the head of the Moscow branch of the UCF, promised him the leadership of the Moscow northwest branch of the movement. Two days later Novikov left Russia.

Soldatov was puzzled. He could not figure out why Novikov decided, as he put it, to "quit the life of the informant and expose everything." Novikov claimed he was tired of living a double life and double-crossing his comrades in the movement.

But Soldatov wondered if the claims were true, and if Novikov were in fact posing as an informer in order to qualify for asylum and secure a good life for himself in Europe. In July 2007, Novikov arrived for the first time in Denmark, where he stayed in a refugee camp, but in August he returned to Moscow.

IN SOVIET TIMES, political investigations were carried out by the famous Fifth Directorate of the KGB, created in 1967 under KGB Chairman Yuri Andropov. Andropov's note to the Central Committee of the Communist Party on April 17, 1968, read: "Unlike previous sub-units we have had in the state security organizations, which dealt with questions of combatting harmful elements in the ideological area who were mainly inside the country, the newly created fifth sub-units have been called upon to combat ideological subversion inspired by our enemies abroad."[2]

The Fifth Directorate comprised fifteen separate departments working to quash dissent. The First department was in charge of work through trade unions, the Second planned operations against émigré organizations that were critical of the Soviet Union, the Third worked among students, and so on. Among the departments was one charged with handling foreign journalists (the Fourteenth), one that dealt with punks and unofficial groups (the Thirteenth), and one that served as a liaison with the Jewish community (the Eighth). No fewer than 2,500 employees served in the Fifth Directorate, as Fillip Bobkov, longtime chief of the Directorate, later recalled.[3]

In the middle of Gorbachev's perestroika era, in an effort to improve their image, the Fifth Directorate was renamed the "Directorate to Defend the Soviet Constitutional System" (Directorate Z). However, it did not survive the fall of the Soviet Union and was eliminated in September 1991. Even so, experienced officers remained on active service.

In Yeltsin's time, the FSB resurrected the unit. The FSB's Directorate to Protect the Constitution was created on July 6, 1998, the same month that Putin was named FSB director. In an interview with *Nezavisimaya Gazeta* in November of that year, its chief, Gennady Zotov, described his Directorate's role: "The state pursued the goal of creating a sub-unit 'specialized' in fighting threats to the security of the Russian Federation in the sociopolitical sphere. Due to a number of objective factors connected with Russia's fundamental nature, it has always devoted special attention to the protection of the country from 'internal sedition,' for 'internal sedition' has always been more terrible for Russia than any military invasion."[4]

To date, this is the most honest and open comment made by any FSB general on the need for political investigation.

But not all political surveillance was conducted by the central authorities. Regional offices and units also played a role. In the FSB, one of the largest of these regional departments was in Moscow.[5]

Under Russian law, the special services are not supposed to engage in direct investigations using covert agents implanted in political organizations. That would be illegal under the Act on Operational-Investigative Activity passed in 1995, in which Article 5, Item 2 explicitly states:

> The bodies (officials) carrying out operative-investigative activity are forbidden: . . . to take secret part . . . in the activity of properly registered and non-banned political parties, public and religious movements, with the purpose of influencing the character of their activities.

To Soldatov, several details in Novikov's story seemed strange, such as the contract that he signed, instead of a signed statement of collaboration, which was typical for the KGB. But Soldatov thought perhaps this was just one more of the many indicators of the new economic regime in Russia. But other details rang true. According to former FSB officers interviewed by Soldatov, the behavior described is typical of the employees of the Moscow department of the FSB. By contrast to the officers of the Central Apparatus, they do prefer to hold meetings near their headquarters, and they require written accounts and receipts as proof to their leadership that they have not pocketed the money given.

The most convincing detail in Novikov's claims was his description of the building where his initial meeting took place. Novikov told Soldatov the address was Bolshoi Kiselny Lane, 13/15. The public doesn't know much about this place except that the building belongs to the Moscow Department of the FSB. Inside, there is a little-known unit responsible for fighting political extremism.

Soldatov and his Danish journalist colleagues spent countless hours in discussion in Copenhagen about how to check the facts surrounding Novikov's story. Eventually they asked Novikov to call his handler and to record their conversation. Novikov was brought to the beautiful riverbank in the center of Copenhagen on a cold winter day. A TV crew was ready to record the conversation. No other people were in sight.

Novikov dialed the mobile number of his handler:

"Alexei Lvovich?"

"Yes," the voice on the other end of the line confirmed.

Novikov explained to his handler that he was in Denmark.

"Well, you should have informed me. Why didn't you tell me at once?" Alexei Lvovich demanded. Novikov changed the subject, telling his handler that he had called Lolita Tsaria, chief of the Moscow section of the Kasparov movement.

"I called Lolita," he said, nervously. "She has chosen the coordinators of the groups, and now there are commissions to be formed. It is likely that I will be included in one of them, the commission on organized mass events."

"I got it. Okay. But will you be here in a week?"

"Yes, sure."

"Otherwise your money will get lost again," laughed Alexei Lvovich.

"Money will get lost?" Novikov asked.

"Yes. I asked you the question how you disappeared so suddenly."

"Well, it just happened like that."

"But you will be here in a week, won't you?"

"I hope I will," Novikov assured him.

"Well give me a call sometimes. Do you have Internet access there?"

"Yes, I read all your emails," Novikov said.

"I see. And does anything come to your email box? Anything from Lolita?"

"Lolita? Yes, it sure does."

"Send me what you have when the opportunity presents itself," said the handler. He then asked, "And who has become the coordinator now?"

"Coordinator? It seems to be Nemov. I've never heard the name before."

"I got it. OK, you'll send me those last letters, won't you?" It sounded more like an order than a question.

"OK, I will. Thank you and good-bye, Alexei Lvovich."

"Take care!" Alexei Lvovich hung up.

In Copenhagen, Soldatov wrote up an account of Novikov's story and sent it to Borogan in Moscow. The Danish wanted to air the story on television as soon as possible. Soldatov wanted to check more details.

Borogan took the story to the editor of *Novaya Gazeta*, who suggested she go to the FSB for comment. She faxed a formal request for comment on two points: whether the FSB sent agents to infiltrate political parties, and whether they had infiltrated Kasparov's movement. Borogan did not mention Novikov's name, fearing that to do so would trigger an effort by the FSB to stop publication. As it turned out, the FSB didn't respond to the request.

Even before Soldatov flew back to Moscow, he was making frantic efforts to check the story. He asked a colleague at *Novaya Gazeta*, who had once served in the KGB's Fifth Directorate, to listen to the details and give him his opinion on whether the story might be true. After listening, Soldatov's colleague concluded that it sounded a lot like the Moscow department of the FSB, given the locations of the meetings and the details about the building. The colleague also said that the meeting with Alexei Lvovich's supervisor was typical of this department—it was the leadership's way of checking in on their officers, to ensure that recruited agents are real, and worth the money they are allotted. It was common that an informant would know very little about his handler, so it would not help to pressure Novikov for more details on that score.

Soldatov and Borogan debated whether to call Kasparov for comment. They decided against it—they had no reaction from the FSB, and they didn't want it to look as if the story had been inspired by Kasparov's movement.

After much debate, the authors published the Novikov story on February 21, 2008, on the front page of *Novaya Gazeta*, the same day Danish journalists aired their program about the case.[6]

The news was met with a huge public outcry from opposition circles. Roman Dobrokhotov, the leader of an opposition group called the "We" movement, told news agencies that Novikov had been everywhere—he could not remember any political action that Novikov had not taken part in. He added that it seemed strange that an FSB agent would "shine" so much on the events. Still, Dobrokhotov said he suspected that the FSB had infiltrated the political movements, and he was convinced that there were other undercover intelligence officers among Russia's opposition groups.

The Kasparov movement, meanwhile, seemed unruffled by the story. Spokesperson Marina Litvinovich told Soldatov, "Well, that's good you wrote about it, and so?" On the day the story was published, Denis Bilunov, a deputy of Kasparov's, noted, "I never had a doubt that there were people inside our organization and other opposition groups who agreed to inform the secret services about our activity." He added, "Now, it has come to light." He also said the affair was cause for a lawsuit, but added, "I think that this has to be a matter for the prosecutor's office, because it is largely not about the violation of our rights, but about breaking the law by the secret services."

Other media—including the *Moscow Times*, *Le Figaro*, and the BBC—took up Novikov's story. But the FSB refused to comment on the case. The head of the press office of the Moscow department, Yevgeny Kalinovich, was on sick leave beginning the day of publication and other employees refused to comment. The authors got no answer to their written inquiry. But the case was still uncertain. Even after the story was published, Soldatov was accused by colleagues at *Novaya Gazeta* of publishing unchecked information.

Two weeks after publication, Soldatov met an officer of the Moscow department of the FSB. The officer, who had been a source in the past, confirmed that a controversy had been stirred up inside the department by the Novikov case. Why, Soldatov wondered, had the FSB recruited Novikov?

The officer replied that Novikov had been a "swindler" who was in debt.

"You know, we have a plan for recruitment," the officer added. His statement seemed to confirm that Novikov had been an agent. But the source, who was not from the section that might have recruited Novikov, didn't know much more. He said the FSB had been totally surprised by the story and didn't know how to react to it.

It was illegal to infiltrate properly registered political movements. But as one FSB officer explained to the authors, it *was* possible to perform so-called intelligence gathering by presenting the agent as an accidental activist.

The information about Novikov's apparent financial troubles was new to the authors. They contacted another activist in the movement, Mikhail Dmitriev, one of Novikov's close friends, who knew about the financial problems and confirmed them.[7]

Eventually Soldatov called Novikov and asked him directly about the allegations of financial problems. Novikov conceded he had taken a loan for $15,000 and had no intention of returning it. He also revealed he had contacts with criminal gangs from Transnistria and that the FSB was fully aware of these ties.

Now Soldatov and Borogan saw the case more clearly. With his history of debt, Novikov was a more plausible pawn for the FSB: By becoming an informant, he could repay the monies he owed.

Was Novikov's story true? He was clearly a man who had debts and some kind of criminal past, exactly the kind of person who is easily recruited by intelligence services for infiltration work. He provided Soldatov with accurate information—insofar as it could be checked—about his recruitment and handlers. And he had clearly worked within Kasparov's organization, which was of considerable interest to the FSB. So he had both motive and opportunity. In the end he tried to make the most of it—as you would expect from an opportunist seeking asylum in Western Europe on the grounds of political persecution.

For its part, the FSB could claim that Novikov came to them with information and that they gave him "expenses" to cover his costs. The sums were never that great. It is hardly surprising that they remained silent when the story broke, as Novikov was a comparatively low-level figure, not regarded by the Moscow FSB as a major asset.

Nor was this the end of the story. In July 2008, the authors were told by a professor at the FSB Academy that the story had triggered a wave of anger at Soldatov in the Moscow department of the FSB. And only the Russian presidential elections of March 2, 2008, impeded action being taken against the journalists.

In March 2009, Novikov, by then in Finland, was refused political asylum, but he decided to stay in the country, fighting to reopen the case. By spring 2010 his future was still uncertain.[8]

While Novikov's case was unusual in that he had decided to go to the media with his story, it offered a glimpse of how stealthily the FSB operated to achieve its goals. Informants, who were compensated for dutifully reporting back to their handlers and were given careful instructions on how to "read" an organization and act within it, were just one of many tools used to monitor Russia for dissident activity.

TARGETING EXTREMISM
THE RISE OF "WATCHDOG SURVEILLANCE"

O N MAY 6, 2009, Roman Dobrokhotov, 26 years old, a liberal opposition political activist who had taken part in numerous street protests against the Kremlin, took a train from Volgograd to Moscow. At the Paveletsky Station, he stepped off the train and was immediately detained by a policeman who had been waiting for him by the exit.

The police officer told Dobrokhotov to follow him to the police post at the train station. Once there, the officer said he had been sent in advance to have a talk with the young political activist, to warn him against participating in street protests that were forbidden by the authorities. Dobrokhotov asked the policeman to explain. The policeman told Dobrokhotov that he was being detained on the advice of a telegram from the Moscow transit police that indicated that Dobrokhotov was on "watchdog surveillance," a special system to track serious criminals, by the Interior Ministry Department for Countering Extremism. Dobrokhotov then photographed the interesting telegraph with his cell phone. Labelled URGENT, the document indicated that at least three police units had been deployed to track Dobrokhotov's route. The activist had never been indicted on criminal charges, and he was being detained only for what the authorities called a preventive warning.[1]

The warning Dobrokhotov received offers a glimpse into how the Russian security services monitor the country's citizens. They have begun an ambitious surveillance program to control "extremism," which has come to include, among other things, political protest against the regime, writings critical of the Kremlin or security services, and participation in independent trade unions and informal youth groups. This broad definition of extremism, embracing participation in activity that challenges the existing political order in Russia, was put in place when the Kremlin was worried that the 2008 financial crisis might ignite popular protests.

On September 6, 2008, Dmitry Medvedev, the newly elected Russian president, made a key change in the structure of the Interior Ministry, which acts as a national police force. Under Medvedev, the department dedicated to fighting organized crime and terrorism was disbanded and a new department established, charged with countering extremism. Similar changes were made through all regional departments. Thousands of experienced police officers accustomed to dealing with bandits and terrorists were redirected to hunt down a new enemy.

The official reason given for Medvedev's change to the Interior Ministry was offered in February 2009 by Interior Minister Rashid Nurgaliev, who declared victory in the fight against organized crime: "There will be no new criminal revolution in Russia. . . . The number of crimes is decreasing. . . . We can state: An epoch of criminal wars is in the past."[2]

On April 15, 2009, at a public meeting, Yuri Kokov, the head of the new department charged with fighting extremism, was more revealing: "The operative situation might get worse under the conditions of the global crisis, [with] deterioration of the social and economic situation."[3] He was supported by Alexei Sedov, the FSB's chief of the service for protection of the constitutional system and struggle against terrorism. "We need to consider the consequences of the world financial crisis as a possible catalyst for terrorist activity and increasing extremist manifestations, including violent forms of resistance carried out by all kinds of dissenters, unauthorized opposition, youth, and students."[4]

Under Russian law, public utterances inciting racial, social, or other forms of hate are considered extremism—that is, words, not actions. Yet the Interior Ministry's official records suggest that extremism is not nearly as big a problem as organized crime. Official data from the Interior Ministry's Main Information Analysis Center for 2008 show 36,601 incidents that were investigated involving organized criminal groups, but only 460 cases of extremism were registered.[5]

In the campaign against extremism, the authorities placed the emphasis on prevention. Nurgaliev, the interior minister, announced that "the function of the department on countering extremism is first of all operative and recruiting work, aimed at the discovery and suppression of crimes, and also the prevention and monitoring of what is going on in the sphere of extremist activities."[6] Thus the Interior Ministry, which had formerly investigated crime, was driven into the murky area of prevention, which was more traditional for the FSB.

A list of extremist targets was promptly prepared. On December 16, 2008, the General Prosecutor's Office, the FSB, and the Interior Ministry approved a joint decision on extremism. The document stated that "extremism has become one of the major factors posing a threat to the national security of the Russian Federation."

At the top of the list is "extremism under cover of Islam." In most cases this appears to include associations and communities, independent of the so-called traditional Islam that is supervised officially by the Russian government. Next on the list are followers of pagan cults. The list also includes "participants in informal youth groups" and some radical opposition parties and movements. The joint decision prescribed how to work with the target groups, from surveillance methods to criminal prosecution. One of the most important areas of work is "neutralization and disbanding of associations whose members are prone to extremism."[7]

By spring 2009 it was obvious that the security services intended to broaden the list of extremist groups enumerated in the December 2008 order. Now the Interior Ministry is focusing on independent trade unions (lest they launch a wave of strikes) and warning leaders of such groups that they risk being charged with extremism.

In April 2009, Petr Zolotarev, the head of the independent trade union at the sprawling Avtovaz car factory, announced that he was summoned to the prosecutor's office for the town of Togliatti for "explanations about actions aimed at overthrowing the existing order." Earlier, Zolotarev had been questioned by officials at the local center on countering extremism.

Any expressions of public protest, by anyone from deceived stock market investors to residents rallying to keep a park in their area, can fall under the umbrella definition of extremism. On June 5, 2009, in St. Petersburg, for example, police detained six protesters—real estate investors claiming they had been defrauded—and warned them that they ran the risk of being labeled extremists.

Bloggers have similarly been targeted in the new anti-extremism campaign. In March 2009, Dmitri Soloviev, leader of the youth opposition group Oborona in Kemerovo, Siberia, faced criminal charges for criticizing the FSB in his LiveJournal blog. Two of the offending headlines on his blog were "FSB kills Russian children" and "Arbitrary behavior of the FSB and military conscription center." According to experts invited by the prosecution, the information posted by Soloviev "incites hatred, hostility and degrades a social group of people—the police and the FSB." The charges were eventually dropped.

Savva Terentyev, a 22-year-old blogger from the Komi Republic, faced similar charges for inciting hatred after local journalist Boris Suranov posted a comment on his blog in March 2008 criticizing law enforcement. In July 2009 Terentyev was found guilty and received a suspended sentence of one year.

The Interior Ministry created a special system for tracking targets and set up an electronic database of everything from recorded video surveillance to details about the purchase of plane and train tickets to fingerprint records.[8] The security services and law enforcement agencies meanwhile began to combine special databases on extremists and wanted criminals. Why people are entered into the database remains a state secret.

In May 2007, Sergei Shimovolos, a grey-haired, bearded man who worked as a human rights activist for two decades, traveled from his home in Nizhny Novgorod to Samara to take part in an independent investigation of restrictions that had been placed on public protests during the G8 summit in St. Petersburg the year before.

During his trip, he was checked by transport police in Nizhny Novgorod, in Samara Oblasts (a district), and in the Republic of

Mordovia. Each time, an officer of the transport police asked him to explain where he was headed to and what he planned to do upon arrival. The checks were clearly prearranged, but the question remained how they had been organized.

"In Samara I was lucky: the policemen honestly wrote in the report that they were detaining me on the grounds of a telegram they had received, and they were required to question me in line with crime prevention measures for conducting protest actions," Shimovolos told Irina Borogan.

Shimovolos protested his surveillance in court. "At the court, I received materials that bore witness to the fact that I was put under so-called 'watchdog surveillance' by a decision of the Nizhny Novgorod Organized Crime Unit, which allowed them to monitor my movements through the ticket sales database," Shimovolos recalled. He also learned that in 2007, some 3,865 Russians were under this type of watchdog surveillance. Now their names come up in the very same electronic card files that have data on criminals on the wanted list. Shimovolos asked the court to admit that such measures violate a person's rights, and urged the Interior Ministry to destroy all such records on citizens like himself, who had not been deemed extremists by a court but had been entered into the database.

On April 22, 2009, the Nizhny Novgorod District Court refused to eliminate the records and rejected Shimovolos's complaint on all counts. Although Shimovolos lost, his lawsuit offered insight into the ways that surveillance of law-abiding citizens is carried out.[9]

Information about Shimovolos made its way into the electronic database of the Interior Ministry known as "Rozysk-magistral," or the "Wanted Line," on March 19, 2007. The decision to include his information in the database was made by officers in the organized crime unit in the Nizhny Novgorod District. Shimovolos thinks he was flagged for helping to organize a political opposition march in Nizhny Novgorod.

INITIALLY, THE INTERIOR MINISTRY'S "Wanted Line" hardware and software suite, known as PTK, was created to assist in tracking criminals on federal and regional wanted lists. The PTK is connected with the "Express" and "Magistral" databases, which receive information about travel tickets purchased in Russia. When a criminal buys a ticket, the information goes to the PTK server and then is sent along to regional transit police, who can intercept the target at the local train station or airport. The Interior Ministry's overall objective was to cast a wide net in order to apprehend criminals far and wide.

But as Shimovolos's case shows, data about law-abiding citizens was also included in the PTK. The procedure for criminals and ordinary citizens is effectively the same, except that instead of an arrest, policemen receive instructions on how to handle citizens who are not suspected of a criminal offense.

Surveillance operations are carried out using new technologies that the Interior Ministry has at its disposal. This includes a portable, handheld terminal with access to all of the ministry's data on wanted individuals. The device, which resembles a smart phone, weighs less than seven ounces, can transmit photos and videos, and was designed to give police officers real-time access to federal and regional databases like "Wanted Persons," "Passports," "Weapons," "Theft," and "Automotive Transport Wanted by Interpol," among others.

Practically every large rail terminal and airport in Russia (as well as parts of trains and commuter trains) is now equipped with a face-recognition system known as "Videolock." (Cameras are located in rail cars, waiting rooms, cash registers, and platforms.) Dobrokhotov might have been detained with the help of such a system. A policeman could receive his image, marked with a special symbol, on the handheld terminal.

In 2006, there were 32 million fingerprint dossiers. Two years later, the federal and regional automated fingerprint data banks exceeded 71 million dossiers, for a population of 145.2 million.[10] In the last few years, almost all the detainees at protests in Russia were photographed and fingerprinted. According to the Interior Ministry, in 2009 new technological developments enabled police to check fingerprint data in real time and get a rapid response indicating whether a person was in a database.

While entering the names of potential extremists into existing databases, the Interior Ministry simultaneously began to develop new, larger, and more sophisticated databases.

In 2005 the Interior Ministry started to create a "super" database intended to integrate all police data at the local and federal levels into a single system accessible by each regional office. The system, scheduled for completion in 2011, has already succeeded in linking hundreds of Interior Ministry offices across the country.

According to individuals involved in the development of the network, once completed, officers in more than 4,000 units will have access to the database. In time, there will be a single space from which officials can gain instant access to information about an individual—audio, video, photographic, fingerprint, biometric, and text.[11]

While Russia's 2008 financial crisis has forced authorities to make numerous budget cuts, it does not appear to have dampened enthusiasm for the surveillance program. Instead, evidence suggests that officials are expanding efforts in this area. In late 2008, with the aid of data from 120 regional situation centers,[12] a situation center was established that brought together officials from the Interior Ministry and Federal Migration Service to monitor migration, with the goal of preventing the emergence of social tension.

At the same time, the Interior Ministry has begun to develop databases specifically designed to collect information on potential extremists. On April 29, 2009, in Yekaterinburg, Yuri Kokov made his first mention of a system called "Extremist"—a large catchall database of information that could be used in an investigation but has not been included in a formal criminal charge.[13] According to the authors' information, on March 31, 2009, the Sistematica company in Moscow won the state contract to build a "system to automate the line of the fight against extremism."[14] The client is the Interior Ministry, and the sum of the contract is more than $380,000. The system should be completed by November 2010. As stated in the contract, the "automated system is to improve the quality of information support to combat extremist activities." The development of the system, the document states, will allow for the creation of a database on countering extremist activity, as well as automate the processes of the exchange of information between the Interior Ministry, the FSB, and Federal Protective Service.[15]

The system will have branches in every regional situation center fighting against extremism and will allow fifty users to work simultaneously. The Interior Ministry has said that it is "currently not possible" to estimate the size of the database: In other words, the ministry cannot say even approximately how many people might be entered into the database and will be subject to monitoring.

Russia's expanded surveillance efforts seem to be directly at odds with the spirit of the 1993 Russian Constitution, which states in Article 23:"1. Everyone shall have the right to the inviolability of private life, personal and family secrets, the protection of honor and good name. 2. Everyone shall have the right to privacy in correspondence, telephone conversations, and postal, telegraph, and other messages. Limitations of this right shall be allowed only by court decision."[16]

UNDER RUSSIA'S WATCHFUL eye, individuals as well as organizations have increasingly come under a sophisticated system of surveillance. Those with the earmarks of extremism are put on a watch list, and the details of their personal lives may be scoured by FSB personnel. According to Russian law, public utterances inciting racial, social, or other forms of hate are considered forms of extremism. In 2006–2007, yet under Putin, "extremism" was expanded to include media criticism of state officials—a distinction that in turn required the media to label as extremist any organization the government deemed to be so.[17] Another amendment to the law made under Putin extended the definition of extremism to include"public justification of terrorism or other terrorist activity," but without defining"justification."Additional amendments regulate the production and distribution of"extremist"material without specifying what constitutes such material and introduce new penalties for journalists, media outlets, and printers found guilty of the offense. Penalties range from fines and confiscation of production equipment to the outright suspension of media outlets for up to ninety days.[18]

Lyudmila Alekseeva, the head of the Moscow-based Helsinki Group, compares the current situation in Russia to that of the struggle against the dissident movement in the Soviet Union. "There is a sense of déjà vu: the practice of surveillance of dissidents is back, taking people off trains, preventing conversations. The practice not only returned, but is enriched with new means of pressure on the people."

At a press conference on June 16, 2009, human rights activists from the Movement for Human Rights and the Moscow Helsinki Group demanded that Russia disband the Interior Ministry Department for Countering Extremism. In their statement, the groups noted that in creating the new department, Medvedev had established "a system of political surveillance consisting of people who, accustomed to dealing with dangerous criminals ... were given very broad and vague criteria to include people on the lists of targets to counteract."[19]

These measures of surveillance are not precisely comparable with Soviet practice. The Soviet police state tried to control every citizen in the country. The new, more sophisticated Russian system is far more selective than its Soviet-era counterpart; it targets only those individuals who have political ambitions or strong public views. Yet it's hard not to draw a comparison between the two. Increasingly, Russia's measures to closely monitor the lives of its citizens reflect an authoritarian hand—one less interested in the goals of civil society and more concerned with maintaining rigid control.

LIVING OFF THE FAT
OF THE LAND
THE NEW ELITE

I N SOVIET TIMES, loyalty to the secret police was enforced by fear. Stalin-era purges touched the secret police as well—many in the service and the leadership were executed or sent to jail. But service could be well rewarded. In the KGB, the rank and file received bonuses and free apartments, sidestepping long waiting lists. Generals enjoyed being chauffeured in official black Volgas—the roomiest Soviet sedan, used by the upper-echelon bureaucracy—and they qualified for country homes on the elite Rublyovka Road. But it was well understood by the recipients of these privileges that they were only good as long as one held on to one's position. The real owner of the dachas and cars was the KGB itself. Agents, first and foremost, were servants of the state.

In the years after the Soviet collapse, the servants of the state once again developed a taste for luxury. Old-fashioned Volgas were replaced by the largest, most prestigious black Mercedes, BMWs, and Audis, specially equipped with plates, lights, and sirens that allowed drivers to cut through Moscow's enormous traffic jams. (The lights and plates also give the driver the right to roar down the wrong side of the road at high speed, and have become one of

Russia's most visible symbols of privilege.) In Moscow alone, the FSB has ninety-five such vehicles at its disposal, while Foreign Intelligence has only fourteen and the Ministry of Defense has nineteen.[1]

In the 1990s, with unconstrained capitalism in Russia, officers were more focused on money and perks than their predecessors had been. They wanted higher salaries and pensions, and they saw it as their right to benefit from the privatization of state property, including valuable lands along the gold coast of the Rublyovka. This corridor, a collection of villages along the Rublyovo-Uspenskoye Road, has, since the imperial era, been a route for the elite. It was unofficially called the "Road of the Tsar" because Ivan the Terrible used it when he went falcon hunting. And in Soviet times, the pleasant summer homes, or dachas, were reserved for members of the Politburo and Central Committee of the party, famous artists, scientists, and people close to the Kremlin. But the socialist system demanded that these dachas be given to all of them temporarily, with no way of transforming them into personal property. Part of this land was set aside for the KGB's dachas.

After the fall of the Soviet Union the Russian elite continued to occupy the area. The famous villages on Rublyovka—Barvikha, Zhukovka, Nikolina Gora, Usovo, and Gorki became a refuge for enclaves of the newly wealthy and powerful. Yeltsin's family enjoyed a compound in the Rublyovka village of Barvikha. Vladimir Putin chose the state residence near Usovo; the former tycoon Mikhail Khodorkovsky and former prime minister Victor Chernomyrdin built their mansions in the village of Zhukovka; and Russian president Dmitry Medvedev preferred the state residence in Gorki-9.

Construction in the forests surged in the 1990s, and accelerated in the Putin decade. Traditional wooden dachas were replaced by mammoth, columned brick-and-stone mansions. The Rublyovka turned into Russia's refuge for oligarchs and powerful officials. One hundred square meters in a dacha in the Rublyovka was valued at around $200,000.[2]

The FSB ended up a very rich landowner. Although the KGB's dachas on Rublyovka were officially state owned, they had been managed by state security for so long that they were considered to be entirely at the FSB's disposal.

ONE OF THOSE who witnessed the advent of pricey mansions on Rublyovka was Viktor Alksnis, a onetime colonel in the Soviet Air Force whose grandfather had been a founder of the Red Army air force. Alksnis had served in Latvia, but when the Soviet Union collapsed, the military was forced to leave and Alksnis came to Russia, where he lived in a small village outside Moscow. At the time Russia was steamrolling toward democracy and free markets under Yeltsin, Alksnis was a voice from the past, steadfastly opposed to what the new Russia was attempting to become—a capitalist democracy. Alksnis, with wavy grey hair and a calm, self-confident manner, served in the Congress of People's Deputies, the Soviet parliament that was elected in 1989, as one of the leaders of Soyuz, a parliamentary group formed with the goal of preserving the Soviet Union at all costs. Later, he twice served in the new Russian parliament, where he openly criticized the West, capitalism, and liberal ideas. In 2003, he was elected to the State Duma from the district that included the Rublyovka, and he never ceased to be outraged by the rise of the million-dollar mansions.

In 2006, Alksnis discovered that in 2003 and 2004 the state had doled out about ninety-nine acres of its land in Rublyovka to private citizens. These lands consisted of eighty allotments, thirty-eight of them taken from the funds of the FSB Directorate of Material and Technical Support with the consent of the service's leadership.

The land was given outright to former and current high-ranking FSB officials. According to Alksnis, land was granted by the simplest of mechanisms: A letter of request, followed by a letter of approval, was all it took for land to change hands.

For example, he said, Alexei Fedorov, a deputy chief of the FSB's Economic Security Service, sent an application to the top official of the Odintsovo district, including with it a request from Semenenko, the deputy chief of the FSB division for lands and property, asking for land to be granted to Fedorov. Alksnis added that the land was under state ownership and that Semenenko had no right to relinquish it. The top official of the Odintsovo district just rubber-stamped the decision, Alksnis said. By law, he told Borogan, the land should have been transferred to a federal property agency for sale.

In researching the records of property transactions, the authors noticed that the FSB generals listed were not denoted by post or rank. For instance, major generals were merely called "servicemen who have served more than fifteen years." But the authors discovered that a number of high-ranking FSB officials were on the list of those who had been given free land. They included Alexei Fedorov; Mikhail Shkuruk, chief of the Control Department in the FSB Border Guard Service; and Boris Mylnikov, head of the Antiterrorist Center of the Commonwealth of Independent States, a post equivalent to first deputy director of the

FSB. Mylnikov was given his land for the nominal sum of $5 for 100 square meters.[3]

Others who received property free of charge were Yevgeny Lovyrev, the FSB's main personnel officer; Vyacheslav Volokh, former chief of the FSB Antiterrorist Center, who had by then left the service and become assistant to the Minister of Agriculture; and Sergey Shishin, then the head of the Internal Security Directorate of the FSB. Lovyrev, Volokh, and Shishin were all granted allotments in the village Gorki-2.[*]

In the late 1990s Gorki-2 became a fashionable part of the Rublyovka area, and the neighbors of the three FSB generals were captains of the new Russian capitalism: David Yakobashvili, chairman of the board of food-processing giant Wimm-Bill-Dann, and Oleg Deripaska, the owner of Rusal (Russian Aluminum) and at one point the country's richest man, ranked by *Forbes* at number 9 in the world in 2008 (worth $28 billion).[4] Ads like this started to appear on the Web: "The Rublyovo-Uspenskoye Road, two connected allotments, the Gorki-2 village, an exclusive arrangement, access to the Moscow River, guards of the FSB, the entire packet of documents for a cottage building, $4,750,000" (published November 24, 2008).[5] Given the prices in this advertisement, the land given to Shishin and Lovyrev was worth over $2.5 million for each.

---

[*] Once the site of a manor belonging to a prominent Russian merchant named Trapeznikov, the region was nationalized by Soviet authorities after the Bolshevik Revolution. In the 1920s and 1930s the village was tasked with providing eggs, milk, meat, and vegetables for the Kremlin. Because of the sensitive role it played, Gorki-2 was kept under the personal control of Felix Dzerzhinsky himself. After World War II the village continued to provide the leaders of the Soviet state with food, including milk for Soviet leader Nikita Khrushchev.

Alksnis began to hear from his constituents, who were angry about the transactions. He sent a formal inquiry to the local authorities about the deals and forwarded it to the government of the Moscow region, but he was told not to worry. Without a response from the government, he turned to the press. When Irina Borogan's story about the land transactions was published in *Novaya Gazeta* in March 2006, it went all but unnoticed by the authorities.[6]

When the authors sought further investigation with a federal property agency, they were told that the lands had been granted for free under a law designed to guarantee modest apartments for army or security service veterans. In this case, the law had been used to hand some of the most expensive land in Russia to FSB officials.[7]

Had law enforcement agencies performed an investigation, the practice of giving out precious lands to FSB leadership might have been described as unauthorized generals' initiative. Instead, in this case, it seemed to be state policy.

In 2007, Alksnis lost his seat in the parliamentary elections. The Kremlin changed the rules governing parliamentary elections, so that independent candidates were no longer permitted to run. Only officially registered parties were eligible to compete—and Alksnis's name was simply dropped from the party list.

WHILE GENERALS WERE showered with free property in the elite district, discontent was brewing among lower-level FSB agents. Tensions reached a boiling point over a decision to introduce a new salary system known as "Factor 2.2," under which FSB administrative officers would receive 2.2 times more pay than case officers of equal rank. By 2008, FSB officers had started to sue their leadership in Moscow military courts, demanding apartments and benefits, as promised by Russian law.

In response, the FSB created a department aimed at protecting high-ranking generals from such lawsuits. An FSB colonel told the authors: "This department was established to protect FSB leadership, not ordinary officers. At one meeting, generals of my section were asked why there was such a big difference in salaries. They answered that the Motherland once had no money. Now, the country had the resources and so they should be paid adequately for their work." In 2008, the authors learned that a number of FSB officers had turned to the European Court of Human Rights in Strasbourg, declaring that the leadership of the FSB was discriminating against them.[8] The first decision in the cases came on January 14, 2010, and found in favor of the petitioners.[9]

IN ADDITION TO amassing physical property, FSB leaders were also keen to enrich members of their families. Land in the Rublyovka corridor was granted to Alexander and Vladislav Ugryumov, two sons of German Ugryumov, the chief of the FSB's counterterrorism department in the early 2000s.[10]

Andrei Patrushev, whose father Nikolai was director of the FSB from 1999 to 2008, was granted a full-time position as adviser to Igor Sechin, the chairman of the Rosneft state oil company. In 2007, President Putin gave Patrushev, 26, an award for his service to the state.[11] Patrushev had been working as an adviser to the chairman of Rosneft for seven months, and before that had served for three years at the Economic Security Service of the FSB.[12]

On the same day, Nikolai Patrushev's brother Viktor, who worked for seven years with the mobile-phone operator Megafon, was awarded the Order of Friendship. This apparently strange choice of the order, usually awarded to artists and foreign sportsmen "for strengthening friendship and cooperation between the Russian Federation and other countries," might be explained by the fact that early in 2006 Victor had already been given the Order of Honor by Putin "for his merits in development of physical culture and sports." The FSB director's brother served as an adviser to the chairman of Dynamo, a sports club that had been patronized by the state security services since the 1920s.[13]

Whether in the form of valuable land, luxury cars, or merit awards, the perks afforded FSB employees (especially those in particularly good standing) offer significant means of personal advancement. Russia's new security services are more than simply servants of the state—they are landed property owners and powerful players, capable of influencing hiring decisions and planting cronies and relatives in positions of power.

THE LOVE OF THE GAME
THE FSB AND NATIONAL SPORT

WITHIN THE VEILED world of the Russian security services, sport has proven far more than a means of entertainment. The services' close affiliation with particular sports associations is both more sinister and more pragmatic. The clubs, which have maintained intimate ties with the security services since the Soviet era, offer elite training grounds for special operations forces as well as a bevy of useful contacts for servicemen.

On Wednesday, October 23, 2002, several FSB generals were called to the Lubyanka headquarters for a big celebration. The leadership, including director Nikolai Patrushev and two of his deputies, Vladimir Pronichev and Victor Komogorov, presented awards to the trainers and members of the Dynamo volleyball team for distinguished results in the Eleventh National Championship of the Russian Super League.[1] (Volleyball, which Patrushev himself played, was his favorite sport.) Pronichev, Patrushev's closest deputy, headed the Dynamo Sports Association, which at this point consisted of a soccer club, two ice hockey teams, basketball and volleyball teams, stadiums, and other clubs. The security services and Dynamo have been inseparable since 1923 when the club was founded; Pronichev served as head of association beginning in

2000, and Victor Komogorov held another top position in the sports organization. For his part, Patrushev led Dynamo's volleyball club.

A few hours after the ceremony, Chechen terrorists seized a theater in the center of Moscow that was packed with more than eight hundred people, in what would prove one of Russia's worst terrorist attacks of the decade.

But the attack did not deflect the FSB leadership's fondness for sport. On Saturday, October 26, in the chaotic aftermath of the siege, the FSB director appeared at a stadium in Moscow to cheer on Dynamo's volleyball team against Neftyanik Bashkirii in the opening game of the season.[2]

PATRUSHEV'S ATTENTION TO volleyball opens a window on how the security services managed to regain some of their lost prestige in the decade of Putin's rule. In Soviet times it was common for the KGB and the military to enjoy extremely close relations with sports clubs. After the uncertain challenges of the 1990s—during which the FSB lost control of Dynamo—Patrushev and his generals regained control after 2000.

The Soviet tradition was to tightly weave together the ranks of the security services and army with specific sport clubs. Dynamo was a club for the KGB and Interior Ministry, while the Central Army Sports Club (CSKA) was tied to the army. It was not a matter of choice: All the athletes in the army were automatically members of CSKA, just as their counterparts in state security were part of Dynamo. When KGB officers passed physical training they sported the Dynamo insignia on their clothing. In turn, all professional athletes competing in national and international championships representing Dynamo or CSKA displayed their military ranks. Lieutenants became majors and colonels on the strength of their sporting prowess. Vyacheslav Fetisov, the Russian minister of sport from 2004 to 2008, was a famous Soviet ice hockey defenseman and a longtime captain of the Soviet Union national team who subsequently played for CSKA, the New Jersey Devils, and the Detroit Red Wings. He won the Stanley Cup twice and held the rank of major in the Soviet army. Victor Shilov, a famous Dynamo wing in the 1960s and 1970s, was given the rank of lieutenant captain in the KGB.[3] At the same time, in the late 1970s and early 1980s, Dynamo's facilities were used for ultra-secret training of KGB commandos.

In November 1978 two Cuban officers, Raúl Rizo and Ramiro Chirino, secretly went to Moscow. Prominent karate instructors, they were invited to the Soviet Union because Vladimir Pirozhkov, deputy chairman of the KGB, had been impressed by the Cuban martial arts training system.* The Cubans showed him so-called "operative karate," suitable for special operations forces.

In the Soviet Union karate was considered the most dangerous martial art, and training or competitions were permitted only for the KGB elite personnel. For three months Rizo and Chirino trained more than a hundred KGB officers in the Dynamo club on Petrovka Street in central Moscow. Only fifteen were given the rank of instructor. Their skills were considered so secret that KGB officers were only allowed to take part in internal competitions at

---

* Pirozhkov was in charge of the KGB antiterrorist group Alpha (the Russian version of the U.S. Delta Force), and he persuaded Yuri Andropov to ask Fidel Castro to send some instructors to the KGB.

Dynamo and were forbidden from competing with sportsmen from other clubs. Until 1991 there were two versions of karate in Russia: the Dynamo type, which was martial; and the non-Dynamo type, which was for competitions.

At Dynamo, trainers, staff, and administrators were appointed and monitored by the state security organizations for generations. By the end of the 1950s, all leading positions at the club were filled on the orders of the security services. For many years Dynamo served as a training base for both the KGB and the Interior Ministry. KGB officers from the active reserve were given jobs throughout the club.

After the Soviet collapse, those officers who had been assigned to the club from the KGB were called back,[4] and funding to the club was cut. The secret services formally retained their interest in Dynamo, but control over the club fell to the Interior Ministry.

Yeltsin brought the security services officers back into the Dynamo organization with a 1996 decree establishing the "Dynamo State Sports Association," an umbrella group overseeing different sports and arenas. Security service officers began to filter back into the club apparatus. Out of 500 officers attached to the club, 226 came from the Ministry of Internal Affairs, 78 from the FSB, 52 from the Border Service, 11 from the foreign intelligence service, 90 from the tax police, and 43 from the communications agency.[5]

The decree was not fully executed until December 1999, although the reason for the delay has never been revealed.[6] The FSB openly took over Dynamo in 2000, when the FSB deputy director, Pronichev, a muscular general popular in the ranks because of his experience in special operations, was appointed chairman of Dynamo's national association. Sergei Stepashin, who had served as head of the FSB in 1994–1995 and as prime minister briefly in 1999, was named chairman of the club's board of trustees. The links were reinforced by appointments at the regional level. For example, Victor Zakharov, the chief of the Moscow department of the FSB, headed Moscow city's Dynamo organization.

With the FSB as its patron, Dynamo, which for a decade had suffered from a shortage of cash, saw its financial problems disappear. In 2001 the club signed a sponsorship deal with Mikhail Khodorkovsky's Yukos, then the country's largest oil company. When Khodorkovsky was arrested in 2003 and Yukos began to sink under the weight of official pressure, Dynamo turned to another investor, signing a new sponsorship contract in 2004 with Monaco-based Russian businessman Alexei Fedorychev, head of the sulfur supplier Fedcominvest. Fedorychev lost no time in pumping an estimated $200 million into the club. Dynamo's next sponsor, under a pact signed in February 2008, was Metalloinvest, owned by steel magnate Alisher Usmanov, a Dynamo fan for many years. In April 2009 the Russian state bank Vneshtorgbank announced that it had become Dynamo's general sponsor, replacing Metalloinvest, to help the financially strapped club repay a loan to the bank for construction of a new stadium.

Sponsors are critical to the success of sports clubs in Russia, which draw less revenue from ticket sales. According to Dynamo, in 2009 outside sponsors were expected to provide 1 billion out of a budget of 1.8 billion rubles.[7]

To sports clubs, having the FSB's protection means an end to their funding problems, open doors to governors in the regions, and even occasional access to the Kremlin. That is much better than the sports clubs' situation in the 1990s, when criminal authorities offered clubs their money and friendship in exchange for an improved public image.

More prestige than business, sport became an easy and convenient way for FSB generals to establish unofficial contacts with important people. The national volleyball federation was long controlled by FSB generals, including Patrushev after 2004. The next seat at the federation's leadership table, after Patrushev, was occupied by Oleg Dobrodeev, a general director of the All Russia State Television and Radio Company, who was elected vice president. In October 2009, Russian president Dmitry Medvedev ordered state security officials to leave their posts as heads of sport federations, saying the sports groups should be led by professionals. Most of the government officials complied. Officially the FSB also complied, but in fact the agency managed to maintain control. On November 18, 2009, Patrushev retired as president of the federation but was immediately elected chairman of its advisory council, while two FSB generals retained their federation positions.[8]

While Dynamo was carefully passed from hand to hand among tycoons willing to support the FSB-backed club, former state security officers were placed in crucial posts in other sports organizations. In 2003, Vladimir Plushev was appointed main trainer of the Russian national hockey team; he was also a lieutenant colonel in the counterterrorism section of the KGB. In 2004, another counterterrorism expert, Mikhail Golovatov, was named chairman of the Russian ski federation. In the past Golovatov had been a member of the national ski team—and in the early 1990s, Golovatov headed the KGB special operations unit Alpha.[9]

In October 2006 colonel Nikolai Malikov, director of the central sports club of the FSB Border Guards service, was chosen to become the main trainer of the Russian national pig team by the Sport Pig Federation, which claims more than a hundred member organizations. Since 2005 the Sport Pig Federation has been hosting Pig Olympics in Moscow, which were attended in 2008 by Vladimir Putin. Piglets competed in three events: pig racing, pig swimming, and "pigball."[10] "We got seventeen applications from different countries," explained Boris Bukalov, the president of the federation, "but at a meeting with candidates, our compatriot [Malikov] won their hearts unconditionally, and the commission could not oppose such a choice. Thus the executive committee has unanimously approved as the deserved trainer of Russia, the doctor of pedagogical sciences Nikolai Malikov."

By meeting in the sports arena, security service officers and influential businessmen, thinkers, and media people maintain close ties in a seemingly innocuous environment.

THE RENAISSANCE
OF YURI ANDROPOV

AS PART OF Putin's strategic campaign to bolster the security services' prestige in the aftermath of the Soviet Union's fall, he carefully devised an embellished narrative of Yuri Andropov, depicting the ruthless KGB head as a competent, effective leader, with an excellent understanding of national and global economics. While leading the FSB into a new era of service—one in which counterterrorism weighed heavily—Putin chose to praise a leader of the old guard, and a leader with a brutal legacy.

After the failed coup attempt against Soviet President Mikhail Gorbachev in August 1991, large crowds outside the KGB's Moscow headquarters toppled the statue of Felix Dzerzinsky, the first head of the Soviet secret police after the Bolshevik Revolution. On one corner of the building was a plaque honoring Yuri Andropov, the longest-serving head of the Soviet secret police and general secretary before his death in 1984. As crowds swarmed over the Dzerzinsky statue, KGB officers, in the dark of the night, quietly removed the Andropov plaque to prevent its destruction.

In the summer of 1999, when Putin was still head of the FSB, the decision was made to restore Andropov's plaque on the building. On December 20, 1999, Putin attended the ceremony reinstalling the plaque, in his new role as prime minister.[1]

The occasion marked the start of an official campaign to promote Andropov's legacy as proof that the security services could lead Russia out of its troubles. The aim was to use his persona to exemplify the state security approach to solving the problems of the state—political as well as social and economic. At the same time, the image of a ruthless champion of discipline and control appealed to a security service eager to define themselves after a decade of uncertainty.

The facts about Andropov were far from laudable. To mask the less savory details of his life, the FSB presented him as a modest, highly intellectual ascetic—a poet who also had a grasp of economics, and a man who worked hard to fight corruption.

In truth, Andropov was a brutal chief of the Soviet secret police for nineteen years. His term as general secretary lasted a scant fifteen months—hardly enough time to allow him to pursue lasting change.

Andropov put himself on the map in 1954 when he was sent as the Soviet ambassador to Hungary, a position he maintained during the 1956 Hungarian uprising. According to the British historian of intelligence services Christopher Andrew, the horrific reaction of the Hungarian resistance left a deep impression on Andropov. He had "watched in horror from the windows of his embassy as officers of the hated Hungarian security service were strung up from lampposts. Andropov was haunted by the speed with which an apparently all-powerful Communist one-party state had begun to topple."[2]

In 1967 Andropov was appointed head of the KGB. Obsessed with the dissident movement, two months after his appointment he created the notorious Fifth Directorate of the KGB, which was responsible for political investigations.[3] In his view, dissidents "violate the law, they supply the West with libelous information, they spread false rumors, and they try to organize various anti-Soviet sorties. These renegades have no foothold and can have none within our country."[4]

As head of the KGB, Andropov expanded the policy of confining dissidents to psychiatric institutions. Vladimir Bukovsky, one of the founders of the dissident movement, was sent to a psychiatric clinic in 1963 for two years for photocopying anti-Soviet literature (an illegal act), namely *The New Class* by Milovan Djilas. Institutionalization was not limited to those guilty of political opposition. Mikhail Shemyakin, a famous Russian sculptor, was subjected to forced psychiatric treatment to "cure" him of views that did not conform to Soviet norms. Bukovsky and Shemyakin were eventually expelled from the Soviet Union in 1976 and 1971, respectively.

As modern security service leaders constructed their image, they studiously avoided Andropov's infamous past. Instead, they borrowed a page from Andropov's own propaganda efforts. Andropov had engaged in a celebratory campaign for Felix Dzerzhinsky, the founder of Soviet state security, by sidestepping the details of Dzerzhinsky's past and highlighting his personal qualities.[5] As Andropov portrayed him, Dzerzhinsky was an extremely shy, ascetic man who slept on a narrow iron bed and ate only the most meager rations of food.

The mythmaking about Andropov borrowed the same approach. When Russia marked the ninetieth anniversary of Andropov's birth in June 2004, celebrations included renaming a school after him, unveiling a ten-foot-tall Andropov statue, and several new scholarships in his name for students wanting to train as intelligence officers. In Andropov's home village of Nagutskaya, celebratory events were attended by Alexander Zhdankov, the deputy head of the FSB, and several local dignitaries.

In the same year, several laudatory books were published as part of the FSB's Andropov campaign, with titles such as *Unknown Andropov, Team of Andropov, Yuri Andropov: Unknown About Known,* and *Andropov.* Nikolai Patrushev, then director of the FSB, wrote a major article in the state-owned newspaper *Rossiyskaya Gazeta* titled "The Mystery of Andropov," in which he stated that the officers of the FSB tend "to keep the best professional, patriotic values, formed by this uncommon person, the professional politician-intellectual who created a structure appropriate to the needs of the [times of Andropov]."[6]

In addition to his strong prowess as a leader, Andropov was celebrated as a great economic mind in an effort to recast the state security services as historically involved in the country's economic policy. In the early 2000s, an exhibition at the FSB museum was changed so that statements by Andropov's predecessor Dzerzhinsky about economics and fighting bureaucracy were hung on a wall. Moscow mayor Yuri Luzhkov proposed in 2002 to restore the monument to Dzerzhinsky on Lubyanka Square: "Dzerzhinsky is primarily associated with the solution of the problems of vagrancy, restoration of the railroads, and economic recovery. The NKVD and KGB were after Dzerzhinsky."[7]

Andropov became the second brilliant economist of the system. The story was widely disseminated that, after the long years of stagnation under Brezhnev, Andropov intended to embark on a program of economic reforms and was in fact the real initiator of perestroika, the restructuring later carried out by Gorbachev.

As the story went, it was only Andropov's death in 1984 that prevented his plans from being realized. Olga Kryshtanovskaya, the head of the Russian Academy of Sciences Institute for Elite Studies, said in a 2007 interview: "Andropov thought that the Communist Party had to keep power in its hands and to conduct an economic liberalization. This was the path China followed. For people in the security services, China is the ideal model. They see this as the correct course. They think that Yeltsin went along the wrong path, as did Gorbachev."[8]

TAKING THE MYTHMAKING to an even grander level, a top FSB official declared that the security services had created a whole pantheon of great managers. In a 2001 interview, Vladimir Shults, then the first deputy director of the FSB, said this band of officials included Felix Dzerzhinsky, Yuri Andropov, Sergei Stepashin (director of the FSB in 1994–1995 and prime minister in 1999), Vladimir Putin, and Nikolai Patrushev (by then director of the FSB).[9]

From the point of view of the FSB, it was important to show the public that the country needed the economic know-how of the security services, in order to justify their rise into high-level positions in government and business. These management positions demand knowledge that isn't taught in the FSB Academy. The generals and colonels have to have an explanation—for themselves as well as for society—of why they are qualified for work not in their background.[10]

Andropov's legacy also furthered the idea promulgated by the FSB that the country's difficulties were caused by external enemies rather than internal problems. One of the key people involved in the Andropov campaign was Oleg Khlobustov, an FSB colonel, lecturer, and senior research fellow at the FSB Academy, and the author of the book *The Unknown Andropov*. In his lecture "The Phenomenon of Andropov," delivered at Lubyanka in December 2004, he quoted Andropov as saying: "Nowadays the source of threats to the security of the USSR lies outside. From the outside the class enemy tries to transfer subversive activities onto our territory, to provoke ideological diversions."[11]

This point of view is widely shared by contemporary FSB officers in Russia. Opposition movements are largely considered to be sponsored by Western donors keen to organize a Russian version of the so-called Orange Revolution—a series of protests in Ukraine from November 2004 to January 2005 in response to what Ukrainians declared was a rigged vote, which ultimately led to a new vote in which pro-Western candidate Viktor Yushchenko emerged victorious. These fears were strengthened on the eve of the Russian presidential elections of 2008.

After it was toppled from in front of the Lubyanka headquarters, the 15-ton statue of Dzerzhinsky was transferred to a small park behind a Moscow arts center. The park became known as the Graveyard of Fallen Monuments.

Every year some Russian politicians, including Communist revanchists, campaign for reinstating the statue. And each time, they are opposed by human rights activists. Some liberals feared Putin would re-establish the statue during his presidential term. But it never happened. During his term, Putin erected new monuments to Andropov and Dzerzhinsky but never attempted to resurrect the large statue in the square.

In reality, the myth of Andropov turned out to be largely directed at the security services' rank and file; in one case, a statue of Dzerzhinsky was restored only inside a courtyard of a national police building at Petrovka 38. Putin and the security services seemed well aware that Russian society was indifferent to the legacy of Soviet state security, and they made no attempt to force it upon the general public. The supposed resurrection of the KGB's pantheon of heroes pleased Putin only when this activity was limited by the secret services. Even as they attempted to create a new version of the Andropov legacy, the security services kept a lid on the evidence of the real history.

Today, archives concerning Soviet state security remain largely closed. Many holdings are available only to people in the secret services, and nineteen years after the fall of the Soviet Union it is still widely debated whether the KGB archives should be opened to the public. Meanwhile, some archives opened in the 1990s were closed down again in the decade Putin was in power.

In the early 1990s the Russian authorities were keen to declassify the KGB archives. In December 1991, a commission on declassifying the records of the Communist Party Central Committee was created under Dmitri Volkogonov, a leading Russian military historian.

In 1992, Yeltsin's government invited the Soviet dissident Vladimir Bukovsky to testify at the trial of the Communist Party of the Soviet Union in the Constitutional Court of Russia. To prepare for his testimony, Bukovsky was granted access to a large number of documents from Soviet archives. Using a small handheld scanner and a laptop computer, he managed to secretly scan many documents—including KGB reports to the Central Committee— and smuggle the files to the West. (As Bukovsky later told the authors, he was allowed to scan these documents simply because archive officials didn't know what the scanner was.)

Bukovsky's efforts resulted in a book, *Judgment in Moscow*, and a Web site.[12]

In 1993 Russia joined the International Council on Archives, which created a group of experts formed to prepare an account of the archives of repressive regimes and offer recommendations for working with such archives. But after the bloody conflict between Yeltsin and the Supreme Soviet in October 1993, the question of transferring the archives of law enforcement ministries and secret services was dropped.

The majority of the Soviet Union–era secret service archives simply remained in the record offices of the FSB, the Ministry of Internal Affairs, and the Military Office of the Public Prosecutor. Finally, an Interagency Commission to Protect State Secrets was created in place of the declassification commission. As a result, the collection of documents that had been publicly available before 1995 was closed. For example, Nikita Petrov, an expert from Memorial, the human rights organization, said that previously declassified Central Committee of the Soviet Communist Party documents have been withdrawn from the Russian State Archive of Recent History by the foreign intelligence service.[13]

IN MAY 2006, in honor of the thirtieth anniversary of the Moscow Helsinki Watch Group, the National Security Archive at George Washington University posted on the Internet a series of documents from the former Soviet Union related to the Moscow Helsinki Group, including the KGB's reports to the Central Committee about the "anti-social elements" who had started the group thirty years earlier, and the various repressive measures the KGB took "to put an end to their hostile activities."

Most of the documents posted by the National Security Archive came from the Volkogonov Collection, which Volkogonov donated to the Library of Congress in the 1990s. Thus these reports documenting the regime's efforts to suppress dissent were available on the Web in 2006 in Russian and in English translation, while in Russia these documents were sealed and classified throughout the decade of the 2000s on the basis of the State Secrets law.[14]

In July 2007 the FSB claimed that 2 million documents about repression between 1920 and 1950 were open to the public. The statement was widely seen as evidence of the FSB's openness and willingness to disclose the contents of the archives. But in fact the documents were unavailable to historians: Access to them is granted only to relatives of victims.

The same deceptive approach was employed with documents concerning the massacre of Katyn, an issue that is still a thorn in the side of Polish-Russian relations. In 1940, throughout Russia and the Ukraine (most notably in the Katyn forest in western Russia), thousands of imprisoned Polish officers were slaughtered. Soviet authorities denied responsibility, laying the blame on the Germans. Only in 1990 did Mikhail Gorbachev admit that the Soviets had killed the Polish prisoners. Yeltsin opened up classified files on the case for investigation, but in the Putin decade Russia's military prosecutor shut down the inquiry.

In January 2009 Russia's high court threw out a bid by campaigners to reopen an investigation on the grounds that all the perpetrators called to account in the inquiry have died, and relatives have failed to offer genetic evidence linking them to those killed in the massacres. According to Anna Stavitskaya, the lawyer for relatives of ten of the Katyn victims, "the decision meant the end of efforts by campaigners to resolve the issue in Russia," and the group would now turn to the European Court of Human Rights in Strasbourg.[15] However, after the Polish president Kaczynski's aircraft crashed near Smolensk on April 10, 2010, Medvedev handed over 67 volumes of documents on the Katyn massacre to Poland.

At the end of 2008, the FSB department in Tver, a region outside of Moscow, published a book celebrating the department's ninetieth anniversary. In it, Dmitri Tokarev, a major in the NKVD (a predecessor to the KGB) was portrayed as having played a key role in the leadership of local state security. Tokarev led Tver's NKVD in 1938–1945 and was shown as a war hero and effective German spy catcher. But his department was also responsible for the execution of 6,000 Polish officers in the Ostashkov camp in the spring of 1940. The reports on executions—called "implementations"—were signed by Tokarev.[16] No mention of the tragedy was made within the book.

THERE HAS NEVER been a full accounting of the misdeeds of the Soviet secret police. Any such airing of history would inevitably point to many who served in the KGB. The archives that would reveal these secrets have been steadfastly closed. The FSB, veterans of the KGB, want to keep it that way. In so doing, they perpetuate a more innocent history of Soviet-era events, while positioning Andropov as a hero to be celebrated.

THE PROPAGANDA MACHINE
IMAGE-MAKING AND THE FSB

I N DEALING WITH public opinion, the security services of Russia had their work cut out for them. They were the heirs of organizations—the KGB in particular—that had been paragons of secrecy and had never needed to explain themselves to the public. In the Soviet system, the state and party dominated all: There was no civil society to link the people with their rulers. But in the new Russia, a noisy, imperfect democracy was on the rise—green shoots of civil society that the security services could neither ignore nor hide.

In the decade of Putin, one way the FSB handled the tension between past and present was through propaganda films that portrayed security services as they wanted to see themselves—as special agents performing heroic deeds. Although there were many possible channels for influencing the public such as books, news media, and the Internet the FSB decided to put an emphasis on cinema and television. These efforts offer another window into how the resurgent security services operate in the new Russia.

In 2001, a series, *The Special Department*, appeared on television. In it, FSB agents in St. Petersburg prevented the theft and smuggling of valuable Russian artworks. The main hero of the show is a descendent of the city's old intelligentsia who served in special forces in Afghanistan and has returned to protect the artifacts of Russian museums like the Hermitage. *Secret Watch*, a television series about the FSB Surveillance Service, began airing in the fall of 2005. The show, which featured secret agents following people and tracking down terrorists, was also produced with the support of the FSB. In 2007 Russian TV broadcast *Special Group*, a 16-part television movie about the Moscow FSB's heroic acts, such as preventing a terrorist plot and investigating financial transactions. Once again, the FSB was behind the production.

In December 2004, the FSB's biggest blockbuster premiered— the $7 million *Lichnyy Nomer* (or *Dogtag*, but titled *Countdown* in English).[1] The movie, a fictionalized account of two actual terrorist attacks (the 1999 Moscow apartment building bombings and the 2002 Dubrovka Theater siege), was intended to shed favorable light on the FSB.

The portrayal of the bombings in Moscow were left largely unaltered, but in the case of the Nord-Ost hostage crisis, the film's producers replaced the actual theater with a circus. The protagonist was an FSB officer who was captured in Chechnya and forced to admit he had taken part in the bombings. (This was a fictionalized version of a real and controversial story of the military intelligence officer Alexei Galtin, who was captured by Chechens and had made a similar statement on video. Galtin was later to escape and to disavow his claims as made under torture.)[2]

In the film, an oligarch named Pokrovsky, living in exile in the West, defied the Russian president and colluded with Arab terrorists and Chechens on a hostage-taking plan targeting the Moscow circus. Pokrovsky's details bore a striking resemblance to those of

Russian tycoon Boris Berezovsky, who fled to London in 2001. But the hostage taking is only the first stage of a much bigger terrorist attack—the planned bombing of the G8 summit in Rome. The main character, an FSB officer, saves the day by rescuing the hostages and defeating the terrorists.

The producers of the film made no secret of the fact that they were advised by Vladimir Anisimov, who was then deputy director of the FSB, or that the project was filmed with the service's support.[3] Yuri Gladilshikov, a leading film critic, said, "We face the first private commercial counterterrorism blockbuster that appears to be made with the support of the secret services." He added, "It was the first time since Soviet times that the state understood the power of cinematography."[4]

IN FEBRUARY 2006, the FSB reestablished a competition that had existed under Andropov, for the best literary and artistic works about state security operatives.[5] Oleg Matveyev, the officer of the FSB Center for Public Communications, acknowledged that the service was openly returning to KGB traditions. He told the newspaper *Kommersant*, "This is returning to past experience. From 1978 to 1988 there was a KGB award for art. It was also awarded to those who created a positive image of KGB employees. . . . Nowadays, whether in the cinema, in TV serials, or in detective series, it's common for special services to be shown in a negative light, so we have decided to revive this competition, to reward those who do not discredit employees of the secret services, and to create a positive image of the defenders."[6]

The first year, the award went to *Lichnyy Nomer*.

The next movie hit was *Kod Apokalipsisa* (Apocalypse Code), in which the female protagonist—an attractive FSB colonel—saves seven world capitals. It was given the FSB award in 2007, and the movie *Likvidacia* (*Liquidation*), about the security service struggle against criminal gangs in Odessa soon after World War II, won in 2008.[7]

Following the success of *Lichnyy Nomer*, the FSB turned to Russian state TV. Documentaries were considered the best propaganda vehicle, because they are cheaper, can be produced more quickly, and can be presented as an independent journalistic investigation, thereby relieving the FSB of connections. Best of all, they guarantee direct access to millions of viewers.

In January 2006, the documentary titled *Shpioni* (*The Spies*), devoted to British spy activity in Russia, offered the FSB a boost. The film's director, journalist Arkady Mamontov, showed a video taken by an FSB surveillance team of a British embassy official walking on an unnamed Moscow Street. The FSB claimed in the film that the British diplomat, identified as Marc Doe, was trying to retrieve data from a spy communications device disguised as a rock, later widely known as the "spy rock."[8]

An X-ray of the rock shown in the film, displaying four big batteries and a radio transmitter tightly packed together, was offered as proof of Doe's involvement in espionage. Then Mamontov's documentary investigated Doe's ties with Russian nongovernmental organizations: The names of the most respectable Russian NGOs were shown in the list of the organizations financially supported by the British government, and Doe was called the handler of the NGOs.

The documentary, which aired two weeks after Putin signed legislation toughening the rules for nongovernmental organizations, was used to show that the largest such organizations working in Russia are in touch with British intelligence.[9]

The FSB's Center for Public Communications gladly displayed an example of such a spy rock to journalists. Sergei Ignatchenko, the spokesman for the FSB, said, "According to our experts, this device cost millions of pounds. It's a miracle of technology."[10] The FSB claimed that one Russian was suspected of espionage for England, but it turned out that no foreign spies had been detained. The FSB said that the Russian was arrested, but no trial followed. What is more, the FSB did not even seize the spy rock as proof of espionage. (According to Ignatchenko, the rock presented at the press conference was later found in a different part of Moscow.)[11] In the end, four members of the British embassy staff were accused of taking part in a spy ring, but they were not expelled from Russia, which is highly unusual for true espionage cases.[12]

While *Shpioni* was seen by many as transparent propaganda, it nonetheless intimidated nongovernmental organizations, which feared they could be accused of harboring spies.

Shpioni set the tone for subsequent documentaries. In one called *Plan Kavkaz* (*Caucasus Plan*), shown in April 2008, a journalist claimed to have found evidence of the CIA's backing for the first Chechen war.[13]

IN 2000, THE authors of this book worked at the daily newspaper *Izvestia*. That summer, Soldatov was called by Olga Kostina, a public relations officer who had once worked for MENATEP, a bank owned by oligarch Mikhail Khodorkovsky. She explained that the FSB had created an "unofficial" press service to which journalists could turn more freely than to the agency's official public communications center, and she was hired to organize this work. She told Soldatov that there was also a high-level commission being formed within the FSB to oversee the new approach.[14]

Kostina soon organized an interview for Soldatov with Victor Zakharov, the newly appointed chief of the FSB's Moscow department. (At the time, rumors were circulating that Putin was planning to make changes at the FSB, and an interview with a top official might be a chance to get some real information.) But once he arrived, Soldatov found himself seated in a large conference room with a gigantic extended table. Nine or ten consultants sat around the table, hindering Soldatov from addressing Zakharov. At the far end of the table sat the FSB general, in uniform, with a chubby, inexpressive look.

He was holding a few sheets of paper. They carried the questions that Soldatov had submitted in advance and the previously approved answers.

Zakharov started to read the papers aloud, and Soldatov, frustrated, attempted to ask him some questions, but his response was formal: "There is nothing special about my destiny," the FSB general said. "I was born into a family of workers, and in 1973 I graduated from the Moscow Institute of Railway Engineers." He had entered the KGB in 1975. At the end of the meeting Zakharov brightened when he gave Soldatov a tape containing songs about the FSB. All of them had been written by Vasily Stavitsky, then the chief of the center of public communications of the FSB and a recognized poet of the secret services.

The general had given an interview, but had failed to supply any information.

One of the songs became an FSB official hymn, with the words:

Always at the front,
Always at one's post,

Don't touch Russia—
A Chekist is always vigilant.[15]

The following week Kostina invited Soldatov to join the "pool" of journalists briefed by the FSB. Soldatov was told that there were five journalists from different newspapers in the pool, who were briefed regularly at the Lubyanka headquarters. They were all briefed at the same time, and that is exactly how their stories appeared: simultaneously, in their respective publications. After his experience with Zakharov, Soldatov declined. Soon afterwards the authors left *Izvestia*, which was becoming increasingly pro-government. But the pool remained active for years as an instrument for steering press coverage.

On January 29 and 30, 2001, the two biggest Russian daily papers *Izvestia* and *Komsomolskaya Pravda*, published front-page stories about a former Russian army noncommissioned officer, Vasily Kalinkin.[16] The articles claimed that he had deserted the Russian army to join the Chechen rebels in 1991 and had subsequently been trained in terrorist tactics in Afghanistan by an instructor named "Bill," (a thinly veiled hint at CIA involvement). The story claimed that Kalinkin had signed a document of cooperation with American intelligence before returning in 1994 to Russia, where he became an undercover agent. According to the newspaper accounts, Kalinkin waited six years for orders to blow up the Volga Hydroelectric Station—the largest of its kind in Europe, a 725-meter-long, 44-meter-high concrete dam that crosses the Volga River.

Both articles stated that in July 2000 representatives of the Chechen rebels went to Kalinkin with orders to carry out a terrorist attack on the Volgograd dam. In November of that year, Kalinkin gave himself up to a military counterintelligence unit.

These stories apparently planted by the FSB were full of holes: There was no explanation as to why Kalinkin had to spend six years as a stay-behind agent, why he was ordered to carry out a terrorist attack as late as 2000, or how he intended to blow up the hydroelectric station. A few days later, Kalinkin repeated his account in a press conference. He gave interviews to the Russian press in which he claimed the "recruiting document" he had signed had "in the left corner the Statue of Liberty and in [the] right the title 'Osama bin Laden Diversion School.'"[17] What was most telling was that the story appears to have been printed by two of the largest newspapers in Russia almost exactly as the FSB had wanted it to read, despite the lack of supporting evidence.

The Kalinkin case was an example of a tactic invented by the Soviet KGB and primarily used for operations abroad, known as "active measures," or political warfare usually aiming to influence the course of events in a particular country. A related tactic called "assistance programs" or "assistance operations" was intended to change the policy or position of the foreign government in a way that would "assist" the Soviet position.

To Sergei Tretyakov, a former Russian foreign intelligence officer in New York who defected to the United States in 2000, there is no difference between "active measures" and "assistance operations." He said to Soldatov, "In the First Chief Directorate of the KGB, a Section 'A' (for 'active measures') handled these operations. When the First Chief Directorate was renamed the Foreign Intelligence Service, its Section A was renamed the Section of Assistance Operations. In the early 1990s, the CIA had asked the foreign intelligence service to stop carrying out 'active measures' that undermined the national security of the United States. As a result, the section was given a new name, but its methods, structure, and employees were retained."[18]

Active measures were based on 95 percent objective information to which something was added to turn the data into targeted information or disinformation. In 1999 this approach was openly acknowledged when Zdanovich, then chief of the FSB's Center for Public Communications, presented himself as head of the new department for assistance programs. It embarrassed many FSB case officers, who were not happy that Zdanovich had revealed what was presumably a confidential term, and that he clearly presented himself as a chief of a disinformation unit.[19]

ON SEPTEMBER 9, 1999, shortly after midnight, between 600 and 800 pounds of explosives detonated on the ground floor of an apartment building on Guryanova Street in southeast Moscow. The nine-story building was destroyed, killing 94 people and injuring 249. On September 13 a large bomb exploded at 5:00 A.M. in the basement of an apartment block on Kashirskoye Highway in southern Moscow, about 3.7 miles from the site of the first attack: 118 people died and 200 were injured.

The bombings terrified the city, and Putin immediately blamed Chechen terrorists and prepared to launch a major military offensive into the republic. The bombings were a critical turning point in Putin's rise to power—his resolute response to the events, his deployment of troops, and his crude vow to "wipe out" the Chechens "in the outhouse" made him extremely popular. The question of who was responsible for the bombings—Chechens or someone else—has sparked debate that will not die. The debate mushroomed into a crisis of confidence in the FSB.

The terror the bombings inspired was so great that the authorities responded with frantic, widespread security measures, including stationing one soldier from the Interior Ministry in every building in the capital. (Soldiers were hastily deployed without rations, and in many cases Muscovites offered them food.) The panic deepened on September 22 in the wake of media reports that another terrorist attack on an apartment building had been foiled in the city of Ryazan, south of Moscow. According to initial media reports, an ignition device and explosives were found in the cellar of a Ryazan building on Novoselova Street, and the explosive material was similar to the hexogen used in Moscow. The Ryazan FSB department opened a criminal investigation immediately.

The same day, in Moscow, Alexander Zdanovich, the FSB's main spokesman, was a guest on the NTV interview show *Hero of the Day*. When asked about the details of the Ryazan investigation, he said, "According to preliminary conclusions, there was no hexogen found in Ryazan. There was no ignition device, just elements of an ignition device." But on September 24 the FSB director, Nikolai Patrushev, made the surprising statement in a television interview that the Ryazan episode had been an FSB training exercise. "First of all, there was no explosion. Second, an explosion was not prevented. But I think they didn't do their job very adeptly. It was a training: It was sugar, not explosives—and this training was carried out not only in Ryazan—and we must praise Ryazan's law enforcement and local population. They reacted appropriately. I believe this training should be close to what happens in the real situation." Zdanovich then said on television,

"Yes, in the framework of the counterterrorism operation, the FSB carried out a series of exercises in some Russian cities, including Ryazan. I want to say that in the other cities, which I don't want to identify, the measures didn't work, and the FSB officials, local law enforcement, and local authorities didn't do their job, nor did we get any signals from local residents." He added, "The next step in these exercises was Ryazan and first of all I have to say thank you to its citizens, and to the inhabitants of this specific building, for the vigilance they showed when they discovered these supposed explosives. And at the same time, I want to apologize to them."[20]

With these remarks, the leadership of the FSB utterly confused Russia's citizens. Since then, there have been persistent questions about the role of the FSB in the training exercise and the explosions. The authors believe that there were indeed exercises carried out in Ryazan. Such exercises are typical for Vympel, a special unit of the FSB with the mission of verifying the efficacy of counterterrorism measures at locales like nuclear plants. But it is also the authors' impression that the FSB needlessly bungled the crisis by giving an explanation that raised more questions than it answered. The idea that the FSB might have been involved in the bombings to help bring Putin to power became a runaway conspiracy theory. To date, the FSB has failed to counteract this speculation with convincing evidence of what did happen in Ryazan.

In 2002, some details of the Ryazan exercise were leaked to the monthly paper *Sovershenno Sekretno*, which has long been closely connected to the security services, but the story went almost unnoticed. The story said that two FSB special operations units, known as Alpha and Vympel, had been sent to Ryazan on September 20,

1999, to prevent a possible attack and check the preparedness of cities in the face of terrorism.[21]

Instead of providing the public with exhaustive explanations, the FSB did its best to silence questions. Former FSB officer Mikhail Trepashkin, now a lawyer, was invited by Sergei Kovalev, a member of the State Duma and famous dissident, to assist in an independent inquiry of the apartment bombings. Trepashkin had also been hired by two sisters whose mother had been killed in one of the buildings to represent them in the trial of two Russian suspects accused of transporting explosives. Trepashkin began to raise his own questions about the case, suggesting that the FSB might have been involved.[22] On October 22, 2003, Trepashkin was arrested for illegal arms possession, convicted, and sentenced by a closed military court to four years in jail in what appeared to be a setup.[23]

Shortly thereafter a disgruntled former FSB officer, Aleksander Litvinenko, who had fled Russia, and co-author Yuri Feltshinsky published a book, *Blowing Up Russia: Terror from Within,* in which they directly blamed the FSB for organizing a campaign of terrorism. On December 28, 2003, as the book was being shipped to Russia, 4,376 copies were seized by the FSB.

On January 28, 2004, former dissident Aleksander Podrabinek, who had imported the books to Russia, was called to Lefortovo and interrogated by the FSB.[24] In the authors' opinion, the book contained no new evidence against the FSB, and Trepashkin's claims of FSB involvement proved to be highly dubious.[25] But the FSB's response to Trepashkin and their ban of the book only served to strengthen the suspicions that the FSB was somehow complicit in the plot.

∞∞∞∞

UNDER YELTSIN THE 1990s were a period of remarkable openness in Russia when journalists were free to explore areas that had long been off-limits. Under Putin, the FSB returned to police state methods to deal with foreign journalists, using the threat of with-holding visas and access to the country as leverage in an effort to influence their coverage.[26]

In May 2002 Nikolai Volobuev, then the chief of the FSB's counterintelligence department, said thirty-one foreign journalists had had their press passes revoked because they were "conducting illegal journalist activity," and eighteen among them were refused entry to Russia and had their visas blocked for five years.[27] Since then this method has become common practice. According to the Center for Journalism in Extreme Situations, which is based in Moscow, more than forty journalists were refused entry to Russia between 2000 and 2007.

In July 2006 Russian authorities refused an entry visa to the British journalist Thomas de Waal.[28] The Russian Federal Migration Service explained that de Waal's application had been denied under a 1996 security law. The explanation might be that de Waal wrote ex-tensively on the war in Chechnya: In 1993–1997 he had worked in Russia covering the North Caucasus, and he co-authored the book *Chechnya: A Small Victorious War*. In 2003, he testified as an ex-pert witness for the defense at the extradition trial in Britain of Chechen rebel leader Akhmed Zakayev. In June 2008, British journal-ist Simon Pirani was refused entry to Russia, although he had a valid visa in his passport. Pirani, who writes about trade union issues, was told by Russian authorities he was deemed a security threat.[29]

Natalia Morar, a Moldovan citizen who works for the independent Russian weekly newsmagazine *New Times*, and who had lived in Moscow for six years, was refused re-entry to Russia in December 2007 after a business trip to Israel. Morar had covered corruption and written articles critical of high-level FSB officials. She was forced to fly to the capital of Moldova, where she was told by Russian embassy officials that she posed a threat to Russian national security. In February 2008 she arrived at Domodedovo airport in Moscow with her Russian husband, Ilya Barabanov (who also works with *New Times*), whom she had married since she had last been refused entry. But she was stopped at passport control at Domodedovo airport and told that her status had not changed despite her marriage.[30] Although she has continued to work for *New Times* covering corruption issues, her job has become increasingly difficult without access to Russian sources of information.

Meanwhile, the security services closed the doors of their press offices. By the mid-2000s the Federal Protective Service responded only to requests for filming or photographing inside the Kremlin. Military intelligence has no press office at all, the foreign intelligence service refuses to comment on anything that happened after 1961, and the FSB's Center for Public Communications has tended not to answer media requests even under the threat of legal prosecution.

In 2009 the Directorate of Assistance Programs (which includes the Center for Public Communications) was given new powers. On July 15 Alexander Bortnikov, then director of the FSB, expanded the list of FSB generals allowed to "initiate petitions to conduct counterintelligence measures that restrict the constitutional rights of citizens" (in other words, that compromise the right to privacy of correspondence and communications, as well as the inviolability of the home).[31] Under Bortnikov's direction, these generals now have the authority to order wiretapping, surveillance, and the searching of premises.

The list, first established in 2007, was originally limited to heads of counterintelligence sections, the department of economic security, and the border guards, as well as FSB leadership. The order signed by Bortnikov in 2009 significantly expanded it to include the FSB Directorate for Assistance Programs.

According to the law, the FSB may carry out counterintelligence measures under the following conditions: There is information regarding signs of intelligence and other activity by foreign states' secret services or by individuals aimed at damaging Russia's security; there is a need to gather information about the activities posing a threat to Russia, protect state secrets, or monitor people who provide or have provided the FSB with confidential assistance; or it is necessary to ensure the FSB's own security or fulfill the requests of the secret services of other countries with which it is on good terms.

Russia's journalists obviously are not "clients" of the list—no bearers of state secrets, they might divulge secrets or names of agents only if they are told this information by FSB officers or other officials with access to such material. But to protect well-guarded secrets, the FSB has special units, from its main Counterintelligence Service to the Military Counterintelligence unit, which typically initiate prosecutions after journalists divulge sensitive information in print.

The lawyers and FSB officers the authors questioned related that the Directorate of Assistance Programs might have asked for a surveillance permit not to initiate criminal proceedings but to keep a closer eye on journalists. (Previously the chief of the directorate had to request permission from the head of the counterintelligence department to intercept journalists' correspondence. Now the head of the FSB's directorate in charge of dealing with journalists is able to carry out an order on his own.)

Bortnikov's order raises another question. FSB units are divided into operational and support units. The first (for instance, counterintelligence or counterterrorism) consist of operatives who recruit agents. Support units include, for example, the FSB's capital construction directorate, department of medicine, human resources, and (it was long believed) its directorate in charge of dealing with journalists.

The ability to order eavesdropping is obviously a method of operational units. Responding to Soldatov's question as to whether the Directorate of Assistance Programs is an operational unit, the officer on duty at the FSB Center for Public Communications replied, "It is defined by our internal regulatory documents, and nobody will [tell] you."[32]

While under Yeltsin journalists had experienced a certain breadth of freedom, Putin's desire to portray the security services in a positive light and to maintain strict control over what could and could not be investigated (or published) renewed Soviet-era policies of closed-door operations and no questions asked.

THE SECRET UNDERGROUND

MUCH ABOUT THE security services in Russia has been kept well cloaked, either locked in impenetrable archives, quite literally hidden in plain sight, or stashed below the very streets. A secret rabbit warren of tunnels, constructed during the Cold War years, continues to serve the security services today. When the KGB spread out through the Lubyanka Square neighborhood of Moscow, the buildings were often hidden. Passersby were confused by the absence of signs and the unusually high fences throughout the city that served to hide KGB and military facilities. But such obfuscations told only part of the story. The most secret sites were hidden beneath Moscow's streets.

From a hill near Moscow State University, Michurinsky Prospect runs southwest from the city center. A large part of Michurinsky Prospect—a tree-lined avenue in a desirable residential area—is occupied by an important secret services facility, the FSB Academy. A short distance from the academy are several empty fields. Underneath these open expanses is a maze of tunnels, rails, chambers, and secret entryways.

During the Cold War, in anticipation of nuclear conflict, Great Britain, the United States, and the Soviet Union built special underground bunkers where their respective leadership could seek refuge in the event of a nuclear attack. The Soviet Union built up its underground system far beyond those of the United States or England. Bunkers, underground factories, and tank tunnels turned Moscow's subsoil into Swiss cheese: According to independent experts, twelve levels of underground tunnels lie beneath the Russian capital. The largest of all is an underground subway system, known informally as Metro-2 and officially as D-6.[1] Running parallel to the public Moscow Metro, D-6 is used only by high-ranking officials. D-6 has been an ongoing project since the 1940s; its construction has never stopped. Although no official records are available, it is estimated that when the Soviet Union collapsed, D-6 consisted of four lines, seven stories below ground level. A special section in the KGB, the 15th Directorate, established in 1977, was placed in charge of its safety.[2] But in 1991, when the KGB was disbanded, the 15th Directorate was not included in the FSB or in the Federal Protective Service, responsible for the protection of senior state officials.

For three years, the 15th Directorate appeared to be nowhere. Finally, in 1994, came the first open document to mention the directorate's new title: the Main Directorate of Special Programs of the President (GUSP). This was a separate security service with a peculiar status; it was not given the status of an independent agency like most of the secret services, but rather was included in the Administration of the President. GUSP's guidelines were not established until 1996, and were promulgated by presidential decree.[3] GUSP was not sanctioned by any act of Parliament and came into existence without being subject to parliamentary scrutiny.

The leadership of GUSP was so determined to maintain maximum secrecy that it sometimes created problems for itself. Because it was not included in the list of Russian special services, GUSP's personnel did not have the right to carry weapons. Only in 1999 was this obstacle resolved. By the end of the 1990s GUSP followed the example of the FSB and started to expand its activity and resources. In 2000 it was reported that GUSP staff totaled 20,000 people.[4] To date, GUSP leaders have never made public statements; GUSP has no press office, and its Web site offers only official documents and its insignia.

GUSP's low profile has not, however, deterred public interest in Moscow's secret underground. Since the early 1990s unauthorized exploration of passages was popularized by the group Diggers of the Underground Planet, a loose collection of subterranean explorers formed by Vadim Mikhailov. A tall man with a pale, pockmarked face, Mikhailov began his underground adventure at an early age: His father, a train driver for the Moscow metro, would often take him into the operator's cabin. When he was 12, Mikhailov and some friends undertook their first journeys into the sprawling mass of tunnels, sewer systems, and natural passages beneath Moscow. It wasn't long before they made their first major discovery: a Stalin-era underground bunker deep below Leningradsky Prospect.

In the mid-1990s Mikhailov was an international media celebrity. He had become an underground guide whose signature tours ended with his emergence through a tunnel into prominent Moscow locations such as the center of Red Square.

The first disclosures of the underground system by the Russian press came after the Soviet collapse, in the newspaper *Argumenti I Fakti*. The 1992 article prompted a stream of stories about the secret metro underneath Moscow, and overnight Mikhailov found himself the only available expert.

But his group's activity was not limited to comments and interviews. Soon after the secret underground was revealed, Mikhailov started a campaign against the city government for allowing historically significant city sites to be disturbed by construction projects and for failing to properly maintain the water mains below many of the city's aging buildings. Mikhailov warned the authorities that many of the buildings, like the famed Durov Animal Theater, which suffered severe structural damage when pipes burst under it, were in danger of collapse.

In 1998 the Moscow authorities started to retaliate: Yuri Luzhkov, the mayor of Moscow, irritated by Mikhailov's prodding, ordered that the security of underground communications be improved, noting, "The penetration of these underground constructions by extraneous persons, including the so-called Diggers of the Underground Planet, has caused cables to be plundered, and arson attacks to take place. The mass media quite often publish unverified data, causing an unhealthy degree of public agitation."[5] The edict of the mayor stipulated the creation of groups to guard the entries to Moscow's underground.

Despite his adversarial relationship with Moscow's authorities, Mikhailov was often called upon when situations required his expertise. The Diggers helped the authorities in a successful manhunt for three convicted murderers who dug their way out of Butyrka Prison, and Mikhailov's team assisted in the rescue following the 1999 apartment bombings.

But the authorities increased their harassment. In June 2000 Irina Borogan was preparing a story about Moscow State University's underground for the newspaper *Izvestia*. She was accompanied by Mikhailov beneath the university's main building on

Sparrow Hills in the southwest of Moscow. The building, one of seven huge tiered neoclassical towers built in the Stalin era, was finished in 1953. The central tower is 240 meters tall, 36 stories high, and flanked by four huge wings of student and faculty accommodation. It is said to contain a total of 33 kilometers of corridors and 5,000 rooms. But its most impressive feature is the multilevel labyrinth that lies beneath the building, designed to shelter thousands of teachers and students should a nuclear attack ever occur.

Borogan and Mikhailov climbed down through a fountain near the main entrance to the university, via a ventilation shaft. A number of corridors spread out in all directions. Some of them, Borogan noted, were more than five meters high. According to the Diggers, there is an entrance to the secret metro D-6 in the third level of the bunker. As far as is known, it is the entrance to the D-6's first line, which was built in the 1950s, and which led from the Kremlin to the government airport Vnukovo-2 via the Russian State (Lenin) Library, past the underground town in Ramenki, Moscow State University, and the Academy of the General Staff. (D-6 was designed to save the Kremlin's inhabitants in case of attack.)[6]

Mikhailov admitted to Borogan that his unauthorized visits to areas so close to the most sensitive underground facilities in Russia meant that he was subject to constant pressure from the secret services. Mikhailov told Borogan that the Federal Protective Service, responsible for the safety of the president, had become his main persecutor. He was often detained, interrogated, and threatened with prison terms for his illegal penetration of the secret underground.

Seeking protection, Mikhailov appealed to the Ministry of Emergency Situations, hoping it could shield him from the pressure. In

July 2000 it was officially announced that the Diggers movement would be given the status of an associated organization of the ministry. But in the end, the ministry failed to fulfill its promises. Mikhailov found himself in an uneasy position when he was forced to establish unofficial contacts with the secret services in order to guarantee his own security. As a result, since 2000 Mikhailov has almost ceased to accompany foreign journalists to sensitive areas and has refused to make comments about underground, supposedly secret facilities.

In October 2002 Mikhailov's group was called upon by the FSB during the Nord-Ost hostage crisis. The Diggers helped the anti-terrorist Alpha unit to enter the Dubrovka Theater, which had been captured by Chechen terrorists, through the sewage system. Mikhailov later said he was fascinated by the opportunity to work with the secret services. After the crisis ended, Mikhailov told *Izvestia:* "It would be surprising if for twenty-five years of existence, the Diggers movement were not scrutinized by the FSB. It is absolutely correct. Such control over activity near confidential sites is necessary."[7]

Mikhailov accused other diggers, not in his group, of conducting "absolutely illegal activity in the city's systems: They seize state objects, they damage them. . . . These people reveal, first, a lot of false and twisted information about those vaults. And second, there are things that must not be removed because they concern national security. If we've been there, we never leak it to the press or on the Internet."[8]

By securing the loyalty of Mikhailov's group, the secret services had eliminated the only possible way that outside activists had of monitoring their underground activity. Soon afterward GUSP and the FSB put pressure on the press. In May 2002 Soldatov published a story in the weekly *Versiya* about the construction of residential apartment complexes on the premises of former FSB special facilities.[9] The story was illustrated by a map Soldatov had made based on open sources. The map showed GUSP facilities and those of other secret services in Moscow. Six months later, the FSB brought criminal charges against Soldatov and *Versiya* for revealing state secrets about GUSP's facilities. After a series of interrogations the charges were dropped in December 2002.[10]

Meanwhile, GUSP has kept building new facilities. According to independent information, the construction of D-6 continues.[11] Since the mid-2000s more than a dozen governors of Russian regions have been given awards by GUSP's leadership for "assistance in maintenance of special programs." The list of recipients includes the governors of Omsk, Chelyabinsk, and Kirovsk regions, and the districts of Belgorodskaya Oblast, Karelia, Voronezh, Stavropolye, Krasnoyarsk, and Kaliningrad. GUSP also gave awards to officials from the St. Petersburg government and the president of Russian Railways.[12] The only reason for this stream of GUSP awards might be the support provided by regional authorities for maintenance or reconstruction of GUSP's regional facilities (bunkers and communications). It was also known that in 2006 a GUSP special commission was sent to Kazan, the capital of Tatarstan, apparently to check "special sites" located in this region.[13]

By the mid-2000s, GUSP, the secret service established in true Cold War tradition, had managed to keep the Soviet underground empire intact and top secret. Although the service was designed to function independently from the FSB, the latter appears to have had a decisive role in running the organization. Two of the last directors came from top positions in the FSB—Victor Zorin was the head of the FSB counterterrorism department, and Alexander Tsarenko headed its Moscow department prior to being sent to

GUSP. It is not possible to establish whether Tsarenko left the FSB or whether he is subordinated to the FSB director. In the years after his appointment in 2000, Tsarenko continued to be called a "colonel general of the FSB" in media reports.[14]

By the end of the decade, the FSB followed GUSP's example and returned to the Soviet practice, with a few state security facilities made known to the public while the exact location of the others is kept secret.

LEFORTOVO PRISON

CAREFULLY UNMAPPED, notorious for a history of ruthless attitudes toward its inmates and a legacy of torture, Lefortovo is the only Russian prison not to have had its full history unveiled. Formerly a KGB prison, Lefortovo has since been handed down to the FSB. Given its hateful past, it's hardly surprising that its name alone can strike fear into a Russian citizen's heart.

The week after one of the biggest terrorist attacks in recent Russian history, when Chechens had seized a theater and held the audience hostage, the authors were preparing an article highly critical of the Russian response: The authorities had stormed the Nord-Ost theater, spraying fentanyl gas throughout the hall, with disastrous results.

One evening that week, on November 1, 2002, several FSB officers arrived at the newspaper *Versiya*, where Soldatov and Borogan worked, to confiscate Soldatov's computer and the paper's server. The article had just that day been sent to the printer. The agents left a summons for Soldatov to appear at the FSB department of military counterintelligence to answer questions about an article he'd written the previous spring. But Soldatov felt certain that what the officers really wanted was to prevent an independent investigation of the theater siege.

After his first interrogation, Soldatov was told he needed to report to the FSB investigative branch on Energeticheskaya Street, a few blocks from Lefortovo Park, named after Franz Lefort, a close associate of Tsar Peter the Great. The author reported to the infamous Lefortovo prison. The prison is difficult to find, hidden behind the gloomy apartment buildings. It is not identified by tourist guides, nor does it appear in books devoted to the city's history.

The decision to interrogate Soldatov within the confines of the FSB's intimidating prison was hardly arbitrary. It was not unreasonable to assume that, under pressure, in the claustrophobic environment of a ruthless and much feared prison, subjects would be more likely to divulge information. Those invited for questioning to Lefortovo never knew whether they would be freed or just moved to another part of the same building—to the prison. Psychologically, it has proven to be an effective method of persuasion.

Soldatov walked up to Checkpoint N2, an unremarkable entrance to a yellow brick building. This was the entrance for witnesses in investigations, families, and suspects, but not for prisoners.

Inside, he saw no people, just CCTV cameras. Visitors are ordered to wait in a hall for their guide. Outsiders are only allowed into the prison accompanied by an FSB officer. The visitor cannot see any human faces; instructions are issued over a loudspeaker. The entrance is flanked by two heavy doors that are opened simultaneously.

Walking down the pale blue and beige corridors, Soldatov was led to the third floor. Inside, it felt like a rabbit warren—and it was impossible to ascertain just where one was. White paper veils the office windows, which face an interior rectangular court.

On the day Soldatov went to Lefortovo, he was led to the small study of a young FSB investigator. The investigator started a belabored process of filling out a form on Soldatov's identity. Anxious, Soldatov wanted to answer the investigator's questions as quickly as possible and get out of there. But the investigator would not be hurried. In a few days, Soldatov was followed by Borogan, and the interrogators repeated the same slow, agonizing process.

During the Soviet years, when it had been run by the KGB, Lefortovo induced fear and trembling in the populace. Today, it remains at the heart of the FSB's empire, a symbol of the security agency's power.[1] With the collapse of the Soviet Union, the hulking prison was at the center of a struggle for control—a battle the FSB eventually won, but far from openly, in a contest of strength among Russia's security services.

WHILE ALL OF Moscow's main prisons have been documented by historians or experts—even the internal jail in the FSB's Lubyanka headquarters—this is not the case with Lefortovo. Even the prison's design remains a mystery: Nobody knows exactly why architect P. N. Kozlov in 1881 chose to build the military prison in the form of the letter "K." (Some speculated it might be in honor of the Russian empress Catherine II the Great—Katerina, in Russian.) Historically, Lefortovo has had close ties with the regime. It is the jail typically used to hold the political enemies of a regime, by Soviet and Russian rulers alike.[2]

The radical opposition leader and writer Eduard Limonov, who was imprisoned at Lefortovo on a charge of illegal weapons possession, gave a detailed account of the prison in his 2002 book *A Captive of Dead Men*: "In a place where three parts of the letter K . . . all converge, there is a command and control room. . . . There are always five, six, ten jailers, there are screens of computers, and there are microphones."

Former inmates have reported that Lefortovo's guards make every effort to prevent inmates from seeing one another. Escorting prisoners, guards use little clackers—a circular piece of metal—or snap their fingers to make their presence known to the other guards. The other way they communicate is by knocking on hollow pipes attached to the walls at each door and along corridors. If two escorts meet, one puts his charge into one of many wooden cabinets lining Lefortovo's corridors. This has been the practice since Tsarist times. In the nineteenth century, special boxes were put to use in the prison's church to prevent inmates from seeing one another during the service. (Under the Soviets, the church was turned into an execution chamber.)

By Limonov's estimate, there are fifteen exercise yards on the prison roof, used by three separate groups of prisoners each day. Each of the prison's four floors holds fifty cells, but only two floors are occupied. Although the prison has a capacity of up to two hundred, it usually contains no more than fifty detainees.

Most cells are designed to house three people but rarely are there more than two. There are a few solitary cells and two cells for six inmates. This is in striking contrast to other Moscow prisons where inmates are crammed into cells. Even lawyers note that it is practically the only corrective establishment in the country where drugs cannot be found and where there is no "rope telegraph"— the Russian prison tradition of using a crude "mail rope" for transmitting notes and small packets of tea and tobacco from cell to cell.

Natalia Denisova, the wife of Valentin Moiseev, a diplomat condemned for espionage, describes Lefortovo from personal experience: "Though conditions in Lefortovo at first sight were not bad, the rules are very strict. I was not allowed to see my husband for ten months, even though under the law two meetings of at least three hours a month are allowed. But I was never allowed to talk to my husband for more than an hour. It is really hard to transfer anything to prisoners, especially money. Relatives are supposed to send it by mail, and it takes a month. Money is necessary to buy products in prison."[3]

In Soviet times, Lefortovo prison was used by the KGB for the detention of political enemies and suspected spies. As the main KGB successor in the early 1990s, the FSB inherited Lefortovo. But it had to fight hard to hold on to the prison.

In 1993, in the throes of the early effort to weaken the former KGB, the FSB temporarily lost its investigative apparatus in a reorganization ordered by Yeltsin. In turn, the prison was handed over to the Interior Ministry in January 1994. Nine months into this new arrangement, two prisoners escaped—the first in Lefortovo's history, and an undeniable black eye for the Interior Ministry. With the ministry now seen as incapable of effectively running the prison, Lefortovo was returned to its former overseer by 1997. (Along with Lefortovo, thirteen regional prisons were handed back to the FSB.)[4]

In 1996, Russia joined the Council of Europe. In so doing, the Kremlin promised, among other things, to "revise the law on federal security service in order to bring it into line with Council of Europe principles and standards within one year from the time of accession: in particular, [to withdraw] the right of the Federal Security Service (FSB) to possess and run pretrial detention centers."[5]

The Council of Europe demanded that Russia separate its investigating agencies from their detention facilities on the grounds that inmates could be subject to pressure from investigators. While the Interior Ministry transferred its prisons and other penitentiary facilities to the Justice Ministry in 1998, the FSB struggled fiercely against the European pressure.

In 2004 Vyacheslav Ushakov, the deputy director of the FSB, explained at a meeting with representatives of the Council of Europe's Parliamentary Assembly that it was absolutely crucial for the FSB to possess a prison guaranteeing" a high level of safety."[6] Only Lefortovo, according to Ushakov, met these requirements. (In March 2005, Ushakov's argument was tested by a young 27-year-old prisoner from Kyrgyzstan, Talgat Kukuev, who had easily made it past Lefortovo's perimeter fence. He was not caught until May of that year.)

Finally, in July 2005 Putin signed a decree to transfer all FSB prisons (Lefortovo included) to the Ministry of Justice by January 2006.[7]

At first it seemed that the FSB intended to comply. The FSB jails were reported to have been transferred to the Federal Penal Service, where a special department was created for them.

But in late 2005 the authors were given information by reliable sources inside the FSB Investigative Directorate that the FSB prison personnel would be transferred to the penal service on temporary assignment. While they were formally on the staff of the penal service, these officers actually remained subordinate to the FSB. This information came from different sources, and the authors published it in the independent online magazine *Ezhednevny Journal* in January 2006.[8] The story was never challenged by the FSB, and in 2008 it was confirmed officially, but in a peculiar way.

In March 2008 the Saint Petersburg military court sanctioned the arrest of two FSB officers who turned out to be the chief and deputy chief of the number three pretrial detention center in the city. This prison had been previously attached to St. Petersburg's FSB department and according to presidential decree had been transferred to the penal service in 2006. Both officers had previously served in the regional department of the FSB, but when the penal service took over, the prison retained their posts. Officially, they had been transferred to the penal service, but they kept their FSB ranks all the same, according to the information disclosed at the trial and then reported in the media.[9]

Russia's defiance of its promise to Europe drew no action from Putin. Ultimately, the FSB even managed to expand its prison facilities. In June 2006, in a new decree, Putin allowed the FSB to create its own "temporary" detention facilities.[10] Few believed that the so-called temporary detention facilities were anything other than the very prisons the FSB was supposed to relinquish. The presidential decree clearly claimed that the accused being investigated who already had been charged could also be held in the FSB temporary detention facilities.

It was a smart trick carried out by the FSB's leadership. Until recently only the Interior Ministry and the border guards possessed temporary detention centers, intended to hold people arrested for a few days until official accusations could be presented. So it was quite logical that such centers were used only by the Ministry of Internal Affairs, whose employees caught criminals in the streets, and by border guards, who apprehended people who infringed on state borders.

In 2003 the border guards were absorbed into the FSB, offering an incentive and an excellent excuse to extend the practice of the

Federal Border Service, which keeps border violators behind bars, to the entire secret service. Now the FSB had temporary detention facilities not only near the border but throughout the entire country.[11] With the addition of such facilities, the FSB cleverly maneuvered around its promise to turn its prisons over to the Ministry of Justice while expanding its ever-widening reach within Russia.

PART II

RESPONSE TO TERRORISM

THE NORD-OST SIEGE

I N THE FALL of 2002, during one of the most serious terrorist attacks on Russian soil since 1995, Russia's security services' ability to counter a hostage situation under extreme pressure proved
disastrously inadequate.

In September 2002 several small groups of Chechens, three or
four each, began arriving in Moscow by bus from Makhachkala
and Khasavyurt in the republic of Dagestan. For many years this
route was taken by North Caucasian traders who moved between
Moscow and the regions. It was faster than a train, and there was
no need to buy a railway ticket, which required a passport. Most of
them came on September 16, and some came a few days later, on
September 19.[1] Simultaneously, a vehicle laden with explosives hidden under apple crates and another carrying three bombs disguised
as brake mechanisms for Kamaz trucks were driven into the city.

The Chechens gathered in three rented apartments outside the
city center, which were to house them for the weeks ahead. Their
explosives were carefully hidden in garages in different districts of
Moscow. There were fifty-two people in total, most in their twenties. The women among them were instructed to await orders in
the apartments while the men, disguised as construction workers,
were sent to a huge building at no. 7 Melnikova Street, in the

southeastern part of the city. Once the theater of the Moscow Ball Bearing Factory, it was known as the theater on Dubrovka.

The hall and nearby premises were rented by the Link Production Company, which had launched Russia's first Broadway-style musical *Nord-Ost* in October 2001. The show was a hit. A significant part of the building was occupied by the Institute for Human Self-Restoration and a gay club frequented by members of Parliament, prominent businessmen, and politicians.

In its heyday, the three-story club was visited by more than 1,500 people a night, but starting in May 2002, it was under construction. Chechens were hired as workers in the last stage of the reconstruction. Few paid attention to what they were doing. The door between the gay club and the theater hall was never closed.

On October 19, 2002, a small car exploded near a McDonald's restaurant on Pokryshkina Street; one Muscovite was killed and eight people were wounded. A second car bomb near the Chaykovsky Concert Hall failed to explode. This tactic of a diversionary attack was to be repeated many times over the years ahead, notably in 2004, when the Beslan tragedy was preceded by the suicide bombing attack in the Rizhskaya metro station in Moscow. But in October 2002 it was the first time the FSB had come across such tactics.

On Wednesday, October 23, the first act of *Nord-Ost* was coming to a close at 8:45 P.M. when three minivans approached the main entrance of the theater: a Ford Transit, a Volkswagen Caravelle, and a Dodge. In a few seconds a large group of Chechens armed with Kalashnikovs and pistols rushed into the theater shooting in the air. Some members of the Chechen group were already inside, disguised as normal theatergoers.

The Chechens, with only forty-one people, didn't have the manpower to capture and guard the whole building. Instead they focused solely on the area occupied by Link Productions, about 40 percent of the structure.

The entire audience of 920 people, 67 foreigners among them, was taken hostage by the Chechens, who ordered the captives to call relatives to ask them to organize a demonstration against the Chechen war. Amongst the hostages were journalists and law enforcement officers, who promptly called the news media and the secret services. When the Chechens understood that Russian authorities knew what was going on inside the theater, they ordered all hostages to relinquish their phones. A few managed to hide them.

At about this time the FSB leadership was celebrating the achievements of its Dynamo volleyball club at the Lubyanka headquarters. They were called away from the celebration for what was to become one of the gravest terrorist attacks in Russia during the decade.

At the outset, it was unclear to the authorities how many terrorists were in the theater and how many guns they had. (The forty-one hostage takers included nineteen women and were armed with seventeen Kalashnikovs and twenty pistols.) The terrorists had brought dozens of explosive charges, including twenty-one explosive belts and two massive bombs that could easily have destroyed the theater hall and everyone in it. During the preceding weeks these had been carefully collected in the premises of the gay club.

On the first day of the siege, a 22-year-old Chechen named Movsar Barayev declared himself the leader of the terrorists.

Barayev was the nephew of the notorious Chechen warlord Arbi Barayev, who had been killed in 2001. (Movsar, whose real name was Movsar Salamov, adopted the name Barayev after the killing of his uncle.) The Nord-Ost attack, as it came to be known, appeared at first to be an act of personal revenge. Barayev had two deputies: experienced Chechen fighter Ruslan Elmurzayev, 29, nephew of the Akhmadov brothers, who were famous warlords; and "Yaseer the Assyrian" (no further identity was ever established). Elmurza-yev turned out to be the real commander of the operation. The women were headed by Esira Vitalieva, a 42-year-old Chechen who had been a cook for another nationalist leader, Shamil Basayev, during the first Chechen war.

The attackers made hundreds of calls to different countries, which led to rumors that they were being controlled from outside. Barayev said he was subordinate to the famous Chechen warlord Shamil Basayev, and a week after the storming, Shamil Basayev took responsibility for planning the attack.[2]

The Chechens' strategy at Dubrovka was similar to Basayev's approach in a notorious terrorist attack in 1995 on a hospital in the southern Russian town of Budennovsk.[3] First, Chechens intimidated authorities with threats to kill hostages while appealing to public opinion. The Chechens allowed a few people to visit the theater during the siege. Some were journalists, including Mark Franchetti of the *Sunday Times* of London, an NTV crew, and Anna Politkovskaya of *Novaya Gazeta*; the others were famous Russian doctor Leonid Roshal, politician Irina Khakamada, and popular singer Joseph Kobzon.[4]

The terrorists chose Marina Shkolnikova, a physician who happened to be at the performance, to make statements on their behalf. She left the theater repeatedly with lists of demands before returning to the building. The terrorists soon adopted the practice of releasing a few hostages with every visitor. By the end of the second day of the crisis, more than 150 people had been freed, mostly children, women, and foreigners.

In 1995 in Budennovsk, having taken hostages in the hospital, Basayev immediately killed some men to show that he was serious in his claims and didn't intend to stop. Basayev's fighters were also able to sustain the storming, which turned into a fierce battle with special forces. Basayev eventually took the hostages and fled with them. But Movsar Barayev's group was unable to sustain its initial impetus. It could not turn the theater into a fortress, as Shamil Basayev had done with the Budennovsk hospital, when his two hundred fighters placed hostages as human shields in every window.

Within hours of the start of the siege, most of the building was occupied by special forces. For Movsar Barayev, the only real option was to convince the Kremlin that the terrorists were ready to destroy the theater and die alongside the hostages. To frighten the authorities and demonstrate their will, Barayev posed for the television cameras accompanied by women dressed as female suicide bombers, wearing suicide belts and black veils.

The Chechens' number one demand was to end the war in the republic within a week. They hoped to repeat the success of Basayev, who had taken some 1,500 hostages in Buddenovsk and leveraged the attack to negotiate with the Russian leaders by telephone in Moscow. By the end of that crisis, Basayev had succeeded in garnering a promise from Moscow to cease its military presence in Chechen territory. Russia's leadership, however, was criticized for its handling of the incident, in which more than one hundred hostages died—a number at the hands of Russian special forces—and more than four hundred were wounded. In Chechnya, Basayev was credited with having brought the first Chechen war to a close.[5] In Moscow, Budennovsk was viewed by the authorities as an enormous defeat.

As they gathered at the theater on the first day of the Nord-Ost attack, Russian authorities realized that they must avoid anything like the events at Budennovsk seven years earlier. Putin appointed Vladimir Pronichev, deputy director of the FSB, and Vladimir Vasiliev, deputy minister of the Interior Ministry, to lead the operation at the theater. They were given a free hand by the Kremlin to plan an assault on the theater, and to negotiate if necessary.

The Russian troops assembled in the area included hundreds of soldiers from the Interior Ministry, who were used to establish a security perimeter around the theater building. Dozens of FSB officers meanwhile set about interrogating all people everyone found in the area, in case there might be terrorist informers. A screening checkpoint was established in a nearby school.

The only forces to come face-to-face with the terrorists were officers from the FSB special purpose center, headed by General Alexander Tikhonov. The special purpose center comprised three departments: antiterrorist Group Alpha (or A department), which is the Russian equivalent of the elite U.S. Delta Force; Group Vympel (V department), a second antiterrorist unit; and the service of special operations, a small elite FSB team formed to pursue criminals in dangerous situations.[6] Only departments A and V had the training for an operation to free hostages.

Traditionally, servicemen at departments A and V held the rank of officers of the FSB. These were powerful organizations far different from regular military units. Department A had four sections; Department V had five. In times of crisis, the sections become assault groups, with more than thirty fighters each. At the time of the Dubrovka siege, two sections were on permanent deployment in Chechnya, with one section left in reserve. The special purpose center deployed all the remaining sections to the operation—three from Department A and three from Department V. The commander of one Department V group was Colonel Sergei Shavrin.

Tall, reserved, and soft-spoken, with a mustache and angular face, Shavrin, then 37 years old, was no typical FSB man. He had come to the special purpose center in the 1980s from the border guards. Although considered to be part of the old KGB, the border guards always kept their distance from the Lubyanka, being more soldiers than operatives. Shavrin was a decorated officer and a deputy commander of the section at the Vympel.

During the Cold War, Vympel members had been trained to operate abroad, received education in foreign languages, and traveled widely, including in Latin America and Europe. At home their training included penetrating the most heavily guarded strategic points (such as nuclear stations) to find breaches in security. In most cases they succeeded. As a rule, they despised their colleagues in other KGB departments responsible for internal security.

The Vympel had suffered after the Cold War. During Yeltsin's violent clashes with hard-liners in Parliament in October 1993, Vympel officers had refused orders to storm the Russian White House, then the location of Parliament. As a result of such insubordination, the Vympel was handed over to the Interior Ministry for two years: Only fifty officers out of a few hundred, however, were actually transferred; the rest simply left. In 1995 the remnants of the unit were returned to the FSB.[7] Shavrin did not leave the

Vympel and was sent to Chechnya. By the time of the Dubrovka crisis, Shavrin had made fourteen trips to hot spots and had received the Hero of Russia medal in 1996 after he led his troops safely out of a siege during the storming of Grozny.

But in the cold, slushy rain outside the Dubrovka, Shavrin was uncertain he would be able to save his troops. "Everybody feared that the terrorists would let us into the theater and then someone on the outside would blow the place up with a remote," Shavrin told Soldatov. "That would have been the end. We were waiting for it. We even said goodbye to one another. But it turned out differently."[8]

The special troops had orders to kill all the terrorists. Shavrin recalled, "The order was signed prior to the beginning of the storming.* Knowing that the building is mined, that the explosives would be enough to raze the building to the ground, and that the mining system setup had duplicating systems so that one surviving terrorist could set it all in motion, trying to catch someone alive could lead to tragic events. Somebody would have time to ignite an explosive, and in that case we would rescue nobody," Shavrin recalled.

On Friday night, October 25, at about 11:00 P.M., the authors entered the school building next to the theater, where the relatives of the hostages were waiting.[9] A list displayed on one of the walls enabled us to establish the exact number of hostages that had been reported missing by relatives. At the time it was 698, though that figure eventually rose to 920. At about 2:00 A.M. on the

---

* The order was signed by the general public prosecutor and by all the leadership in the operations staff from the Ministry of Internal Affairs and from the FSB.

morning of the 26th, a friend got a call from one of the hostages, a journalist from *Moskovskaya Pravda*. She relayed that the terrorists had announced their plan to start shooting captives at six in the morning.

In an effort to move closer to the theater, the authors with two colleagues gained entrance to a neighboring apartment building. Fifteen minutes later we were welcomed into one of the apartments of the building situated to the right of the main entrance of the theater, on the corner of Melnikova and First Dubrovskaya Streets. From the windows of the upper floors we had an excellent view of the theater and the square in front of it. We had a pair of binoculars and two cameras. We didn't notice any particular changes in the distribution of the armored vehicles and troops as compared to the previous night, when the terrorists had insisted that the special forces be kept away from the area. Right in front of the theater entrance were two minivans, a red one and a white one, in which the terrorists had arrived. The only difference was that the van headlights had finally gone out. The terrorists had left the minivans with their engines on, which meant that they could have been mined. An attempt by two Internal Ministry troopers on the second night of the crisis to switch off the engines led to tragic consequences: One was wounded by a terrorist who fired at them from a theater window.

The following is based on notes taken by Soldatov and Borogan at the time:

3–4 A.M. A silence pervades the illuminated square.

5:00 A.M. Suddenly the theater's entrance lights go out, which is a bad sign: The previous day, the Chechen terrorists

stated that if these lights were turned off, they would regard it as the beginning of an attempt to storm the building, and they would start shooting the hostages.

5:35 A.M. A grenade explosion is heard, followed by the sound
of shattered glass. The storming of the theater has begun.
Bursts of gunfire come from the factory facade opposite the
side entrances of the theater, about 200 meters away, followed by machine-gun fire.

6:05 A.M. The radio says that the operations staff claims to have
received a call from a hostage. He says the terrorists have run
out of patience and are beginning to execute hostages. According to the official version, all the shooting comes from
the terrorists. By now it is obvious to us that this is the beginning of a storming on the initiative of the Russian
forces. For a while everything is still; we can see the internal troops being repositioned. Temporarily, the theater is
silent. A blue Jeep with its lights off and engine running
comes up to the main entrance, and four fully armed soldiers appear on a bridge to the left of the building. Their
uniforms indicate that they belong to Vitiaz, the special
troops of the Internal Troops (the armed forces subordinated to the Interior Ministry).

6:35 A.M. A group of six to eight soldiers from the Internal
Troops runs across the square to the main entrance, kicks it
in, and fires at the glass.

Meanwhile, vehicles and ambulances have been filling
the square. A minute later they are joined by the armored
carrier that had been waiting on the corner of the First
Dubrovskaya and Melnikova Streets. It stops about 120
meters away from the theater entrance. Two shots are audi-

ble from within the building. The shots are answered by heavy machine-gun fire from the armored carrier.

The FSB special purpose center troop appear to be accompanying two women out of the building when all of a sudden the building is lit up and the sound of gunfire fills the air. About ten soldiers are hiding in the grass to the right of the building, with another group to the left of the theater.

We hear two explosions inside the building, accompanied by a white light. These must have been grenades. After that the groups located around the car park all run across the square to the main entrance.

6:40 A.M. Three explosions follow one after another inside the building, accompanied by a red light, followed by bursts of gunfire.

6:45 A.M. A small group of soldiers carrying a powerful torch sets out across the hall of the ground floor in the direction of the wing of the building where there is a library.

6:47 A.M. At three points inside soldiers begin to break out the theater's windows and cut the poster with the enormous letters "Nord-Ost," which covered the glass walls of the entrance hall of the first floor.

6:50 A.M. Someone is dragged out of the building. A few seconds later we can see two soldiers carrying a young man dressed in a gray sweater. We can't understand whether the man is a disguised terrorist, a hostage, or a journalist.

7:00 A.M. The doors of the main entrance are thrust wide open. Three Defender Jeeps are being driven up to the building. Empty buses are moving along Melnikov Street right below our windows. In front of the main entrance there are now dozens of people. Shouts of "Come on!" can be heard from all around. A woman hostage can be seen almost creeping out of the building. Someone else can hardly walk. A body is carried out, followed by another one.

7:03 A.M. Shooting can be heard. At the same time a group of people is being accompanied out of the building. A girl is being carried out, then a few bodies.

7:06 A.M. Bodies are still being carried out. Now rescue forces in white helmets join special forces troopers in the rescue. The bodies are being placed in a line right in front of the main entrance of the theater. There are more than twenty of them. Judging by their clothes and the way they are being carried mostly across the rescuers' shoulders, most appear to be women or even young girls. Thank God, we think, because finally after all these dead, they've managed to find someone alive. A few ambulances packed with the wounded leave the square.

Four buses stop to the right of the building; we can clearly see them from our vantage point. In the meantime, to the left of the main entrance the rescuers continue placing bodies; there are dozens, and the number of corpses increases rapidly. A few minutes later they occupy the whole area; all the steps on the left are covered with multicolour sweaters worn by the hostages. Just three days before these women dressed up in order to look good at the theater. There isn't enough room, and the corpses are now placed one over another. We wonder if there is any hope left that among those bodies there could still be someone alive. It doesn't look possible.

The first bus with freed hostages on board leaves from the entrance area. But the hostages looked strange, as though they are asleep or unconscious. A few minutes later some rags are carried out of the building (possibly table-cloths or curtains) and thrown over the inert passengers on another bus.

At the main entrance the row of corpses is growing longer. Another bus leaves.

Meanwhile, television is reporting that a member of the operations staff has announced the end of the storming: The hostages are free, and the terrorists have been killed. Not a single mention is made of any victims. At the time of this announcement, two more bodies are carried outside the building.

7:43–7:50 A.M. Another two buses with the bodies of hostages, with the same strange look on their faces, are leaving.

7:50 A.M. A screen is placed in front of the theater entrance, blocking the view.

8:00 A.M. Vasiliev, co-chief of the operations staff, claims that thirty-six terrorists have been killed, Movsar Barayev among them. He also says that the operations staff was forced to storm the building after several hostages attempted to escape on their own.

Moments after Vasiliev's announcement, one of our colleagues shouts in alarm, "Look! They're putting dead bodies on the buses—they are falling down from their seats!" And he passes us binoculars. At the same moment an NTV journalist reports that he can see buses passing by and that the hostages' faces are "livid."

8:45 A.M. To the right of the car park we see black body bags being loaded onto a bus. A bus comes up, and the corpses are put on board.

11:00 A.M. The dead are still being carried out of the Dubrovka Theater. Even when we leave the apartment, some corpses still remain on the steps of the main entrance.

FROM THE BEGINNING, Russian authorities had been prepared for a massive explosion from one of the bombs brought in beforehand by the Chechens. But at the time of the storming, there was none. Instead of killing themselves along with the hostages, the female terrorists, loaded down with explosive belts, had simply covered their faces with head scarves and lain down on the floor among the hostages. Since special purpose fighters were under orders to kill all terrorists, there was no chance to later ask the Chechens why they hadn't detonated their bombs. Shavrin said, "When we entered the hall, we saw a female suicide bomber. She was sitting on a chair. Her eyes were open, she was holding the electrodes, all she had to do was to connect them. Why she didn't do that is unclear. Perhaps she was waiting for some instruction or command. She had enough time."[10]

The day after the siege, it became known that the special forces had pumped into the theater fentanyl, an anesthetic gas, which they assumed would put the terrorists to sleep. The gas is three hundred times more powerful than morphine, but the effect on a person takes two minutes.[11] When the gas was pumped into the theater, the terrorists were not knocked out immediately.

According to Shavrin, the operations staff doubted there would be many hostages alive after the storming. Anticipating an explosion, the FSB used the deadly gas in a desperate attempt to support the special troops when they went in, no matter how effective it might be. The operations staff, considering the situation hopeless, had used all available methods. When no explosion occurred, the storming was deemed a victory; at that moment the authorities had not given thought to the consequences of the poisoning for the hostages.

In the end, 130 hostages died, only five at the hands of terrorists.[12] According to Russian authorities, fentanyl was a breath paralyzer, and the number of victims was so great simply because the hostages had been weakened by three days of the crisis. But Pavel Finogenov, who lost his 32-year-old brother in the Nord-Ost siege, told Borogan: "My brother Igor was an officer of the special forces and had recently undergone training, including an imitation gas attack, which he completed successfully. He was in excellent shape."[13] Virtually no preparation had been made for the aftereffects of the gas. No temporary hospital had been set up, there was not enough oxygen on hand, and there was no antidote at the ready for those poisoned. It soon became clear that no one had been briefed on the use of fentanyl. "At headquarters level the prediction was that there would be losses, there would be shooting, there would be an explosion, there would be a lot of casualties. But what actually happened? The storming was over, there was no explosion, and eight hundred people or more had to be resuscitated from the effects of the gas. It turned out that no one was prepared for this," recalled Shavrin. "We anticipated the explosion. We thought less than 10 percent would survive."

The operations staff of the FSB and other services had gravely miscalculated. They did not imagine that the threat to blow up the building might be a bluff. The FSB's laboratory had provided the gas, but no one thought about how it could be ameliorated afterward. The operations staff was ultimately determined not to repeat the disaster of Budennovsk. The generals wanted to make sure Putin would succeed where Yeltsin had failed. On October 24, on the second day of hostage crisis, Mikhail Leontiev, a political commentator for TV Channel One, thought to be very close to Vladimir Putin, said on his show: "The sense of the event is that all of us are paying for Budennovsk—for the shame of the political agreement with gangsters and degenerates. When one speaks about the question of price and negotiations, let's count how many lives we have paid during these seven years for Budennovsk and Khasavyurt. . . . We are guilty—all of us together are guilty who have allowed them to think for a moment that there could be a repeat of Budennovsk."[14]

After the storming the same mantra was repeated by FSB general Alexander Zdanovich, then a member of the operations staff. On October 26, asked to compare the storming of Nord-Ost with that of Budennovsk, Zdanovich replied, "The first thing I would say is that there have been times when our special forces have been ready to solve the problem. In my opinion, this time [in Budennovsk] there was a lack of the political will to make a decision."[15]

Those who questioned the operation were punished. The radio station Echo Moskvy was officially warned by the Media Ministry that it could be closed down for airing interviews with the terrorists. The television channel Moskovia's broadcasts were temporarily halted. The NTV coverage of the crisis was personally criticized by Vladimir Putin.[16] Meanwhile the clinics treating hostages suffering from gas poisoning were prohibited from providing information about the victims to journalists. The authorities officially stated that they would not divulge all the circumstances of the operation.

On Sunday, October 27, the day after the storming of the theater, the authors, then working for the weekly *Versiya*, realized the futility of waiting a week for their story to run and decided to publish it on the Web site Agentura.ru. On Monday, prominent Italian journalist Guilietto Chiesa republished their reportage in *La Stampa*.[17]

The following Friday, November 1, when *Versiya* was going to press, a group of FSB officers arrived at the editorial offices and began a search, claiming they were looking for information published in an article by Soldatov the previous May. A few computers, including the editorial server, were seized, and a number of journalists were ordered to visit the FSB for interrogation. On Sunday, Soldatov received a phone call from Alexei Gorchakov of the FSB's Investigative Directorate and was summoned for questioning.

A MONTH PASSED with a series of interrogations of the authors and others from *Versiya*. It was a difficult time. We felt under intense pressure, and all of the interrogated journalists were asked to sign nondisclosure agreements.

At the end of November 2002, Soldatov was called by Vladimir, a major in the Moscow department of the FSB who worked in the counterterrorism section and a source who was at times useful for obtaining information on terrorist groups. Vladimir asked for a meeting, and chose to meet at the entrance of the Moscow Zoo, situated in the Krasnaya Presnya neighborhood in the center of the city.

When Soldatov met Vladimir at a bus stop, the man who'd been a periodic source for two years refused to sit in the author's car, suggesting instead that they walk alongside the perimeter of the zoo. "Look, Andrei, you know we are all in big trouble," Vladimir said. "I was told to tell you they are ready to finish the investigation, but we have to make a deal. Forget about Nord-Ost." Vladimir was suggesting that we not attempt any further investigation. At the time, there were still many unanswered questions about the operation, including the nature of the gas and the decisions the FSB had made in the face of a terrorist attack. Soldatov and Borogan were still receiving information about the Dubrovka siege and tried to keep the investigation alive.

Soldatov was astonished that his contact with Vladimir was now known to the FSB leadership, and that Vladimir was being used by the FSB to persuade *Versiya* to drop its investigation. (Just a week before the meeting, Soldatov and Borogan had published details provided by an investigator in the Moscow prosecutor's office, who claimed that not all of the terrorists' explosives had been operational, most had been dummies, and furthermore that the Kremlin had been well aware of this.)

The authors had also obtained information suggesting that the number of victims was higher than the official figure of 130. But it was increasingly difficult to gather information in a climate of paranoia; sources feared that all journalists from *Versiya* were under investigation and surveillance.

As they strolled around the zoo, Soldatov flatly refused to give up his investigation.

"Forget it, there is nothing to investigate, and nobody is interested in it—Nord-Ost was a victory!" Vladimir countered. Vladimir explained to Soldatov that the operation was being portrayed as a victory to discourage terrorists from attempting similar attacks in future. This was one of the reasons the FSB was not interested in releasing the exact number of victims: "Andrei, you know, according to the suicides bombers' rules, if you kill six people, you've won."

Vladimir warned Soldatov that if he didn't stop investigating, he would be summoned for interrogation constantly. Soldatov countered that whenever he was questioned, it would be reported by his journalist friends—that it would put pressure on the FSB, not only on himself. In the end, that is exactly what transpired: The FSB continued to call Soldatov for questioning, and the journalists kept writing about it.[18]

After a few weeks, the calls to Soldatov ceased, and the FSB returned *Versiya*'s computers. The FSB never told Soldatov whether the case was closed, but it stopped asking him about the case.

In the weeks after the siege, the Kremlin declared a victory against terrorism, and the generals who planned the operation were rewarded. The country's highest honour—Hero of the Russian Federation—was bestowed upon FSB director Patrushev, his deputy Vladimir Pronichev, who had commanded the operation from the FSB, and Alexander Tikhonov, the commander of the special purpose center. The head of the FSB's Moscow department was promoted.[19] The authorities justified this decision by saying the security services, gravely weakened during the 1990s, now needed support, not criticism.

Despite the authorities' attempts to portray the Nord-Ost theater siege as a victory for Russia, in fact the operation illustrated the security services' frightening lack of preparedness for a grave hostage situation. In addition to the devastating loss of life it caused, Nord-Ost revealed a shameful truth: Even when armed to handle the threat of terrorism, the FSB had mounted an ill-coordinated operation and managed to bungle it.

THE BESLAN CRISIS

TWO YEARS AFTER the disastrous Nord-Ost siege in Moscow, Chechen terrorists launched a series of brutal attacks in the North Caucasus. Once again, the security services' inability to respond quickly and effectively (despite changes to the structure of the security services themselves) demonstrated a perilous absence of the sort of commanding direction necessary in a crisis situation.

The first attack occurred on June 21, 2004, when more than two hundred insurgents arrived in Nazran and Karabulak, in the republic of Ingushetia, bordering Chechnya.[1] Militants divided into groups of twenty or thirty and stormed fifteen government buildings, including the 503rd Army Regiment headquarters, the Interior Ministry headquarters, the base of an FSB border guard unit, an arms depot, and the local police headquarters.

The insurgents, Chechen and Ingush fighters, were led once again by Chechen warlord Shamil Basayev.[2] Their main target was law enforcement personnel. Dressed in camouflage uniforms and masks, the insurgents stopped people in the streets, demanded identification, and killed anyone carrying law enforcement personnel identification. They even established their own checkpoints during the raid.

According to official data, the insurgents killed sixty-two law enforcement officials, including the Ingush minister of internal affairs, two prosecutors, and nine FSB regional officers.[3] The attack was well coordinated: While insurgents were combing both towns for law enforcement, thirty-five militants headed to the Ministry of Internal Affairs arms depot in Nazran, where they found more than 1,500 Kalashnikovs and a large quantity of ammunition. Appropriating the ministry's trucks, the rebels loaded up with weapons and left the area. The loading took three to four hours, during which time the insurgents continued to attack military facilities and prevented any attempts to recapture the guns. The entire raid lasted less than five hours, and federal army troops did not arrive in Nazran until the following day, when the fighting was over.

The attack in Nazran opened a new front in the Russian conflict in the North Caucasus. It was the first such military foray by Chechens outside Chechnya's border in many years. The action was a direct strike on law enforcement and the FSB and control over a whole region was lost for nearly a day. Just when many had thought the second Chechen war was over, the Nazran attack posed difficult new challenges to Russia's security services.

The Nazran attack came at a time of change and paralysis in the organization of the security services. In Moscow, the top brass wanted to show that the war had indeed ended and that all that was needed was some kind of police action. This attitude prompted a change in the way the security services handled events in the volatile region. More responsibility was given to the Interior Ministry, which was essentially a police organization. The FSB kept its hand in, as did the military, but by the summer of 2004 it had been determined that police action would be left to the police agency. Under the new structure, jurisdiction was unclear, security services were overlapping, and problems with coordination soon reached a critical level. By July 2004, in the North Caucasus the situation was extremely complicated: At least three divisions of the national FSB as well as regional offices, military intelligence, and Interior Ministry units were all operating in the same area. There was little or no coordination between them.[4]

In August, the Kremlin made a key organizational change. Twelve "operational management groups" were created for the troubled North Caucasus region, all of them under the purview of the Interior Ministry. The groups were to coordinate security services in the region in the event of a terrorist attack. The change put responsibility for dealing with an attack in the hands of the police rather than the military or the FSB.[5] Each of the twelve groups was headed by a colonel of the Internal Troops at the Interior Ministry who had the rank of head of the regional antiterrorist forces—making him the second-highest official in the region after the governor in the fight against terrorism. In the event of hostage taking or insurgent attacks, the commanders of the twelve groups were expected to assume control. They could make decisions independently from Moscow. The creation of the twelve groups was also significant as a shift in power. During the 1990s, responses to all major terrorist attacks had been managed from Moscow by the central authorities.[6] The new system was intended to decentralize control, giving regional commanders an increased role. (Nonetheless, the Kremlin kept the identities of the commanders secret, so the public could not hold them accountable in the event of failure.)

On August 24, 2004, two domestic passenger planes, a Tu-134 and a Tu-154, took off at Moscow's Domodedovo International Airport at 10:30 P.M. and 9:35 P.M., respectively. At around 11 P.M. they crashed almost simultaneously, hundreds of miles apart: In both incidents eighty-nine people were killed. Within days it became clear that the planes had been blown up in the air by two female suicide bombers.

On Tuesday, August 31, another woman blew herself up near the Rizhskaya metro station in the center of Moscow. Ten people were killed and fifty-one wounded. It was a Tuesday night, and the area surrounding the station was full of high-ranking officials, including the mayor of Moscow. All these attacks appeared to have been organized as a diversion for a far bigger assault that would follow within twenty-four hours.

On September 1, 2004, more than forty terrorists armed with guns stolen during the raid in Ingushetia captured a school in Beslan, in North Ossetia. More than 1,100 people, including some 770 children, were taken hostage.[7] Over the first two days of the crisis, the terrorists hounded the authorities with demands to deal directly with prominent politicians, releasing a few hostages with every visit to show their willingness to negotiate. They allowed the former president of Ingushetia, Ruslan Aushev, to enter the school. In exchange, twenty-six hostages were released as a sign of goodwill. But the hostage takers refused to deal with journalists, claiming they might be FSB informers. (The well-known journalist Anna Politkovskaya might have been allowed into the school, but she was mysteriously poisoned on the plane while flying to the region on September 1. The results of her medical tests have disappeared, strengthening the view that she was poisoned by the security services.)[8] Nevertheless, in the first hours of the hostage crisis, they executed more than a dozen men whose bodies they dumped out the windows of the school.

On Friday, September 3, the third day of the hostage crisis, there were no signs of an impending assault by government forces. The security perimeter around the school was porous; no new army deployments were in evidence.

By Friday morning rumors were circulating among journalists that the terrorists might allow medical staff to remove the bodies of the men who had been shot and thrown out of the windows.

As the gunmen allowed four medical workers from the Ministry of Emergency Situations to approach the school in two ambulances, two bombs went off inside the sport hall of the school, where the hostages were gathered. It was 1:05 P.M. on September 3.

The explosions almost destroyed the roof of the sports hall and part of the wall. In panic, some children saw an opportunity to flee. The terrorists responded by opening fire, which prompted the security forces to storm the building.

When the shooting began, the special purpose center of the FSB, comprised of the elite officers who had been trained for terrorist attacks, was not prepared. Although there were enough troops on the ground, two assault groups out of ten were not at the immediate site but were undergoing training for an assault on a similar building thirty kilometers from Beslan.[9] The officers of the special purpose center who were near the school were not even wearing bulletproof vests. As they watched the children fleeing and the terrorists shooting, they had no choice but to storm the school. Ten officers were killed, the biggest loss ever for the special purpose center.

The Beslan operation quickly turned into a city battle. Some local armed men ran from the school, taking freed children with them. Others ran in the opposite direction with guns. Around

2:00 P.M. one of them shouted to us: "We need hunting cartridges; please, find some!" By then the battle had expanded far beyond the area around the school. Some people had been shooting, some feared the terrorists were in hiding and began frantically searching for anyone who looked out of place. Two local militiamen caught one woman who was thought to be a terrorist, and only the sudden arrival of her husband saved her.

After almost three hours, local troops appeared to be hunting one another. We were surprised how disorganized and fluid the whole situation became. At about 5:00 P.M. we managed to get closer to the school and were standing close to the school with dozens of Ossetian men. But we weren't sure if the operation was still under way. Around this time in Moscow, the state TV channels reported the operation was finished. At 6 P.M. Soldatov was called by radio Echo Moskvy, and at this very moment another explosion took place: "What's going on?" he was asked. "We were told the operation is long over. Could you explain that sound?" In fact, the last explosion didn't come until 11:15 P.M. It was a shell from a tank of the 58th Army attached to the operations staff, firing on the last three insurgents holed up in the school's cellar. In total, 334 hostages were killed, including 186 children. It was a disaster.

THE BESLAN SIEGE cast a harsh light on the ability of the Russian security services to cope with large-scale hostage-taking and terrorism. All the various ministries and elite forces had been called, but they seemed to be parts of a broken watch: They were all in one place, all involved in the same movement, but the whole mechanism was out of order.

From the beginning, the hostage crisis in Beslan was clearly of national scale. But fearing responsibility for possible failure, FSB generals in Moscow deliberately framed the event as a local crisis. The reorganized system, approved only one month earlier, was supposed to put one of the twelve commanders in charge of such an event. But during the Beslan siege, the commander was made subordinate to the FSB chief in North Ossetia. On the first day of the crisis, Putin sent FSB director Nikolai Patrushev and Minister of Internal Affairs Rashid Nurgaliev to Beslan, but they left the republic as soon as possible.[10] The two officials did not even make it to the town of Beslan. They landed at the airport just long enough to get another flight back to Moscow.[11] The school was captured at 8:00 A.M., and by noon the heads of the FSB and the Ministry of Internal Affairs managed to fly to Beslan and get all the way back to Moscow, 932 miles north, to meet Putin.[12] "I did not meet Patrushev and Nurgaliev in Beslan," testified Valery Andreev, the FSB chief in North Ossetia who was put in charge of the operation. He spoke at the trial of the only surviving terrorist, Nurpashi Kulaev, in the Supreme Court of North Ossetia on December 15, 2005.[13]

A year after the tragedy, on September 2, 2005, Putin met with members of the committee "Mothers of Beslan," and he was asked, "Why did Patrushev and Nurgaliev not appear in Beslan on September 1? They were at the airport, and they departed. Why did some of them not remain?" Putin responded, "It happens sometimes that there are a lot of generals, and they impede each other. Therefore, they departed."[14]

To make matters worse, two operations staffs were established, the first and official one headed by Andreev, and the second and semi-official one consisting of FSB generals from Moscow. Two generals, Vladimir Pronichev and Vladimir Anisimov, deputy directors of the FSB, were presented as "consultants" to Andreev, with no clear delegation of responsibility. In his statement at the trial on December 15, 2005, Andreev remarked that it was the FSB director, Patrushev, who had told him that Pronichev was coming to provide "practical help for the operation," while the purpose of Anisimov's presence was not stated.

In fear of alienating the local population, authorities failed to erect an effective security perimeter around the captured school.

This led to the shooting-turned-storming, which surprised both special troops and terrorists. That locals were the first to mobilize people and cars to take children away from the burning school was the best illustration of the operations staff's inability to lead the rescue operation. The scene in Beslan was crawling with top officials, including two deputies from the FSB director and a number of other Moscow FSB generals, among them Alexander Zdanovich, whom the authors met on September 3 near the operations staff. But with all these bigwigs on the area, the commanding authority seemed to have no clear powers, and the supposed special troops operation turned into a sort of anarchic street fighting that ended only with the help of tanks and only hours after the storming had begun. The operation to free the hostages appeared to be led by nobody. At 2:00 P.M., after almost an hour of shooting, we saw Eduard Kokoity, the president of South Ossetia, the breakaway province of Georgia, ordering Russian soldiers to strengthen the cordon.[15] He was the president of another country, but he was one of the people making decisions.

Beslan brutally exposed the Russian security services' utter fail-ure to react quickly and effectively to a crisis. The decentralization of power from Moscow, and the assignment of a dozen officers specifically designated to the troubled region, had failed to avert a dire scenario. In the end, after three chaotic, terrifying days, 334 hostages (186 children among them) lost their lives.

THE RUSSIAN RESPONSE

AFTER THE NORD-OST and Beslan crises, repeated calls were made for parliamentary investigations into the events and the security services' chaotic responses to them.

During the Nord-Ost siege, Irina Khakamada, a liberal politician with the Union of Right Forces and deputy speaker of the State Duma, was among those invited into the theater by the Chechen assailants. She realized on seeing the Chechens for the first time that it would be very difficult to negotiate with them. "You know, I had an impression, they are martyrs not by words, but by their eyes. I looked in their eyes and sensed that they are really ready to die, if it came to that." Khakamada wanted them to release the children before they were harmed. "I wanted to take the children out. I began to ask them and explain that the children should be out of here. And I had the impression that I managed to convince one of them, I saw his eyes glisten, and he started to tell me that he has his own small children. But at this moment the leader appeared and cut him off and said, 'That's all; don't annoy me with your requests!'"[1]

After the storming of the theater and the deaths from the gas, Khakamada and others in her party began to push for a parliamentary investigation. Boris Nemtsov, another leader of the party and formerly a high-ranking official under Yeltsin, hoped the investigation would yield firm answers to three main questions: How had armed bandits turned up in the center of Moscow? How timely and complete was the medical help provided to the released hostages? And why are the authorities hiding this information?

On October 29, just days after the siege, Khakamada demanded a full parliamentary inquiry into the disaster. But only 44 of the 441 members of the lower house of Parliament supported her request. "We blame no one, but we believe that we need an investigation by Parliament as well as by the state," she said.[2] The leader of a pro-Kremlin faction in Parliament, Vyacheslav Volodin, called her proposal "untimely" and went on to say: "Any parallel steps carried out before the official conclusion of investigations can only be seen as a pretext for self-promotion and an effort to gain political points from people's tragedy."[3]

So within days, it was decided that Parliament would not hold a full inquiry. The initiative crumbled because another democratic faction, Yabloko, did not support it. On October 29, Putin invited Grigory Yavlinsky, the leader of Yabloko, to the Kremlin and thanked him for his support of the authorities during the hostage crisis. "You are one of the few who took part, played a positive role," Putin said, "and unlike many others, did not use it as PR for yourself."[4]

The party of Khakamada and Nemtsov, a small one that included the economic reformer Anatoly Chubais, decided to create its own commission. For three days in late October and early November the party gathered experts together to address the remaining questions about the siege. The results of the inquiry, published on November 20, dealt largely with the medical issues of the fentanyl gas. One of the paramedics interviewed said, "Nobody warned us what we would find inside. We were just told there would be many wounded; nobody told us that gas had been used and that we should bring some means of defense with us to protect ourselves from the lingering gas fumes. We were forced to assess the conditions of the wounded ourselves." The report of the commission concluded, "The main reason for the increase in the number of casualties among the rescued hostages during the assault was negligence on the part of the officials responsible for arranging first aid to the victims and transporting them to hospitals, as well as the overall coordination of the rescue effort." Among other things, the panel found that many deaths might have been avoided had the rescued hostages been physically positioned in ways that would have aided their ability to breathe in their weakened state.[5]

Authorities opened a criminal case against the Chechen terrorists, but no further effort was made to probe on the way the security services or the Kremlin had responded. Family members of victims tried in vain to learn more about what had happened during the siege, but they were largely frustrated. The only channel family members could use to challenge the state was to sue for compensation, but when they did, they were accused of trying to profit from the tragedy. In the end, the only compensation offered was to pay for the belongings of their relatives. Pavel Finogenov, who lost his brother Igor to the gas, told Borogan in an interview, "The authorities do nothing to give us even one grain of information about why our relatives were killed and who's to blame." Finogenov and some other family members appealed to the European Court on Human Rights in Strasbourg. "There is tremendous pressure from the highest authorities, the presidential administration, on the prosecutor's office and all the people involved in investigating the attack," he said. "The objective: not to give any information."[6] The relatives of the Nord-Ost victims established their own commission but said in their report, "The lack of objective legal assessment of the security services' activities at Nord-Ost in the organization and execution of the rescue, and the hiding of facts important to investigating the events of that earlier siege, possiby led to an even more awful tragedy in Beslan."[7]

In the end, no pressure was brought to bear on the Russian authorities to account for their decisions or the deaths at the Dubrovka theater. Neither the Parliament nor relatives of the victims nor the press nor the prosecutors were willing and able to carry out a full and independent investigation. The security services and the Kremlin did not want to face any such investigation—and they did not.

Two years later, after the Beslan siege, the same failure of accountability was repeated. Once again, there were calls for a parliamentary investigation. On September 7, 2004, Putin told a special press conference for foreign journalists that it would be sufficient to conduct an *internal* investigation into the tragedy. When asked about a parliamentary inquiry, he said, "Such an investigation could become the next political sideshow."[8]

But after massive protests in North Ossetia, on September 10 Putin agreed to support the creation of a commission within the Federation Council, the upper house of Parliament, to investigate the Beslan attack. A small circle of senators controlled by the Kremlin wanted to limit the investigation. But Boris Gryzlov, the speaker of the State Duma, announced that that body would create its own Commission of Inquiry into Beslan. On September 20, a parliamentary commission of eleven senators and ten deputies of the

State Duma was finally formed. It was headed by Alexander Torshin, vice speaker of the Federation Council, a onetime bureaucrat in the Soviet Communist Party. The commission presented its report two years later, in December 2006. Largely, the report confirmed the official version of the siege and merely approved all changes in the national antiterrorist system. The report concluded that the security services acted correctly and took "the necessary measures to protect health and lives and to minimize the consequences of a terrorist act." The only mistakes identified were in the organization of the operations staff on the scene (which didn't include the president of North Ossetia) and some training issues.

Relatives of the Beslan victims demanded an independent investigation and punishment of high-ranking security officials. In September 2005, a year after the Beslan tragedy, Putin invited eight people among the families to the Kremlin for a meeting that lasted two hours and forty-five minutes. As reconstructed by the family members, they asked Putin about the responsibility of FSB director Patrushev, Interior Minister Nurgaliev, and all the law enforcement structures.

Putin was pressed by one family member, Azamat Sabanov, as to whether the security service bosses should resign. Putin acknowledged that it would be a human reaction to step down. "If I were in their place, it would have been done," he said. However, neither Patrushev nor Nurgaliev was asked to step down.

Aneta Gadiyeva, another family member, asked Putin about the removal of Valery Andreev, who headed the operations staff at the time. "Did you remove Andreev?" she asked.

"Yes, we removed him from operational work."

She retorted, "So why, then, was he promoted in rank and given a new position? He is now deputy head of the Academy of the FSB. What can he teach?"

When another family member again raised the question of Andreev's fate, Putin simply replied, "I will see."

In spite of significant public pressure, nobody in the secret services was punished for the obvious failures of coordination during the storming of the school in Beslan.

On December 27, 2005, Deputy General Prosecutor Nikolai Shepel said the investigation conducted by his office had found no mistakes in the secret services' response to the hostage taking.[9] But the local population kept up the pressure on the authorities, and finally a few scapegoats were found: Miroslav Aidarov, Taymuras Murtazov, and Guram Dryaev, all three of whom were low-ranking local police officers. The three were accused of criminal negligence but were granted amnesty in May 2007.[10]

IN JUNE 2007, the Russian National Antiterrorist Committee created a special working group, subordinate to Patrushev, to counter "the ideology of terrorism." On April 24, 2008, Patrushev approved the plan. A copy of the plan, obtained by the authors, outlined a set of guidelines for the secret services for 2008–2012. Among the measures included in the plan was a special training course, known as "Bastion," for journalists covering terrorism. The authors believe that the course, established by the security services, is a sort of brainwashing for journalists, aimed at limiting journalistic coverage of scenes of terrorist attacks and counterterrorism operations. Interior Ministry officials said that if a journalist has not attended the courses, he or she may be not allowed access to the area, as the number of press accreditations is limited and priority will be given to graduates of Bastion. The plan signed by Patrushev confirmed this. According to the document, the security services are required "to develop the order of accreditation of journalists who passed the courses and to establish a special diploma that would become the grounds for a journalist's accreditation with the operations staff during the counterterrorist operation." This requirement is at odds with the Russian law on media, in which there is no mention of the course as a prerequisite for journalistic accreditation.

In another point of the document, the FSB, foreign intelligence, and other state bodies were ordered to find an integrated response to "actions of an anti-Russia nature" carried out by the overseas propaganda centers of terrorist organizations, "including prevention of an international public tribunal on war crimes in Chechnya in Berlin." The idea of a tribunal had been proposed by members of the German parliament in the mid-2000s.[11]

OVER AND OVER again, the leadership of the security services in Moscow blamed the terrorist attacks by Chechens on outsiders— on Al Qaeda, or Arab extremists who infiltrated Chechnya, or foreign intelligence services helping the insurgents. After the 9/11 terrorist attacks on the United States, the FSB director stated that Chechnya was another front against Al Qaeda, and that the most horrible terrorist actions were financed by Arabs.[12] Two notorious Arab warlords who fought in Chechnya, Emir Khattab and Abu Al-Walid, were accused of organizing the apartment bombings in Moscow in September 1999.[13] Abu Al-Walid was said by the FSB to have received $4.5 million for a terrorist attack on the Moscow metro in 2004.[14] In October 2004 the FSB spokesman in the North Caucasus claimed that Al Qaeda and the Muslim Brotherhood were the main reason for hostilities in Chechnya.[15]

But the focus on external enemies may have been misplaced. Arabs were present in Chechnya, but they were always subordinate to Chechens. The tactics and methods used by terrorists in Russia were largely masterminded by Shamil Basayev. Despite his undisputed skills in guerrilla warfare, his first love was hostage taking.

When in November 1991 Chechen nationalist president Dzhokhar Dudaev unilaterally declared independence, Boris Yeltsin announced a state of emergency and dispatched troops to the border of Chechnya. In response Basayev, then 26 years old, and two friends hijacked a plane that had left Mineralnyye Vody in Russia, diverted it to Ankara, and threatened to blow up the aircraft unless the state of emergency was lifted. The hijacking was resolved peacefully in Turkey, and Basayev was allowed to return safely to Chechnya. His mark was on many of the biggest attacks that followed over the next fifteen years. The most spectacular actions carried out by terrorists on Russian soil were not suicide bombings but hostage takings: the hospital in Budennovsk in 1995, the village of Pervomayskoye in 1996, the Moscow theater in 2002, and the Beslan school in 2004, all organized by Chechens.

In the early 2000s Chechen terrorists used suicide bombers, but their method was different from Al Qaeda's: In Russia, female suicide bombers were primarily used, and would-be "martyrs" were never trained or used in pairs, as was common practice for Al Qaeda in Iraq and Afghanistan. The use of female *shahidas* ("black widows") appears to have been Basayev's tactic, predating the use of women as suicide bombers in Palestine.*

---

* The first attack carried out by female suicide bombers in Chechnya took place on June 7, 2000, when Khava Barayeva and Luiza Magomadova blew themselves up in a truck near the military base in the village of Alkhan-Yourt. Wafa Idris, the first Palestinian female suicide bomber, detonated a bomb in Jerusalem on January 27, 2002.

Russian officials also seem to have shifted their definition of terrorism quite markedly in recent years, so that the effort to combat it is geared less toward preventing acts of violence aimed at civilians and more toward preserving the state against external threats.

The 1998 Russian antiterrorist law called "On Fighting Terrorism," signed by Boris Yeltsin, defined terrorism in these terms:

Violence or the threat of violence against individuals or organizations, and also the destruction (damaging) of or threat to destroy (damage) property and other material objects, such as threatening to cause loss of life, significant damage to property, or other socially dangerous consequences and implemented with a view to violating public security, intimidating the population, or influencing the adoption of decisions advantageous to terrorists by organs of power, or satisfying their unlawful material and (or) other interests; attempts on the lives of statesmen or public figures perpetrated with a view to ending their state or other political activity or out of revenge for such activity.[16]

But in 2006 a new antiterrorism law called "On Countering Terrorism" replaced the 1998 version and offered a quite different definition of terrorism:

Terrorism is an ideology of violence and practice of influence on decision making by bodies of the government, institutions of local government, or international organizations, by means of intimidation of the population and (or) other forms of illegal violent actions.[17]

THE NEW POLICY put a strong emphasis on terrorism as something aimed at the *state*, while the earlier policy had defined it as something directed at *civilians*. It is worth remembering that the full name of the FSB unit responsible for counterterrorism is the "Service for Defense of the Constitutional System and Combatting Terrorism," where the term "the constitutional system" is understood as the political regime existing in the country.

In Putin's day, with a weakened political opposition and timid press, the Russian secret services had no fear of accusing fingers being pointed at them. Putin was the only customer who had to be pleased. The chronicle of the FSB's failures and the Kremlin's reaction in these years followed a clear "red line": If the failure led to human tragedy but didn't threaten the position of the authorities, the generals were to be forgiven. However, if the same failure did endanger the authority structure, then those responsible would be found and punished, even if they occupied the highest positions in the FSB.

The Nord-Ost hostage taking of 2002 did not threaten the Kremlin's position, and afterward FSB generals not only avoided punishment but were rewarded. Victor Zakharov, the head of the FSB department responsible for prevention of terrorist attacks in the capital, was promoted to the rank of colonel general, and FSB director Patrushev was given the country's highest award.[18]

The awards streamed in so thick and fast that none of the Moscow Duma's thirty-five members could avoid one. All were recognized in February 2003 for being "participants in the special action at Nord-Ost" at a solemn ceremony at the city council building.[19] The first award went to Yuri Luzhkov, Moscow's mayor.

But the situation was far different when insurgents raided Ingushetia in June 2004. For a brief period, the entire region fell into the hands of Basayev's militants. This time Putin was quick to make tough decisions: On July 19, he fired Anatoly Yezhkov, deputy director of the FSB and chief of the regional operations staff in the North Caucasus; Vyacheslav Tikhomirov, a commander of the Interior Ministry internal troops; and Mikhail Labunets, a commander of the North Caucasus internal troops.[20] Within a month Alexander Zhdankov, another high-ranking FSB general, was quietly transferred out of his post as a chief in the counterterrorism department, and by the end of 2004 the head of the local FSB department, Sergei Koryakov, was transferred to a region in Siberia.[21]

In the Soviet and later Russian armed forces, the second-highest rank is general of the army, the equivalent of four-star general in the United States. FSB director Patrushev received the rank of general of the army in July 2001. It was a remarkable achievement. In the 1990s the rank was a rare mark of prestige and not all FSB directors were awarded it; Putin himself did not achieve such a high rank while he was FSB chief. During the Andropov years, the KGB passed an important milestone with four generals of the army in service all at the same time. This was achieved once again when Putin became president. In May 2005, Pronichev, the FSB deputy director and border guards chief who had been in charge of the operations staff at the Dubrovka siege, was promoted to general of the army. In December 2005, Sergey Smirnov, an FSB first deputy director, was also made a general of the army. In March 2007, two FSB deputy directors—Alexander Bortnikov (in charge of economic security) and Oleg Syromolotov (counterintelligence)—similarly received that same rank.[22] At this point the FSB had four generals of the army, the military intelligence had one, and the Interior Ministry had two.

⚜⚜⚜

IN RUSSIA, THE public usually doesn't know when an FSB officer commits a crime. The service prevents any external investigation without its involvement.

In lieu of outside controls, in the early 1990s all the parts of the old KGB created special bodies, called Internal Security Directorates, as a check against corruption. The KGB successor created one in 1992.[23]

It soon became established practice for Interior Ministry operatives, on discovering employees of the security services complicit in criminal activity, to inform the leadership of that service. The service must be in the know from the very beginning: The arrest of the suspect must be conducted by a joint group of operatives from the Interior Ministry and the respective internal security directorate.[24]

The only external control over the security services, established in the 1990s, was the General Prosecutor's Office, a special body responsible for overseeing all the secret services, including the FSB. But the prosecutor's jurisdiction was limited from the beginning by a stipulation in a February 1995 law:

> Information regarding people who provide or have provided FSB organs with confidential assistance regarding the organization, tactics, methods, and means of implementing the activity of FSB organs shall not be subject to oversight by the prosecutor's office.[25]

The FSB restricted the general prosecutor's jurisdiction even further in April 2002, when General Prosecutor Vladimir Ustinov and FSB director Patrushev signed a joint decree establishing new boundaries for the prosecutor's oversight. The document under-lined that "oversight must equally ensure both the guarantee of human rights and the order of conducting operations," and estab-lished that "official operational and other work-related documents are to be examined according to the laws governing the estab-lished procedure for classified records, and as a rule, on the prem-ises of the Federal Security Service (the FSB), fulfilling the secrecy requirements. Only in exceptional cases is the Prosecutor's office allowed to demand access to such documents."[26]

On February 11, 2006, Putin signed a new decree on informa-tion considered to be a state secret. While the old version had con-sisted of 87 points, the new one included 113. Three new points, numbered 90, 91, and 92, stipulated that the identities of personnel serving with intelligence, counterintelligence, and units fighting organized crime were all secret. The stipulations, allegedly aimed at protecting officers working undercover in criminal or terrorist groups, were soon put to another use.

In 2007 the authors of this book were preparing a story for the *Novaya Gazeta* on the criminal records of individuals within the Rus-sian secret services. The authors sent an official request to the General Prosecutor's Office asking for statistics on criminal cases involving officials in the FSB, Federal Protective Service, and for-eign intelligence. No names were requested, only details of crim-inal activity. In response the authors received a letter from the Military Prosecutor's Office claiming that "all requested information is in accordance with points 90–92 of the list of information cov-ered by the State Secret Privilege [decree], which is considered to be a state secret, and thus cannot be presented." In turn Alexan-der Beznasyuk, chairman of the Moscow District Military Court, responded to the same request by saying that data about verdicts on the personnel of the secret services are classified "Top Secret."[27]

In the end, the authors wrote the story about the problem, but without the information they sought.

IN PUTIN'S FIRST speech as president to a joint session of Parliament, he declared, "We insist on the only possible dictatorship—a dictatorship of law."[28] Eight years later, when Dmitry Medvedev succeeded Putin, he declared in his inaugural speech, "We must gain full respect for the law and overcome legal nihilism."[29] Both comments pointed to one of the most profound failures of Russia in the years after the end of Communism—the establishment of the rule of law. The Soviet Union was a state ruled by a party, but it was supposed to be different in Russia, where a democracy would be founded on the rule of law, in which the rules would bind everyone and there would be no arbitrary use of power and no individuals above the law. New laws governing capitalism, crime, and the conduct of government were passed in these years. But the rule of law was exceedingly difficult to establish. Along with outlining the laws and determining the judicial system, another integral part of the rule of law was the role of the security agencies—they had the power to enforce the law and to investigate violations of it. But the services were far from effective in their task. They were still caught up in the practices of earlier times, escaping accountability and serving as an agent of the state rather than of the law.

EXTRAJUDICIAL KILLINGS

ISTORICALLY, THE KGB had very little experience dealing with terrorists because of the almost complete absence of terrorist attacks on Soviet soil. The KGB had focused instead on hunting down spies and dissidents. The violent actions that might be considered terrorism were mostly carried out by criminals. In the 1980s, only six terrorist attacks occurred in the Soviet Union, all of them plane hijackings by individuals trying to escape the country. The most famous incident was the attempt on March 8, 1988, by the Ovechkin family—a mother with ten sons—who tried to force the crew to take them to London. Instead of the British capital, the plane landed at a military airbase near Leningrad, where it was stormed. Three passengers, a flight attendant, and five members of the family were killed.[1]

The new decade of terrorism began in earnest in 1991 with the hijacking of a plane by Shamil Basayev, who carried out the action in the name of Chechen independence. Thereafter attacks took place annually. Terrorists captured planes, helicopters, buses, and even a kindergarten. The attacks grew even more spectacular in 1995 when the entire city hospital in Budennovsk was captured by Basayev, who wanted to push Russian forces out of Chechnya.

The security services that replaced the KGB were faced with new challenges as terrorism increased; they had to change their structure and methods to deal with the new reality. The first problem was to find people to create a counterterrorism section. The Soviet KGB had had two departments designated to deal with terrorists: The first was a part of the Fifth Directorate, responsible for political investigations and keeping an eye on domestic terrorist groups; the second was included in the K Directorate, responsible for overseas counterintelligence and preventing penetration by foreign terrorists.

When a new directorate on combatting terrorism was formed in 1991, employees were drawn from the old Fifth Directorate. Many officers previously involved in the disruption of dissident groups were given the new task of fighting terrorists. The skills and practices of the old KGB may not have been a good match for the years of battling terrorists. As a rule, KGB agents played out their strategies over long periods, while the effort to prevent and combat terrorism often demanded rapid action and reaction.

On August 13, 1998, the lobby of the FSB headquarters at Lubyanka was blown up, with two FSB guards slightly wounded. On April 3, 1999, a second attack occurred at almost exactly the same place when a bomb containing the equivalent of 1.5 kilos of TNT was detonated, although this time without deaths or injuries. Both bombings were executed by left-wing extremists from the group called "New Revolutionary Initiative," headed by four idealistic young women in their twenties and inspired by the German Red Army Faction. The culprits were identified soon after the first explosion, but the FSB preferred to keep the group under surveillance rather than apprehend them—a measure that would most likely have prevented the second bombing.[2] At their trial the FSB claimed it had discovered a powerful terrorist organization of nearly 500 members that intended to overthrow the government.

By the mid-1990s the FSB was desperate to find new personnel to fight terrorism. Historically suspicious of ethnic North Caucasians, the FSB had largely failed to recruit Chechens.[3] Eager to add fresh blood to its desk-office staff, it turned to the Interior Ministry, whose officers were regarded as more ruthless, given their history of fighting Chechen and other ethnic organized crime groups in Moscow. This experience was considered to be helpful, since the FSB believed Chechen warlords obtained financing and weapons through Chechen organized crime groups based in Moscow.

Special departments at both the FSB and the Interior Ministry were tasked to deal with Chechens. The FSB unit attempted to infiltrate the groups by any means necessary, including protecting loyal ringleaders. Not surprisingly, the department was accused of being highly corrupt.[4] At the same time, it was highly efficient—fat with priceless information.

As a result, by the end of the 1990s the Russian security services had adopted harsh methods to deal with terrorism. The emphasis was on using ruthless, brutal extrajudicial operations that, for fear of leaks, were to be conducted by ultra-secret and out-of-control special units.[5] These methods were to be expanded in Chechnya when in 1999 the second Chechen war started.

After a short period of Army operations, the FSB took control of Chechnya in January 2001. The FSB was in charge for only thirty-one months—from January 2001 to July 2003—and then control and responsibility were handed over to the Interior Ministry.

During its Chechen reign and afterward, the FSB's special units in Chechnya carried out extrajudicial killings. The Interior Ministry and the military intelligence agency simultaneously deployed units with similar objectives.

Military intelligence conducted these operations with two *spetsnaz* (special ops) brigades, named East and West, comprised of ethnic Chechens. Their primary role was the elimination of suspected insurgents. In August 2004 Minister of Defense Sergei Ivanov met with the *spetsnaz* commanders to declare his support and supply them with more advanced weapons.[6]

The Interior Ministry also sent elimination groups to the region, usually for one-month tours. These so-called "temporary operation groups" were deployed in the Chechen Republic but also in Dagestan and Ingushetia. One officer involved in such activities told the authors: "Our group consisted of only four people: a driver and three operatives with the rank of major and higher. We were required to report only to our leadership in Moscow. We were sent to the area with a list of targets, and when the mission was accomplished, all we had to present as proof were Polaroid photographs of the bodies."[7]

The FSB had two different structures engaged in this area. First, the so-called summary special groups (SSG) consisting of operatives of regional FSB divisions and soldiers from *spetsnaz* groups of the Interior Ministry. Ten of the SSG groups were created in April 2002 to target and kill Chechen rebel leaders. To carry out liquidations of insurgents, they operated independently of the FSB Department in Chechnya.[8]

On April 4, 2004, three Chechen brothers—Rustam Ilaev (30) and his younger siblings Inver (21) and Adlan (17)—as well as a fourth man, Kazbek Bataev (20), were seized in the Chechen village of Assinovskaya. All four were refugees from Bamut, a village destroyed by bombing during the war. At 4:30 A.M. around twenty armed people, most in balaclavas, arrived in three armored personnel carriers at the home of Jahita Ilaeva, the mother of the Ilaev

brothers, to take them away. The captors did not identify themselves, but they spoke Russian without an accent, and those whose
faces weren't covered by masks looked like Russians. The four
Chechen men have never been seen again.

Despite the requests of the relatives to the Ministry of Internal
Affairs of Chechnya and the local prosecutor, no explanation for
the capture was offered. A few months after the event, the relatives
of the kidnapped men received letters from Alexander Stepanov,
the investigator attached to the village of Achkoy-Martan, confirm-
ing that the four men had indeed been taken away "by unidentified persons" in armored vehicles. He wrote that a criminal case
had been filed and that he would inform the relatives about the
outcome of the investigation. According to *Novaya Gazeta*, the four
men were captured by FSB's summary special group SSG-12, and
the case was mentioned in a report of the International Helsinki
Federation for Human Rights.[9]

Two of the disappeared, Rustam and Inver, had served in Chechen president Ramzan Kadyrov's security service—a department
distrusted by Russian security services because Kadyrov encouraged former insurgents to join its ranks. Their bodies might never
be found. In general, Russian special forces made it a practice to
use drastic methods to eliminate evidence. One such method,
known as pulverization, involved strapping artillery shells to a
body, loading it down with TNT. The trick, as explained by two
special forces officers who had fought militants in Chechnya for a
decade, was to "make sure absolutely nothing is left. No body, no
proof, no problem."[10]

Without doubt, the Russians were not the only forces who
turned to brutality in the Chechen wars. The Chechen rebels
fought with equally harsh tactics, often targeting Russian soldiers

and carrying out terrorist attacks against innocent civilians beyond the war zone.

THE FSB HAD also deployed units from its special purpose center to Chechnya. According to Colonel Sergei Shavrin, deputy commander of Vympel Department, two sections with more than thirty operatives each were deployed full-time in Chechnya.[11] These groups carried out one of the most high-profile eliminations of the decade. On March 8, 2005, Aslan Maskhadov, the last legitimate president of separatist Chechnya, was hunted down and killed in the Chechen village of Tolstoy-Yurt by the special purpose center's assault group. One of the officers was awarded the Hero of Russia medal for his role in the assassination.[12]

Russia's unapologetic practice of extrajudicial killings has continued in recent years. On September 2, 2009, leading Russian human rights organizations called a press conference to declare that death squads were still in use in the North Caucasus.[13] "We can describe their method as 'death squads.' We shouldn't be afraid of using this term, because they kill civilians and push the Caucasus toward war," said prominent activist Lev Ponomarev, head of the organization called For Human Rights. "The death squads are used illegally . . . since 2000, Memorial has been tracking such methods: illegal prisons, torture, and extrajudicial executions," said Alexander Cherkasov of the human rights group Memorial. According to Memorial's tally, in Chechnya seventy-nine people were victims of kidnappings in 2009. "After two years of some sort of calm in Chechnya, we have a new wave of suicide bombings, kidnappings, and murders. . . . We've gone backward three years," Cherkasov lamented.

Neighboring Dagestan has seen twenty-five kidnappings since February 2009 by Memorial's count, twelve of which resulted in the murder of victims. A week after the press conference, Sirazhudin Umarov, 32, a construction worker, was kidnapped from Qala, a Derbent district of Dagestan. On September 9 he was called to a meeting by an acquaintance named Azer, a police officer. There Umarov was captured by unidentified masked men. The following day his badly mutilated body was discovered. The security forces confirmed that he had been killed by the authorities, though they claimed he had died during an antiterrorism operation. "His face was so badly smashed from beating that I had difficulty recognizing him," said Gulbenis Badurova, 33, his wife. "His eye was missing, and both hands had been broken."[14]

A few months earlier, Umarov and his uncle had been detained by local law enforcement officials for suspected involvement in the insurgency. Umarov's uncle was tried and convicted. Umarov was released and returned to Dagestan. Two months later, he was dead.[15]

Extrajudicial killing would seem to be at odds with the law. In Chechnya, there was no declared war with Russia, only a counterterrorism operation. During counterterrorism operations, law enforcement agencies are supposed to operate according to the Criminal Code of Russia. Terrorism is a crime listed in the Criminal Code, meaning that terrorists should be detained, charged, and tried. If proven guilty, they should be sent to prison. (The death penalty is not used in Russia.) There is no place in the criminal code for summary execution without charge. Valery Dyatlenko, a former FSB general and deputy chief of the Security Committee at the State Duma, commented to the authors on the "shoot to kill" policy at the end of 2005: "You speak about liquidators, but this is not correct," he said. "No one has permitted anyone to do such a thing." Small insurgent groups, he added, "hide out in forests, and a tactic is in place to combat such groups. . . . There is a unit tasked to check any individual found in a forest. The principle is that no one has a legitimate reason to be roaming the woods. And if shooting begins, then our units, to protect themselves, excuse me, they are at war. . . . But this is not liquidation; liquidation is a term from the SS lexicon."[16]

When asked what he would call the practice, he replied: "Elimination. Or armed struggle. . . . For me this term [direct liquidations] is equivalent to murder. It is wrong. But there is a war, no matter what you call it. These groups are not instruments of punishment or retaliation; it is one of the forms of the struggle."[17] Russian security services in Chechnya adopted other new tactics as well. One, called "counter-capture," was a highly controversial practice of seizing terrorists' relatives to pressure suspected terrorists to surrender. The term "counter-capture" was publicly used for the first time by general prosecutor Vladimir Ustinov before the State Duma on October 29, 2004, when he said that "counter-capture" would have a deterrent effect on future terrorism. "If people—if you can call them human beings—have turned to such an act as terrorism, the detention of relatives, to show the terrorists what could happen to these families, may to some degree save people."[18]

Though the Russian legislature has never approved the policy of counter-capture, it is actively employed. The first capture occurred in March 2004, when more than forty relatives of Chechen field commander Magomed Hambiev were taken into custody. As a result, Hambiev surrendered to the federal authorities. The second capture of relatives occurred during the siege in Beslan. Relatives of the wife of Aslan Maskhadov, including her father, were detained. Similarly, on August 12, 2005, Natasha Humadova, the sister of Chechen field commander Doku Umarov, was taken by the authorities.[19]

In a new wrinkle to the long, bloody conflict between Russia and Chechnya, in May 2004 Putin ordered the creation of a special unit to serve the pro-Kremlin Chechen president. The "Kadyrov guards"—former bodyguards of Chechen President Akhmad Kadyrov—were assigned to the Chechen Ministry of Internal Affairs and used the same tactics of kidnapping and counter-capture.[20] According to Memorial, the capture of seven relatives of Aslan Maskhadov in December 2004 was carried out by Kadyrov guards.[21]

IN 2006, SEVERAL months before he was killed in an explosion, Basayev reorganized the military structure of the Chechen insurgents. Previously, they had been a rather conventional military organization with brigades, regiments, battalions, the Ministry of Sharia's state security, and even an antiterrorist center. Faced with Russian squads carrying out extrajudicial killings, Chechens shifted from a quasi-military structure to a system of small three- to five-person groups tasked with attacking Russian law enforcement personnel.

In November 2006 Ali Taziev (nom-de-guerre Magas), a Chechen commander, stated in an interview on a separatist Web site that the formation of such groups was designed "to target specific people and to prepare and execute military operations for their elimination."[22] These changes were confirmed by the authors'

sources in the Russian secret services, which face a new generation of militants: By 2008, Chechen youth were being drawn to
jihad, replacing experienced insurgents in their mid-thirties. Ji-
hadist groups extended their reach beyond the borders of Chechnya to the internal republics of Ingushetia, Kabardino-Balkaria,
and Dagestan. The tactic of large insurgent raids were replaced by
ambushes.

Between 2007 and 2009 a number of high-ranking Russian
officials were ambushed and killed by Chechen terrorists. On
January 12, 2008, Colonel Anatoly Kyarov, the head of the
Kabardino-Balkaria republic's organized crime unit, was assassinated in Nalchik. On March 7, Mark Metsaev, the head of the
same unit in North Ossetia, was machine-gunned to death. On
June 12, 2009, General Adilgerei Magomedtagirov, Dagestan's interior minister, was killed in the capital, Makhachkala. The militants also returned to suicide bombing; in November 2008 a
female suicide bomber killed eleven people and wounded as
many as forty others in an attack in Vladikavkaz, the capital of
North Ossetia, and in June 2009 a suicide bomber killed two police officers in Grozny.[23] On March 29, 2010, female suicide terrorism returned to Moscow: Two women from Dagestan almost
simultaneously blew themselves up in the capital's metro. The attack killed forty people.

Military operations led by Russian troops, meanwhile, were in
decline: In 2007, Putin cut the federal presence in Chechnya from
50,000 to 25,000 troops. Federal forces now had the same number
of personnel as Kadyrov's formations.

For three years, Kadyrov urged the Russian security agencies
and military to withdraw. He largely succeeded in pushing out (by

persuasion and other means) the extrajudicial hit squads and other remnants of the Russian attack on Chechnya.

In April 2009 the Kremlin declared the decade-and-a-half-long war in Chechnya over. President Dmitry Medvedev ordered the lifting of the "special security regime" in the region and announced the end of the counterterrorism operation in Chechnya.[24]

PART III

ACTIVITY ABROAD

ASSASSINATIONS

I N RESPONSE TO Chechen terrorism, Russia's security forces had gradually expanded their counteroffensive beyond national boundaries to carry out extrajudicial assassinations of terrorists abroad.

At 12:45 P.M. on February 13, 2004, a white Toyota Land Cruiser carrying Zelimkhan Yandarbiyev, a Chechen warlord and vice president of the breakaway republic, and his 13-year-old son was blown up in the Qatari capital of Doha as they were driving away from a mosque after Friday prayers. Yandarbiyev had driven only 300 yards from the mosque when the blast occurred. Gravely wounded, Yandarbiyev was pronounced dead several hours later. No one took responsibility for the attack, by far the most serious blow to the Chechen insurgency since the killing in 1996 of Dzhokhar Dudaev, the separatist president of Chechnya, when Russian military intelligence successfully homed in on Dudaev's cell phone signal and fired a missile in his direction.

Yandarbiyev's assassination was a sign of new tactics adopted by the Russian secret services in their fight against Chechen rebels. In the 1990s the battlefield was largely in Chechnya, but now Russian services were hunting down Chechen leaders anywhere in the world. The Russian authorities had openly declared Yandarbiyev a terrorist because of his role in the Nord-Ost theater attack, but they had little hope that he would be extradited from an Arab capital. Most of the Muslim world was sympathetic to the Chechen cause.

Yandarbiyev was born in 1952 into a Chechen family expelled by Stalin from Chechnya to Kazakhstan. In the late 1980s the intelligentsia in the North Caucasus were the first to be inflamed by nationalism, and Yandarbiyev, in Soviet times a poet and writer, became involved in local politics. He founded his own nationalist party and in 1993 was appointed vice president of Chechnya under Dudaev, serving as acting president during Chechnya's de facto independence in 1996–1997, a period of chaos and rising warlordism. In 1997 he came third in Chechnya's presidential elections, behind Aslan Maskhadov and Shamil Basayev.

Yandarbiyev left Chechnya in 1999 for the United Arab Emirates, having been appointed by Maskhadov as a representative of Chechnya in Muslim countries. (In his new role, he opened a Chechen embassy in Kabul and a consulate in Kandahar.) In the early 2000s Yandarbiyev came to Qatar as a personal guest of the emir, despite having been on the Interpol wanted list since 2001.[1] In May 2003 Russia formally requested Yandarbiyev's extradition from Qatar, and in June the U.N. Security Council's counterterrorist committee added him to its "sanctions list."[2] The week after the attack on Yandarbiyev, on the night of February 18, Qatari authorities arrested three Russians in a rented villa near the Russian embassy. The arrests became known because of a statement by Igor Ivanov, the Russian minister of foreign affairs. Ivanov admitted that all three were agents of the Russian secret services:

"The Russian citizens, one of which has a diplomatic passport, are employees of the Russian secret services. Within the limits of the status attached to the embassy, they were in Qatar on legal grounds, and they fulfilled the tasks without any violation of local legislation, tasks of an information-analytical character, connected to counteraction of international terrorism.[3]

Although he claimed Russia "has no involvement in this incident," Ivanov pointed out that Russian authorities had "repeatedly, including at the highest level, addressed Qatar with urgent requirements to extradite Yandarbiyev, who was personally responsible for the deaths of hundreds of citizens of Russia, including victims in the Dubrovka theater in Moscow, as a result of acts of terrorism which were supervised directly from Qatar." The Russian authorities accused Yandarbiyev of helping to mastermind the hostage taking, based on two phone calls between Movsar Barayev, a leader of hostage-takers, and Yandarbiyev during the crisis that were intercepted by the secret services.

The Qatari authorities riposted by releasing a statement containing the names of the Russians: Alexander Fetisov, the first secretary of the Russian embassy in Qatar, who was released to the Russian embassy due to his diplomatic status but was not allowed to leave the country; Anatoly Yablochkov (sometimes pronounced as Belashkov); and Vasily Pugachev (or Bogachyov). Yablochkov and Pugachev were charged by Qatar with the assassination of Yandarbiyev, the attempted assassination of his son, Daud, and with smuggling weapons into Qatar. Both agents gave detailed confessions that were included in the Qatari prosecution case during the trial. Russia said their confessions were extracted by torture.[4]

The way the operation was carried out can be gleaned from information published by Chechens, who described it as the result of the Qatari interrogation of the suspects.[5] There are still unanswered questions and gaps, but the trial was closed to the public at Russia's request, and further details could not be obtained.

At 7:30 A.M. on January 22, 2004, Yablochkov and Pugachev landed at Doha airport. The authors' sources provided information that both officers were agents of Russian military intelligence. The Russian newspaper *Kommersant* later reported that it had learned from sources in the Qatari prosecutors office that the order to kill Yandarbiyev had been issued directly by Sergei Ivanov, the Russian defense minister.[6]

Two hours later a Jeep Cherokee and Nissan Primera, both bearing diplomatic plates, crossed the border into Qatar from the UAE. The cars held a batch of explosives. Yablochkov and Pugachev stayed in a villa rented by the Russian embassy, where they were met by the first secretary of the embassy, Fetisov.

Preparation for the operation had taken three weeks. On February 13, three Russians in a Mitsubishi Pajero with diplomatic plates arrived in the parking lot of the Sheraton hotel in Doha. Yablochkov traded the Pajero for a rented van and headed to the mosque, where he was to wait for Yandarbiyev. When the Toyota Land Cruiser, with Yandarbiyev inside, pulled up in front of the mosque, Yablochkov returned to the Sheraton for Fetisov. Back at the mosque, Yablochkov planted the bomb beneath Yandarbiyev's vehicle. After the explosion the agents returned to the Sheraton parking lot, where Pugachev was waiting for them. They changed cars once again before retuning to their villa.

Because of their obvious Slavic appearance Yablochkov and Fetisov were noticed and later identified by the security guard of the mosque's parking lot. Crucial evidence was found in their rented villa, including details of explosives and photographs of Yandarbiyev taken during surveillance.

At the time of the attack, Qatar lacked a professional counter-intelligence service. The emir turned for help to U.S. intelligence, which may have helped to track the cellular phones used by the Russian agents. U.S. Deputy Assistant Secretary of State Steven Pifer confirmed in an interview with the Moscow-based news-paper *Vremya Novostei* that the United States did provide Qatar with "very insignificant technical assistance" in tracking down the alleged assassins.[7] Asked by the Associated Press to comment on this statement, an official of the U.S. embassy in Moscow replied that Washington had sent a team of explosives experts to Qatar at the emir's request, adding that the U.S. experts "played no role in the arrest or investigation of any suspects."[8]

The Kremlin made strenuous efforts—from visits by high-ranking personnel and presidential calls to pressure on the media—to get the detainees back to Russia. At a diplomatic level, Putin repeatedly sent Igor Ivanov, the secretary of Russia's Security Council and a former minister of foreign affairs, to Qatar for nego-tiations. In Qatar the captured agents were provided with attor-neys from the famous Russian law office of Yegorov, Puginsky, Afanasiev, and Partners. This was a clear sign of direct support from Putin, because the head of the firm, Nikolai Yegorov, had studied at university with Putin and maintained close ties with him. Leonid Parfenov, a host on NTV television in Moscow, obtained an inter-view with Yandarbiyev's widow after the bombing. It went on the air in May as part of the Sunday program *Namedni*, one of NTV's most highly rated and well-respected programs. The program aired in eastern Russia, but as the hours passed, NTV management pulled the interview before it was seen in western and central Russia including Moscow. In a letter to Parfenov, NTV's management said the FSB had ordered that the interview be dropped, arguing that it could negatively impact the ongoing trial in Qatar. Parfenov protested and sent the letter to the newspaper *Kommersant*. Two days later Parfenov was fired and the program was shut down.[9] According to NTV's Web site, Parfenov had breached his contract with the network by "not supporting the company's leadership."[10]

On February 26, 2004, two Qatari citizens were detained at Moscow's Sheremetievo airport. FSB officials claimed they were suspected of having ties with the Chechen rebels, although both the detainees, Ibat Akhmedov and Naser Ibragim Midahi, were members of Qatar's national Olympic team. They had traveled from Belarus to Serbia through Moscow, and were sent to Lefortovo prison. The detention of two of its national athletes was a clear attempt on Russia's part to make a bargain with the Qataris.[11]

On March 23, Putin personally called the Emir of Qatar. After the call, Fetisov was allowed to come back to Moscow and the two Qatari citizens in Moscow were released.[12] In April the trial in Qatar began, but at Russia's request it was held behind closed doors.[13] In the months that followed, the Russian secret agents were tried and convicted of murder. Both men were sentenced to life in prison—not to death, as had been requested by prosecutor.[14] In the summer Qatari authorities promised to hand the officers over to Russia, ostensibly to serve out their sentences in a Russian jail. For that to happen, Qatar approved a new version of its Criminal Code that allowed the convicts to be transferred to their homeland.[15] Not long afterward, Russia and Qatar signed a prisoner exchange agreement.

On the night of December 23, a Russian government plane, one that usually carried high-ranking officials but this time with both prisoners onboard, landed at Moscow's Vnukovo airport. Vnukovo was chosen because it is a VIP airport, used by Putin for traveling all over the world. There the two prisoners were met by Russian officials, and although no press was allowed to attend the meeting, it became known that the proverbial red carpet was rolled out for them. The secret agents had come home to a hero's welcome.[16]

The same day the official news agency of Qatar declared:

The State of Qatar has granted the Russian government's request to hand over two citizens of Russia to serve the remaining term of their sentences, determined at trial in Qatar, in a Russian prison. Consent has been given according to an agreement concluded by the two states on the basis of rules and laws appropriate to the specific case.[17]

In Moscow, members of Parliament and government officials were busy arguing what kind of awards should be granted to national heroes, and nobody even pretended to comply with the conditions imposed by Qatari authorities.[18] "In Russia's eyes they are innocent. There is no need for any further court procedure," said Dmitri Peskov, a deputy press secretary to Putin, in January 2005.[19] In February 2005 the head of Russia's Federal Penal Service, Yuri Kalinin, claimed he had no information on the whereabouts of the agents convicted in Qatar. "As for our citizens who were delivered from Qatar, they are not being held in our institutions," Kalinin said in comments carried by the Ren-TV television channel. "I have no further information. Maybe they are receiving medical treatment somewhere. Maybe some procedural issues are being resolved. You see, a sentence passed by a Qatar court does not serve as grounds for holding somebody in prison in Russia."[20]

The Qatari operation was intended to be a showcase for the Russian secret services. The consequent arrest of three Russian suspects, their eventual conviction by a Qatari court, and their triumphal return to Moscow helped to create a new strategy—one that would launch operations beyond the borders of the country. Russian officials said they were impressed by the Israeli example of hunting down terrorists abroad. After Yandarbiyev's assassination, one FSB colonel in the elite group Vympel asked Soldatov: "Take a look at the Mossad. Why cannot we do the same with our terrorists?"

Vympel, which consists only of officers, was created inside the KGB in August 1981 to carry out deep penetration, sabotage, and liquidations in times of war. In the 1980s the Vympel officers, highly skilled and fluent in different languages, were sent undercover to the West.[21] However, in the mid-1990s, Vympel was turned into an antiterrorist unit, and later it focused on hunting down rebels in Chechnya, in the process losing priceless skills—a matter for constant regret for its officers. At the same time the Kremlin appeared to have learned the lessons of its predecessors, namely that killings would be most effective in countries more willing to rewrite their policy in favor of the states resorting to such tactics. From the beginning, Qatar was regarded by the Kremlin as a state that might be convinced, a hunch that proved correct.

Two years after the Qatari incident, on June 3, 2006, shortly before 3:00 P.M. a Chevrolet Tahoe carrying five Russian diplomats was cut off by a minivan and a sedan 1,200 feet from the Russian embassy in Baghdad. Gunmen attacked the diplomats' car in the upscale Mansour neighborhood. One of the diplomats, Vitaly Titov, was severely wounded and died later that day. The other four men were kidnapped. On June 19, the Iraqi insurgents demanded Russian troops withdraw from Chechnya and free all Muslim prisoners in Russia within forty-eight hours, or the diplomats would be executed. On June 25, the terrorists released a hostage video showing one man being beheaded and another shot dead, as well as the body of a third. The next day Russia confirmed that the four diplomats were dead.

On June 28, Putin ordered Russia's secret services to find and kill the insurgents responsible for kidnapping and killing Russian embassy employees in Iraq.[22] Patrushev, then FSB director, stated that the special services would do everything possible to eliminate the terrorists: "We should ensure that any terrorist who has committed a crime will not avoid the responsibility," he said. Patrushev added: "This is not a casual assignment. It is in the logic of what we do [i.e., how counterterrorism is understood by the Russian secret services]."[23]

Although it was presented in news reports as an emotional reaction to the diplomats' murders, Russia's policy of carrying out assassinations abroad had been under preparation for some time. The Russian parliament spent months discussing the new legislative initiative that allows the FSB to kill terrorists on foreign soil.[24] The first draft of the bill, according to Mikhail Grishankov, a deputy chairman of the Security Committee at the State Duma, was presented to the Duma in March of 2006.[25] It took only a week following Putin's declaration of retribution in Iraq before the State Duma and Federation Council approved foreign assassinations by intelligence agencies. The federal law was approved by the

Duma on July 5, and the special decision of the Federation Council (the upper house of the Russian Parliament) was approved on July 7, 2006.[26] According to this package of antiterrorism bills, the president could now order Russian *spetsnaz* or intelligence groups to conduct operations in foreign countries.

The battered republic of Abkhazia appeared to be the first target after the bills were approved. Situated at the northwestern corner of Georgia, Abkhazia had once been a desirable holiday destination, but its war for independence from Georgia has reduced the country's economy to ruins and turned the republic into a close satellite of Russia. Abkhazia is isolated in every sense of the word—except from Russia, which maintains a border crossing and has reopened the railway line to Sukhumi, the capital. To strengthen ties with Abkhazia, Moscow made it easy for local people to obtain Russian citizenship, and most now hold two passports.

At 1:30 P.M. on August 17, 2007, Khamzat Gitsba, a prominent local leader of the radical Muslim community, was shot dead in the center of the tiny town of Gudaouta. Gitsba, nicknamed Rocky because of his intense interest in boxing, was well known in the republic as a war hero during the Georgian-Abkhazian conflict of 1992–1993. He was a member of Shamil Basayev's Chechen battalion during the war and was one of the terrorists who took Russian and foreign tourists hostage on the Avrasia ferry in Turkish waters in January 1996. After 2000, Gitsba returned to Abkhazia, where he led the radical Muslim group in the region. At the same time Gitsba kept close ties with Chechen rebels and personally with Shamil Basayev, who was married to Gitsba's sister.[27]

It was well known that Abkhaz Muslims received financial support from Turkey, where there is a large Abkhaz community, but it is the North Caucasian insurgency that is really interested in this help. Khamzat Gitsba had close ties with the Chechen rebels and their supporters in Turkey, and he was regarded by the Russian secret services as a financial intermediary between the Turkish and Chechen rebels. According to the authors' information, Gitsba was also responsible for providing asylum for the militants who attacked Nalchik in October 2005 and fled to Abkhazia thereafter. Abkhazia tolerated his presence, partly because of his role during the war for independence, partly due to the weakness of the Abkhaz law enforcement agencies.

Khamzat Gitsba was machine-gunned in front of a mosque by two assassins who waited for him in a Chrysler vehicle. An hour later the Chrysler was found burning. The local police established that the car had been driven across the Russian-Abkhazian border at the Psou River some days prior to the murder. Video cameras at the Abkhazian customs station identified the Chrysler's registration plates, but because Abkhazia did not keep records of all those driving into the republic, the identities of the drivers were impossible to prove. The Abkhazians turned to the Russian border guards, but the Russians said that such a vehicle never crossed the border.[28] One official close to government circles in Abkhazia, who asked not to be named, told the authors: "We have no doubt it was the FSB's operation: Gitsba was the head of a Wahhabi radical Muslim community, and the government had no other way to deal with it."[29]

Around the same time, a spate of murders of Chechens occurred in Azerbaijan. Imran Gaziev, deputy chief of the representative office of the unrecognized Chechen Republic of Ichkeria in Azerbaijan, was killed in the capital, Baku, on November 18, 2007. The killer shot as Gaziev was getting out of his car. The gun was left at the crime scene; it turned out to be a Baikal pistol with a silencer. The Baikal is a small, snubnose, black handgun that looks almost like a toy, developed in the 1970s for the top brass of the Army, but Interior Ministry troops and the KGB favored it, too. Fighters from different counterterrorist units use Baikals as an auxiliary weapon, as do many criminals. Due to its ability to pierce bulletproof jackets, this gun became known in the West as "the gangsters' gun."[30]

This first spectacular assassination of a Chechen in Baku was not the only attempt to intimidate the local Chechen diaspora. In early 2007 the Council of Chechen Refugees in Azerbaijan had sent an appeal to the United Nations High Commissioner for Refugees, Antonio Guterres, stating that the situation for Chechen refugees in Azerbaijan had "seriously worsened," particularly as a result of "threats to the personal safety of our citizens who came to this country in search of refuge and protection."[31] The council referred to incidents involving "the abduction of people," specifically citing the case of Ruslan Eliev, who went missing in Baku in November 2006. In March 2007, his dead body was found in Chechnya near the village of Samashki.[32] FSB agents have been conducting operations in Azerbaijan for years. The most famous case occurred in 2002, when relations between the two countries were significantly worse; five FSB officers were caught in Baku with false documents and surveillance equipment.[33] They were expelled to Russia without being charged.

In the past, Azeri authorities had tolerated Chechens on their soil. But after the Nord-Ost siege, the Chechen office in Baku was closed down. Following the murder of Gaziev, the Ministry of National Security in Azerbaijan had no comment. The finger was pointed at Russia by the local Chechen diaspora, and it seemed to be more than just a conspiracy theory.

By 2007 relations between Russia and Azerbaijan had improved, and the authors' sources in the Interior Ministry confirmed the existence of an agreement with the law enforcement bodies of Azerbaijan that allowed actions by Russian special units and free passage across the border.[34] When the authors published this information in *Novaya Gazeta*, no denial was ever made by either Russia or Azerbaijan.

In 2008–2009, a series of assassinations of Chechens took place in Turkey. Turkey had long been accused by the Russian secret services of providing support to Chechen rebels, as many Chechen refugees had found asylum in the country, mostly in Istanbul. In September 2008, Gaji Edilsultanov, a former Chechen field commander, was assassinated in Istanbul. He was shot dead in the street in the Basaksehir district of the city. Three months later, on December 10, 2008, former Chechen warlord Islam Janibekov was assassinated in front of his wife and children there. He received three gunshot wounds to his head and died on the spot. The Russian magazine *Spetsnaz*, which has close ties to Russian special operations forces, alleged that Islam Janibekov was known in Russia as Urasul and was wanted by Russian authorities for terrorist attacks in the cities of Yessentuki and Mineralnyye Vody and in the republic of Karachay-Cherkessia in the early 2000s.[35] Musa Atayev (also known as Ali Osaev), another Chechen rebel, was killed in Istanbul on February 26, 2009.

Russia claimed that these were killings due to financial disputes.[36] But this explanation left many unanswered questions, and there was some evidence that the killings were troubling to officials outside Turkey. On March 21, 2009, the Turkish newspaper *Sabah* reported a confidential meeting between the Turkish and French secret services in Istanbul. The meeting reportedly focused on the series of killings of Chechens.[37] The newspaper quoted the liaison judge Philippe Dorcet from the French delegation, who said: "We have received information from our secret police, the DGSE, that assassinations of Chechens would be carried out in France. . . . Chechen murders that occurred one after another in Turkey attracted our attention; we think the murders in Turkey show similarities to each other. We have established a special intelligence team for Chechens living in France. A Russian connection is being closely examined due to the intelligence that we have received."[38] *Sabah* stated that French intelligence services believed the assassinations were planned by the Russian FSB and that the French had moved some of the Chechen leaders living in France to other locations and changed their identities. Istanbul Deputy Chief Prosecutor Turan Cholakkad, who participated in the meeting with the French delegation, told *Sabah* that the murders of Chechens were unrelated to organized crime. But the assassinations did not damage Russian-Turkish relations.

THE LITVINENKO POISONING made the Russian secret services' image abroad even more sinister. Alexander Litvinenko, a former FSB lieutenant colonel, had been assigned to a unit targeting organized crime; the group was eventually disbanded but questions had long been raised about its brutal methods. Litvinenko also took part in an open press conference in 1998, at which he claimed the FSB had ordered him to kill the oligarch Boris Berezovsky. Two years later, Litvinenko fled to London and sought political asylum. Russia in turn accused him of breaking FSB rules. In London, Litvinenko was supported financially by Berezovsky.[39] Litvinenko kept up the public criticism of the Russian authorities and in a press conference in London he accused the FSB of organizing the 1999

Moscow apartment building bombings. Later he also declared that the FSB was working with Al Qaeda and had been involved in the assassination of Russian journalist Anna Politkovskaya.

Litvinenko died in London in November 2006; British experts determined that he had been poisoned by the highly radioactive substance polonium-210. In his last statement, made from his hospital bed, Litvinenko accused Putin of ordering his killing. The British investigation showed that the nuclear material had come from Russia, and resulted in an extradition request for Andrei Lugovoi, a former KGB officer turned successful businessman in the 1990s, who met with Litvinenko in London on November 1, 2006, and then returned to Russia. The Russian authorities refused to extradite Lugovoi because it was at odds with the Russian constitution. Lugovoi, in turn, flatly denied he was guilty and said someone tried to frame him, and he was deliberately marked with polonium.

The British Crown Prosecution Service has never suggested a motive for Litvinenko's killing. Unofficially, British journalists briefed by the counterintelligence service MI5 were told that the poisoning had been organized by the Kremlin, but the government did not accuse Russia directly.[40] When Russia refused to extradite Lugovoi, the United Kingdom expelled four Russian diplomats from the Russian embassy in London.[41] In response, Russia expelled four British diplomats. A joint Russian-British counterterrorism group was disbanded. In Russia, Lugovoi was elected to Parliament, where he was invited to serve on the Security Committee, the same committee that oversees the Russian secret services and writes the laws that govern them.

Litvinenko's murder was one of the highest-profile examples of a Russian assassinated abroad in a decade. The polonium clearly originated in Russia, and it was impossible to bring the nuclear material into the United Kingdom without the help of Russian officials. But there is no information about whether Litvinenko's death was ordered by the Russian leadership or had been carried out by people who were bribed and hired as mercenaries. Russia's lack of cooperation with the British investigation, as well as the election of Lugovoi to the Russian Parliament, were seen in the West as clear indications of the government's support for the poisoning. But within Russia, the events were interpreted as proof that the country would not be pushed around by the outside world—a sentiment that was effectively turned into a propaganda campaign playing on anti-Western sentiments. No conclusive evidence has been seen by the authors about why Litvinenko was killed and who might have ordered it. Lugovoi's election to Parliament, which granted him immunity, pointed to staunch support from an uncompromising leadership.

FSB INTELLIGENCE

WHEN THE SOVIET KGB was divided into different agencies in the early 1990s, the new Russian leaders were determined to create an intelligence system that resembled its Western counterparts, one in which the jurisdiction of each agency would be both geographically and constitutionally distinct.[1] Foreign intelligence would be handled by one agency and internal security by another. The foreign intelligence agency would resemble the CIA in the United States or MI6 in the United Kingdom. The internal security agency would be analogous to the FBI or the British MI5.

There was speculation early in Putin's presidency that he would allow the FSB to swallow up the foreign intelligence agency. While the FSB did obtain some additional departments, in the end no effort was made to merge them. The FSB seemed not to need it—indeed, over time, it was secretly transformed into the third national external intelligence agency, one largely focused on the countries that had once been part of the Soviet Union.

In Soviet times, intelligence and counterintelligence branches of the KGB were closely interconnected, both in the center at Moscow headquarters and at the regional level across the country. In addition to its espionage abroad, the KGB was always busy collecting "intelligence from the territory," a euphemism for recruiting foreign nationals in the Soviet Union, with an eye to subsequently running them as agents in their home countries. This system worked because the Soviet Union, as a police state, had an opportunity to watch literally every foreign national in the country.

Regional departments of the KGB were tasked with dealing with foreign visitors traveling throughout the country. Each regional department had what was called a First Section in charge of recruiting foreigners. Later, after the Soviet collapse, when the KGB was dismantled and divided up, the First Sections were left at the FSB's disposal, having maintained their functions. But they lacked the overarching coordination that would have made them effective. This lack of an umbrella organization was used by the FSB as a pretext to create a department by which it could dramatically expand its reach—and operate abroad.

In June 2002 the authors received a letter from an FSB official who asked not to be identified. In the letter, he noted that by law the FSB has the right to operate as an intelligence agency.[2] In 1999, he wrote, President Yeltsin signed a confidential decree on intelligence agencies that, among other things, created a directorate to coordinate "operative information" inside the FSB. The new directorate was established inside the Department of Analysis, Forecasting, and Strategic Planning and was headed by Major General Vyacheslav Ushakov, who had once served with Nikolai Patrushev, then director of the FSB, in Karelia.

The authors asked Andrei Laryushin, the official spokesman of the FSB, about the Yeltsin decree. While Laryushin couldn't confirm the existence of the decree, which was classified information, he allowed: "Basically, existence of such a decree is logical. If there were no such decree there would be contradictions between the FSB and SVR [foreign intelligence]. That decree would become necessary as soon as intelligence and counterintelligence were divided into different services. Otherwise there would be contradictions between the SVR and FSB just as the FBI and CIA periodically interfere with each other," he added.[3] It soon became clear that the new directorate's functions were to go far beyond those of a routine coordination effort.

After the fall of the Soviet Union, it was crucial for the Kremlin that Moscow retain its influence in post-Soviet states. Russia's security services sought to maintain special relationships with the former Soviet republics, even helping them to fill the vacuum in their security structures. In April 1992 the Russian foreign intelligence agency signed an agreement with its counterpart in the Commonwealth of Independent States (CIS), the loose confederation of republics that had been established, agreeing not to spy on each other.[4]

Because most of the countries, with the exception of Russia, had little in the way of intelligence operations, the agreement was skewed.[5] In turn, the Russian foreign intelligence agency assumed the posture of "Big Brother," making visits to CIS capitals to attend multilateral meetings or bilateral talks—where they were sometimes received by the heads of state of the host countries. But soon it became evident that the strategy for maintaining the political status quo in post-Soviet republics was ineffective. In the decade of the 2000s, one after another, the old regimes that had been established in the early 1990s fell like dominoes in a series of popular uprisings known as the "color revolutions": the Rose Revolution in Georgia (2003), the Orange Revolution in Ukraine (2004), and the Tulip Revolution in Kyrgyzstan (2005). These regime changes were neither predicted nor prevented by Moscow.

It became clear that at least some former Soviet republics were about to leave Russia's sphere of influence and needed to be watched more carefully. In Moscow, the prevailing concern was with Western intelligence in the region because the color revolutions were viewed in the Kremlin as a direct result of operations by the West. Although Russia's foreign intelligence agency should have had jurisdiction over the former Soviet countries, they had agreed not to spy within the territories. The FSB, however, had never signed any such agreement and felt free from any obligations. The FSB's new directorate was tasked with dealing with Russia's nearest neighbors. According to authors' sources, the structure of the directorate was established along geographical lines and its officers were granted the right to travel abroad. On June 30, 2003, an amendment to the "Law on the Organs of the Federal Security Service" was made, stipulating that the FSB would contain a special body dealing with foreign intelligence.[6] In 2004, the directorate was made a full department, called the Department of Operative Information (DOI), and its chief, Vyacheslav Ushakov, was promoted to deputy director of the FSB. In the newly established full department, Ushakov was replaced by Sergei Beseda, an influential general who had previously served in the section supervising the Administration of the President, where he had established excellent connections.

It is difficult to trace the operations of this department, but its key officials traveled to the newly independent former Soviet republics during political turning points. In 2002 the authors published in the weekly *Versiya* the first of a series of stories concerning the department's activity. (The series was continued in 2004 in *Moskovskie Novosti* and finally in *Novaya Gazeta* in 2006.) By then journalists from the CIS countries had sent the authors informa-tion about the activity of the FSB leadership in their respective countries.[7]

According to these outside reports, the FSB's trail was found in Belarus and Moldova. In Belarus the FSB was accused of attempt-ing to influence the political situation on the eve of presidential elections in 2003.[8] In Moldova, Ushakov was said to have recruited a prominent local politician for his department.[9]

It was also known that the leadership of the department took part in talks with presidential candidates during the 2004 presiden-tial elections in Abkhazia, another breakaway region from Georgia supported by Moscow. FSB generals had gone to Abkhazia to sup-port the pro-Moscow candidate, who lost.[10] The visit seriously un-dermined the intelligence positions of the FSB in Georgia, and the department failed to predict the Georgian invasion of South Osse-tia some four years later.

Meanwhile, the FSB was also active in the politics of countries beyond Russia's borders, although it is not clear how effectively. On May 12, 2005, FSB director Patrushev claimed before the State Duma to have helped unmask a plot against the political regime in Belarus. According to Patrushev, international nongovernmental or-ganizations had met in the Slovak capital Bratislava in late 2004 during Ukraine's Orange Revolution "to plan the downfall of the regime of Belarus president Alexander Lukashenko."[11] Surprisingly, the Belarus KGB didn't express outrage at such open intervention by the FSB into its internal affairs. The following day, the Belarus KGB confirmed the FSB's statement. A few days later the heads of the security services of the CIS countries gathered in Astana, Kaza-khstan. The main subject of discussion became clear at the end of the meeting when Patrushev again remonstrated about the dangers of the "color revolutions." This time, he was supported by the chiefs of the Belarus State Security Committee and Kazakhstan's National Security Committee. Both Belarus and Kazakhstan have sharply restricted political opposition and free speech.

In the decade of Putin's rule, the FSB's overseas ambitions intensified. In spring 2009 one colonel in the department told Soldatov that it had expanded its activity to Afghanistan and Pakistan, a statement that was confirmed by a second source. In May 2009, FSB department chief Sergei Beseda was promoted to chief of the Operative Information and International Relations Service of the FSB. His former post was filled by Oleg Khramov, who was known as a Middle East expert.[12]

At the same time, the *Gorizont* Company, specializing in manufacturing insignia and medals, produced at the FSB's request a special medal for the department. It turned out to depict a globe, the same symbol of world-spanning reach used in the insignia of the Russian foreign intelligence agency.[13]

AFTER THE FALL of the Soviet Union, Russia hoped to preserve a sphere of influence in the former Soviet republics. All but the Baltics had joined the CIS. But not all of its members were equally happy at finding themselves once again beneath the gaze of Big Brother in Moscow.[14]

Belarus, Armenia, Kyrgyzstan, and Tajikistan were allies who allowed Russian military bases to be stationed on their soil. Azerbaijan, Georgia, Moldova, and Ukraine drifted in NATO's direction, in part because Russia had supported separatist movements within the countries' breakaway regions: Nagorny Karabakh from Azerbaijan, Abkhazia and South Ossetia from Georgia, Transnistria from Moldova, and Crimea from Ukraine. At the same time, Kazakhstan, Turkmenistan, and Uzbekistan, long suspicious of ethnic Russians who had migrated during Soviet times, began to purge Russians from the ranks of their security services.

In the second half of the 1990s, the Kremlin was eager to establish special relations with all the security services in these states. Two major efforts were launched, but both flopped. The first attempt was the creation of a Council of the Leaders of CIS Security Organs and Special Services in March 1997.[15] The council was headed by the FSB chief and its executive branch by the chief of the FSB international relations service. But the council's functions were purely consultative and its activities were limited to Moscow's traditional area of influence: The most active members were Belarus and Armenia, the closest Moscow allies, while Uzbekistan and Turkmenistan refused to join. The second attempt was made in 2000 with the establishment of a CIS Antiterrorist Center, headquartered in Moscow with a Central Asian branch in Bishkek, Kyrgyzstan.

Though the center was conceived of as a supranational structure, it was effectively under full FSB control: Russia was in command, filled 50 percent of the staff slots, and provided half of the budget, while the other CIS countries shared the rest. The Antiterrorist Center was headed by the first deputy director of the FSB, and the FSB supervised "collective" antiterrorist exercises in Central Asia, which were held every April. In fact, the center was a mechanism for Russia to keep the CIS countries in its sphere of influence.[16]

But the Antiterrorist Center ultimately failed. Its mandate was to create a database for intelligence sharing among the security services of all the member countries. But the idea of pooling intelligence information was abandoned when members learned that the database would be located in Moscow. Too much distrust existed within the CIS countries to willingly send their data to Russia. Soon, the Antiterrorist Center became just another backwater bureaucratic organization.[17]

Furthermore, some CIS states simply did not buy the notion that Russia had a sincere desire to help with counterterrorism efforts on their soil. Turkmenistan, Azerbaijan, and Uzbekistan refused to send representatives to the center, and after the Rose Revolution in 2005, Georgia stopped sending representatives as well.

The Antiterrorist Center kept trying to expand its influence in Central Asia, even when doing so meant expressing support for local authoritarian regimes that repressed popular uprisings or dissent. In May 2005, riots in the Uzbek city of Andijan were severely suppressed by Uzbek security forces, leading to hundreds of deaths. An FSB general, Boris Mylnikov, then the chief of the center, publicly announced his support for the Uzbek authorities and proposed that the center help Uzbekistan's National Security Service.[18] But in the end, the center was unable to extend Russia's influence beyond the states that had already been secured in the early 1990s.

Meanwhile, the looming presence of U.S. and coalition forces in Central Asia during their Afghan campaign was seen in Moscow as a continuation of the nineteenth century's Great Game between the Russian and British empires over the region, but this time between Russia and NATO. That prompted Moscow to change tactics. Since earlier efforts to control security services in the region had proved ineffective, a new alliance was sought. Key to the new effort was Uzbekistan, ruled by Islam Karimov, a strongman since the Soviet days. Uzbekistan was valuable territory to the United

States as a base for launching unmanned predatory aircraft into Afghanistan; Russia wanted the republic to retain its traditional role as a territory under Moscow's sphere of influence.[19]

In turn, Karimov wanted to suppress his country's internal Islamist opposition, a group known as the Islamic Movement of Uzbekistan (the IMU). Most of its members had fled to Afghanistan, and some to Russia. The idea was quite simple: If the Americans could hunt for the IMU in Afghanistan, the Russian security services might help to hunt down Karimov's enemies on Russian soil.[20]

From the mid-1990s on, Russia had become a safe haven for political opponents of Central Asian regimes. Using old but still valid Soviet passports and taking advantage of porous borders, the flow of people into Russia included refugees, political opponents of the regimes, and Islamic activists from Tajikistan, Azerbaijan, Uzbekistan, Turkmenistan, and Kazakhstan. In most cases refugees were secular opposition activists or Islamists from the party Hizb-ut-Tahrir. The party, founded in Jerusalem in 1953 and brought to Uzbekistan in the mid-1990s, opposes violence but advocates the overthrow of secular governments throughout the Muslim world and their replacement by an Islamic state in the form of a re-created caliphate. By the end of the 1990s Hizb-ut-Tahrir had become so popular that was considered a threat to Karimov's regime in Tashkent. Uzbek security services began arresting its members in 1998. For Russia, Hizb-ut-Tahrir posed no threat: Its activities were generally limited to giving sermons or handing out leaflets.

But Karimov was not willing to tolerate any opposition, fearing that Russia could use dissidents in exile to foster rebellion. Uzbek secret services created a strategy of reaching into Russia to grab people who might pose trouble for Karimov. The Russian security services, including the FSB, either participated in the plan or looked the other way.

Human rights activist Yelena Ryabinina recalled to the authors: "In the early 2000s natives from Uzbekistan living in the Volga region and considered to be members of Hizb-ut-Tahrir by Uzbek secret services started to disappear." The chain-smoking Ryabinina, a project director for the Civic Assistance Committee's Program of Assistance to Political Exiles from Central Asia, a nongovernmental organization based in Moscow, spent many hours in the courts defending refugees from Central Asia against illegal deportation. Some of them were later traced to Uzbek prisons. Alisher Usmanov, a teacher at a madrassa in Kazan, the capital of Tatarstan, had been wanted by Uzbekistan since 1998 for what Uzbeks said was an "attempt to undermine the constitutional regime of the country." But Usmanov had been granted Russian citizenship and thus could not be extradited. In 2004 Usmanov was detained by Russian police and sentenced to several months in prison for illegal possession of ammunition. On July 24, 2005, he was due to be released, but his wife says he simply disappeared. It was later ascertained that he had been abducted directly from prison, delivered to the airport, and flown to Uzbekistan. On October 24, 2005, the Russian state news agency reported, "Usmanov was handed over to Uzbekistan according to a joint plan of the FSB and the National Security Service of Uzbekistan for fighting international terrorism."[21] In November 2005 he was sentenced to an eight-year prison term in Uzbekistan.

Similar tactics were used by security services from Tajikistan, Turkmenistan, and Azerbaijan within Russia.[22] In 2004 the Tajik secret services succeeded in abducting a prominent Tajik politician, Mahmadruzi Iskandarov, who had been a field commander in Tajikistan's civil war in the early 1990s. Following a peace deal in 1998 he entered government and was appointed head of the state gas company. At the same time, he became leader of the opposition Democratic Party. In 2003 he challenged President Emomali Rahmonov's attempt to extend presidential term limits. Soon after, he left Tajikistan for Russia. In November 2004 the General Prosecutor's Office of Tajikistan accused Iskandarov of terrorism and issued a warrant for his arrest. He was promptly detained in Moscow. But the Russian Public Prosecutor's Office turned down an extradition request, and on April 5, 2005, Iskandarov was released.

Two weeks later he disappeared and turned up in a prison in the capital of Tajikistan. According to a letter he managed to smuggle out of prison, Iskandarov had been staying at a friend's house outside Moscow. On the evening of April 15, he went for a walk with his friend and was met by two people wearing uniforms of the Russian transport police. They handcuffed him and pushed him into a car. After driving 500 meters, they changed cars and brought Iskandarov to a sauna. The next day they drove him to a forest and handed him over to unidentified people, who he surmised were from the Russian security services. The men blindfolded him and then put him on a plane. No announcements were made during the flight, and Iskandarov concluded that he was on a military transport aircraft. On the morning on April 17, he arrived at Dushanbe Airport, where he was met by officials of Tajikistan's Ministry of Security. In October 2005, he was sentenced to twenty-three years in prison.

Iskandarov was delivered to Dushanbe under the false name of Gennady Petrovich Balanin.[23] Authorities from the Russian airports told Iskandarov's lawyers that the surname Balanin was not registered in their databases. This admission indicated that Iskandarov's passage from Russia had been aided by the FSB, which is responsible for guarding borders and is the agency that maintains border databases. His lawyers registered a complaint with the European Court of Human Rights about Iskandarov's illegal extradition from Russia. The court in turn sent questions to the Russian authorities asking them to clear up their role in this incident. On September 24, 2005, a Russian official, Georgy Matushkin, responded that the Russian authorities had nothing to do with the abduction of Iskandarov. But this assertion was contradicted by Tajikistan. Borogan obtained a statement from Tajikistan's Ministry of Foreign Affairs to the Office of the U.N. High Commissioner for Human Rights dated November 24, 2005, that claimed: "The accused Iskandarov was handed over officially to Tajikistan's side by the security services of the Russian Federation, and on April 17th, 2005, he was put in the investigatory prison of the Ministry of Security of the Republic of Tajikistan."[24]

In most cases the Russian secret services turn a blind eye on the Central Asian secret services' activities on Russian territory, as Iskandarov's mysterious flight to Dushanbe showed.

But the system of abductions was not yet perfected. It lacked some important elements: a coordination center, a regime of impunity for the secret agents involved in abductions, and legal grounds for transferring the captives. This seemed at odds with Russian law, which maintains an established procedure on formal extradition overseen by the general prosecutor. The new system was an effort to avoid legal extradition entirely.

The broader system was embedded in the Shanghai Cooperation Organization (SCO), an international cooperation group founded in 2001 by China, Kazakhstan, Kyrgyzstan, Russia, Tajikistan, and Uzbekistan. With the exception of Uzbekistan, the other countries had been members of the Shanghai Five, founded in 1996. (Uzbekistan joined the organization in June 2001.) The stated purpose of the SCO was the joint struggle against the "three evils" of terrorism, separatism, and extremism. In 2004, a special antiterrorism structure was created within the organization, called the Regional Antiterrorist Structure, or RATS.

Run by an FSB deputy director, the structure held joint exercises and conferences, and at first the project seemed destined for the same irrelevance as the earlier attempts by Russia to dominate the region. But soon the purpose of the organization changed, as did its main beneficiaries, and it began carrying out abductions across national boundaries and outside standard judicial procedures, much like the infamous CIA practice of extraordinary rendition.

Renditions had been instituted in part due to frustration over the long and cumbersome extradition process.[25] According to the authors' information, the RATS spent years creating its own parallel structure that could be used instead of official extraditions.[26]

As stated in the Shanghai convention on combatting terrorism, separatism, and extremism, cooperation between the special services and enforcing bodies is carried out through direct requests of assistance.[27] A request includes the name of an enforcing body, a purpose and justification, and a description of the action required, such as detention or transfer. The request must be signed by the head or deputy head of the relevant authority, such as the local secret service. In urgent cases, requests can be transmitted orally. The Shanghai convention also allows the laws of another country to apply within Russian territory. This is done for cases in which a person is guilty of an act that is a crime in one country, but is not defined as a crime in Russian law. It is convenient, for example, for the Chinese that supporters of Tibetan independence know that they cannot find refuge in Russia, as Russia is required to act in accordance with Chinese law.

Refugee status has been another obstacle for special services wishing to apprehend a citizen from a neighboring country. The members of the Shanghai Cooperation Organization agree not to provide safe haven to people involved in terrorist, separatist, or extremist activities, thus anyone listed in the general SCO data bank cannot be given refugee status, despite the fact that extremism and separatism may be interpreted differently in different countries. (For instance, the Russian criminal code does not contain the term "separatism.")

The FSB, for example, may advise the Russian Immigration Service about a person who is considered unreliable because his preaching displeased Uzbek authorities in the Ferghana Valley. The person in question will be refused refugee status, after which he may be deported from Russia as an illegal immigrant.

That is what happened to Dilshot Kurbanov, an ethnic Uzbek who moved to Russia in 2002 to avoid an investigation related to his membership in an Islamic organization. He was simply a believer, not an extremist, but had decided to get out of harm's way. In 2007 Kurbanov was detained in Russia at Uzbekistan's request and accused of spreading religious extremism. Only an intervention from the European Court of Human Rights at Strasbourg prevented his extradition.

Activist Yelena Ryabinina holds the FSB responsible for denying Kurbanov refugee status. According to Ryabinina, the head of the security service in the Russian city of Tula had sent a letter to the federal immigration authorities instructing them to reject it. The letter, obtained by the authors, referred to documents sent from Uzbekistan alleging that Kurbanov was guilty of various crimes including "using the Islamic religion to disturb the peace." Although no evidence was submitted, the Immigration Service refused refugee status to Kurbanov.[28]

To increase the new system's scope, the RATS created a database from two sources: the list of terrorist, separatist, and extremist organizations whose activity was forbidden in territories of the member states; and the list of individuals declared by member states' special services and law enforcement bodies to be involved in, or suspected of involvement in, terrorist, separatist, and extremist crimes.

To improve the RATS's ability to detain suspects in the six states, it was necessary to give guarantees of absolute protection to executing officers. The SCO's Convention on Privileges and Immunities, ratified by Russia in 2005, gave the representatives of the organization the equivalent of diplomatic status. They are not subject to criminal liability for any actions committed in the course of their duty, and they are immune from arrest and detention. The same unlimited immunity applies to the RATS "experts," secret service officers from any member country who are attached to the RATS for the time of their mission. Experts are shielded from arrest during and after their business trips, and, notably, their luggage cannot be searched.

RATS buildings are also shielded. The convention states that no one can enter any RATS premises without the consent of its director. The RATS property also has immunity from any interference, regardless of location.

The Russian special services have not had the same problems the CIA encountered with leaks to the press about renditions. In the RATS's case, no one will say anything at all. For example, human rights activists were refused information concerning the way Alisher Usmanov was taken to Uzbekistan or how Iskandarov was taken to Tajikistan. It is not known how many people have been seized and transferred to another country under the RATS system.

By 2008 the guidelines for the RATS were largely established, the system was fully operational, and it was quite clear that the other countries benefited more than Russia did. It appears Russia routinely shipped people off to other countries but received none of the people it sought from them. According to FSB reports, in the 2000s there were almost no Russian detentions in Tajikistan, Kyrgyzstan, Kazakhstan, or China, and no suspect in a terrorism or extremism case had been extradited to Russia from Uzbekistan.

But the system has proved quite profitable for Uzbekistan and China: Uighurs tend to flee to Uzbekistan, Tajikistan, and Turkmenistan, while Uzbeks more often flee to Russia and Tajikistan. In 2006 the Uzbeks handed over to China a Uighur imam with Chinese and Canadian citizenship, Huseyincan Celil.[29] In turn FSB director Patrushev reported at a routine RATS meeting in March 2006 that Russia had handed over nineteen people suspected of membership in Hizb-ut-Tahrir to Uzbekistan.

According to information from Yelena Ryabinina, in 2007 Russia began to deport Chinese members of Falun Gong, a movement banned in China in 1999 as an organized political group "opposed to the Communist Party of China and the central government, that preaches idealism, theism, and feudal superstition."[30] On March 28, 2007, Falun Gong member Ma Hui, 44, and her daughter, 8, were deported to China even though Hui was recognized as a "mandated refugee" by the United Nations High Commissioner for Refugees. On May 13, Gao Chuman, another Falun Gong supporter, was brought to China. That practice has continued.[31]

In 2003 the RATS's headquarters was moved from Bishkek, the capital of Kyrgyzstan, to the Uzbek capital of Tashkent. In 2005 Russia put the Hizb-ut-Tahrir party, which is recognized as legal in Europe and the United States, on its national list of terrorist organizations, at the request of Uzbekistan.

In 2008 the FSB presented another gift to Karimov: Uzbekistan's enemies were deemed a threat to Russian national security. At a meeting with heads of antiterrorist commissions in the Ural Federal District in Khanty-Mansiysk in April 2008,[32] FSB director Patrushev declared: "The international terrorist organization Hizb-ut-Tahrir and the Islamic Movement of Uzbekistan (IMU) have made attempts to spread their activity to Russia."

As of 2009, there was no record of IMU activities in Russia. The movement's leader, Tahir Yuldashev (reportedly killed in a U.S. strike in South Naziristan in August 2009), has threatened to kill the presidents of Uzbekistan, Kyrgyzstan, and Tajikistan, but not the president of Russia.

So far the sole beneficiaries of Russia's dealings with Central Asian states, in exchange for their support for Moscow's regional ambitions, have been Central Asia's security services. Russia's initiative to unite China and Central Asia within a new security alliance led by Moscow has helped facilitate the abduction of suspected terrorists, separatists, and extremists outside normal procedures. All Russia got was some more prestige, but the Kremlin has deliberately turned Russia into a hunting ground for the security services of the most authoritarian regimes in Central Asia.

HACKERS

BEYOND ITS PHYSICAL reach, Russia's security services maintain a sophisticated alliance with unofficial hackers, such as
those who carry out cyber attacks on the Web sites of enemies of
the state.

In 2005, a group of adamantly pro-Kremlin, anti-Western Internet activists started to gather in electronic forums in Russia. One
such forum was maintained on the website Informacia.ru. The activists were not connected to the state, nor were they high-level
experts in computer technology, but they knew their way around
the Internet. Angered by the activities of Chechen rebels on the Internet, they felt the Russian government had been ineffective in
dealing with Web sites that called for violent rebellion, including
the use of weapons and bombs. These activists decided to use their
own methods. They paid an expert $500 to write a program that
would launch what is known as a "denial of service" attack on a
Web site—a simple but effective way to disrupt a site, at least temporarily, by swamping it with outside requests or messages.

In August 2005, the group registered its own Web site, Anti
center.org. It had a striking black background with an insignia depicting crosshairs aimed at what appears to be an Arab man wearing a kaffiyeh. Defining itself as "Civilian Anti-Terror," the site
carried a call to action against what it described as extremist and

terrorist Web sites. At the top of its list were Chechen rebel sites. "The main target of our community is the complete destruction of Web sites that propagate terror and violence, distort facts, and lie to their readers." Five main Web sites of the Chechen rebels were listed. They also announced their intention to attack the Web sites of the National Bolsheviks, a marginal opposition party.

Anticenter.org boasted of twenty-five successful cyber attacks, many of which were aimed at the Chechens. For example, on December 5, 2005, the site proclaimed, "Most of the day the Web site of Chechenpress.info was unavailable. Access to the last mirror of the Web site was made seriously difficult." On December 2, they "closed down the Web site Imam-tk.fastbb.ru." On December 1, "as a result of activities of Civilian Anti-Terror hackers, Chechen press.net has a big problem. In the last few hours, we see failures in the last mirror of the same Web site, Chechenpress.info, which has been targeted by a people's attack. We call for all our visitors to download a program for attacking the last mirror, Chechen press.info."

In 2006, for reasons unknown, the group closed down Anti center.org. But before it disappeared entirely, Anton Moskal, a liberal computer programmer in St. Petersburg, had noticed it and taken the precaution of downloading everything on the Web site. On May 28, 2007, Moskal got a call at his home from a man who identified himself as "Stanislav" from the FSB National Antiterrorism Committee. He had a simple request—he was hunting for the Civilian Anti-Terror group and was interested in learning more from what Moskal had downloaded.[1]

In a twenty-minute conversation, which quickly turned to Moskal's patriotism and an imminent necessity to combat terrorists' websites, the programmer tried to explain to Stanislav that he by no means shared the views of the Anticenter.org site, had no connection to the Web site, and had merely copied its content. But Stanislav, unconvinced, left Moskal his office phone number, ostensibly with the hope of recruiting his help. He seemed to be trying to recruit Moskal for help in tracking the Web sites. He invited Moskal to phone him if he had any more information about the hackers behind Anticenter.org.[2]

DURING THE LONG wars in Chechnya and the periods of calm in between, the Kremlin found it particularly vexing that Chechen rebels could communicate effectively with the press and outside world through the Internet. The first and most important Chechen Web site was Kavkaz.org.[3] Launched by Movladi Udugov, the main Chechen spokesman since the first Chechen war, the Web site soon became the principal mouthpiece for the Chechen leadership's opinions and an effective propaganda tool against Russian troops.

During the first Chechen war, Russian and foreign journalists managed to slip through Russian lines and were well provided with information from the other side. Television and press coverage was welcomed by Chechen rebels, who granted access to scenes of destroyed Russian equipment and dead Russian soldiers. Udugov, meanwhile, made comments online and frequently appeared on television. Russia's defeat in the first Chechen war was explained in Moscow by unpreparedness in the "information war." When the second Chechen war broke out in 1999, Russian troops did their best to prevent journalists from getting information provided by rebels.

In December 1999, when Russian troops stormed Grozny, a few journalists stayed in the city, including Masha Eismont, a Reuters correspondent, and Andrei Babitsky, a journalist for Radio Liberty. Their reports angered the Russian authorities, and FSB spokesperson Alexander Zdanovich accused foreign intelligence agencies of manufacturing the news to undermine support for the war effort.[4] Both journalists were intimidated and detained.[5]

Russian newspapers and television channels seem to have learned the lesson: Journalists were ordered not to report from the Chechen side, due to the danger. Lacking journalists in the field, the media turned to information provided directly by the rebels through Kavkaz.org. For instance, on May 7, 2000, Russian forces denied claims by rebels that they had shot down a Russian Su-24 jet fighter bomber. But then a picture of Chechen fighters holding parts of the plane's wreckage appeared on Kavkaz.org, and the Army was forced to admit the claim was true.[6]

Primarily designed to influence foreigners, Kavkaz.org appeared in Russian, English, and Turkish, and its news, interviews with Chechen warlords, video footage, and photographs drew viewers from news media and specialists around the world. In May 2000 Michael Randall, a Chechnya expert at Britain's Institute for War and Peace Reporting, told Radio Liberty that although Kavkaz.org was prone to exaggeration, its information was usually grounded in fact. He credited the site with helping to keep the Chechen situation in public view, by focusing on issues like the abuse of Chechen civilian and military prisoners held by the Russians.

On August 31, 1999, Kavkaz.org was attacked by hackers for the first time. They displayed on the home page a picture of Mikhail Lermontov, the famous Russian poet and a symbol of Russian empire in the North Caucasus, wearing a commando outfit and holding a Kalishnikov. Messages like "This site has been closed down at the request of Russian citizens," signed "The Siberian Web Brigade," were also posted on the Web site.[7] Kavkaz.org came under attack again in January 2002 when a group of students in the Siberian city of Tomsk launched a "distributed denial of service" (DDoS) attack. The group consisted of seven people and was headed by Dmitry Aleksandrov, who had fled Chechnya for Tomsk in 1996. The students claimed to have pressured the rebel Web site for three years, attacking it and sending warning letters to hosting providers in the United States and Canada.[8] The FSB's department in Tomsk appeared to be fully informed about the activity of the hackers, and put out a press release defending the students' actions as a legitimate "expression of their position as citizens, one worthy of respect."[9]

AT THE TIME the students were acting, the Russian intelligence community possessed highly sophisticated cyberwar abilities. If they had wanted to join in the cyberwar against the Chechen sites, they certainly could have. But they chose not to.

The KGB successor in the electronic intelligence field was the Federal Agency of Government Communications and Information, which had grown out of the eighth and sixteenth departments of the KGB and dealt with encoding/decoding and radio interception, respectively.[10]

Like the U.S. National Security Agency, the communications agency was responsible for information security and signals intelligence. While it did not enjoy the level of resources available to the National Security Agency, the Russian communications agency inherited the KGB's excellent mathematics school, which became the FSB's Institute of Cryptology; its facilities abroad, including two signal intelligence/electronic intelligence bases overseas, in Cam Ranh Bay, Vietnam, and Lourdes, Cuba; and the so-called Third

Chief Directorate, responsible for eavesdropping abroad.[11] Only a few people outside the agency knew the official name of the secretive Third Directorate or were aware of its activities.[12]

The cyber facilities of the communications agency were highly regarded by American experts: It was said to have both the authority and the capability to penetrate all government and private information services in Russia. It also has reportedly been successful in collecting intelligence on foreign business ventures, including confidential bank transactions.[13] Starting in the mid-1990s the communications agency took an interest in controlling the Internet, at least inside Russia. In hearings in 1996, its deputy director, Colonel General Vladimir Markomenko, told the State Duma that "the Internet poses a threat to National Security," and the agency was empowered to monitor electronic, financial, and securities transactions and other communications, including private Internet access.[14] Within this sophisticated agency, the primary concern was not Chechen propaganda but protecting the communications networks from intrusion by foreign intelligence services. The professionals in information security were not interested in being at the vanguard of Russia's cyberwarfare against the Chechens.[15]

The communications agency's Third Directorate was absorbed into the FSB in 2003. By this time, it appeared that hackers with no direct government connections were the most suitable tool for Russian authorities to attack Chechen rebel Web sites. Russian officials publicly announced their displeasure with the Chechen Web sites; unofficial hackers gleaned the message and went into action, allowing the authorities to maintain their distance from the perpetrators.

Soon independent hackers, encouraged by the Kremlin, expanded their attacks far beyond Chechen Web sites; the same hackers' groups began to target the Web sites of opposition media and political groups. They targeted extremist groups like the National Bolshevik Party, opposition groups like that of Garry Kasparov, and mainstream media outlets like the newspaper *Kommersant* and Echo Moskvy radio.

The authors believe it possible that certain groups of these hackers were guided not by the security services but by the administration of the president. Other youth movement groups had been organized by the Kremlin administration, so the hackers might well have been, too. The Kremlin openly showed interest in nontraditional methods on the Internet, including mobilization of youth for spreading propaganda. In May 2009, the "Kremlin school of bloggers" was launched. A forum for teaching bloggers how to disseminate their views, it was headed by political technologist Alexei Chadayev, an associate of Gleb Pavlovsky, who had orchestrated numerous Internet propaganda projects at the request of the Kremlin in Putin's time.[16] The school's personnel consisted of eighty people drawn from all Russian regions, each mentoring several other activists. Upon graduating, its students would be deployed to organize information campaigns on the Internet.[17]

In all these cases, the Kremlin did not have to use FSB resources to attack objectionable Web sites; it could simply steer the growing community of "hacker-patriots" in the right direction.

After a major terrorist attack in Nalchik on October 13, 2005, the Russian Foreign Ministry complained that the Chechen Web site was still going strong on a Swedish server. "Unfortunately," the ministry's site said, "the Swedish authorities up to now have not taken any concrete steps to block the dissemination" of the Chechen Web site, which had now become Kavkaz-Tsentr.[18] The official statement appears to have unleashed the unofficial hackers. Within twenty-four hours, the Russian Web site Mediaactivist.ru launched an attack against Kavkaz-Tsentr as well as Echo Moskvy radio, *Novaya Gazeta*, and Radio Liberty. The campaign was openly declared and had as its slogan "Let's shut the mouths of the helpers of Kavkaz-Tsentr!" It resembled a spam-provoking campaign: Mediaactivist.ru posted a list of email addresses that hackers could attack with their letters.[19]

But that protest quickly fizzled: The attacked media sent a warning to the host through which Mediaactivist.ru had been operating, and the Web site was removed from the Internet for spam activity.

On October 16, 2005, another Web site, called Internet Underground Community vs. Terrorism (www.peace4peace.com), was established and began to launch denial of service attacks on Kavkaz-Tsentr. In a statement the hackers said: "We are hackers of different specialties. Most of us have long been on the other side of the law, but that does not mean we are not patriots who will stand up for peace in the world."[20]

The efforts carried out by Russian diplomacy and unofficial hackers were partly successful. In May 2006 the Swedish authorities closed Kavkaz-Tsentr. The Web site was moved first to Georgia and in 2008 to Estonia.

In April 2007, for the first time, Web sites of a foreign government came under attack. Estonia had angered the Kremlin with its decision to move a Soviet war memorial out of the center of the capital. After a massive nationalistic campaign against Estonia in the Russian press, on April 27 Russian hackers launched a series of cyber attacks on the Web sites of the Estonian government, parliament, banks, ministries, newspapers, and broadcasters. Most of the attacks were the "denial of service" type. The attackers ranged from single individuals, using various low-tech methods like ping floods (a simple denial-of-service attack in which an attacker overwhelms the victim computer with echo request [ping] packets), to expensive rented botnets usually used for spam distribution. Russia denied any involvement, but Estonian Foreign Minister Urmas Paet accused the Kremlin of direct involvement in the cyber attacks, and Estonia then requested and received NATO assistance in responding to this new form of aggression.[21]

Who exactly was behind the attack was never publicly acknowledged. Estonia failed to present proof of the Russian government's involvement, and in September 2007 the country's defense minister admitted he had no evidence linking cyber attacks to the Russian authorities. "Of course, at the moment, I cannot state for certain that the cyber attacks were managed by the Kremlin or other Russian government agencies," Jaak Aaviksoo said in interview on Estonian's Kanal 2 TV channel.[22] Meanwhile, Rafal Rohozhinsky, a leading expert in the field, argued that he had seen signs of government sponsorship in the malicious traffic. He pointed to armies of hijacked computers that started and stopped attacks in exact coordination at one-week intervals, implying that they had been rented for the purpose.[23] In the end, the Russian state was never blamed, and no diplomatic measures ensued.

In June 2008, Lithuania was in the crosshairs. The former Soviet republic incensed Russia when lawmakers voted to ban public display of Nazi German and Soviet symbols. Lithuania's stance prompted a massive cyber attack: On June 30 the National Communication Regulator's office said that some three hundred Web sites, including those of public institutions such as the National Ethics body and the Securities and Exchange Commission, as well as a string of private companies, had found themselves under cyber siege. Their Web sites' content was replaced with images of the red flag of the Soviet Union alongside anti-Lithuanian slogans.[24]

In August 2008, the military conflict with Georgia in South Ossetia also included cyber attacks against Georgia's Internet infrastructure. According to a Project Grey Goose report,[*] members of two Russian forums, StopGeorgia.ru and Xakep.ru, "spent a significant amount of time discussing the merits and drawbacks of different kinds of malware, including DDoS tactics and tools. . . . An analysis of the DDoS tools offered by the forum leaders showed basic but effective tools. Some forum members had difficulty using the tools, reinforcing the idea that many of the forum members had low to medium technical sophistication."[25] The attacks compromised several Georgian government Web sites and prompted the government to switch to hosting locations in the United States. Georgia's Ministry of Foreign Affairs, in order to disseminate real-time information, was forced to move to a BlogSpot account.[26]

IN 2007, Informacia.ru began to attract more attention. It appears to have been used both by hackers and by security services. When in May 2007 Soldatov published a story in *Novaya Gazeta* about the unofficial hackers, the community responded on Informacia.ru. Two years later, in July 2009, the Informacia.ru site was used against a British diplomat. Britain's deputy consul general in Yekaterinburg, James Hudson, was forced to resign when the *Sun* tabloid in Lon-

---

[*] Project Grey Goose is an open source intelligence initiative launched by a group of experts and academics in the fields of Internet security and cyberwar on August 22, 2008, to examine how the Russian cyberwar was conducted against Georgian Web sites.

don published excerpts of a video showing a man resembling Hudson having sex with two prostitutes. The 4-minute, 18-second video first appeared July 6 on Informacia.ru and was picked up by *Komsomolskaya Pravda* in Yekaterinburg and the tabloid Web site Life.ru. The *Sun* published a story about it on July 9, the same day Hudson stepped down.[27] The authors do not know precisely how the video reached Informacia.ru. Russia has had a long tradition of using compromising material to carry such out attacks—called *kompromat*—but it is highly unusual for one to be aimed at a diplomat.

One month later, U.S. diplomat Kyle Hatcher was featured in another such video, also published by Informacia.ru and reprinted by *Komsomolskaya Pravda*. In Hatcher's case, the diplomat was not forced to leave: The U.S. ambassador stood up for his employee, while the FBI conducted an investigation and declared the footage fake. The State Department called the video a fabricated montage that included some real footage: "Mr. Hatcher has been the subject of a smear campaign in the Russian press and on the Internet to discredit him and his work," said State Department spokesman Ian Kelly. "We deplore this type of smear campaign."[28]

Informacia.ru was known earlier for its ties to secret services. Prominent human rights activist and Soviet dissident Sergei Grigoryants told the authors that he was surprised to see that his biography published on the site contained details unavailable from open sources.

In 2008, the community that had once created Anticenter.org launched a new Web site, Antiterror.tv. It boasted that it had closed down two hundred Web sites and tracked down the Internet locations of one hundred authors of illegal Web sites, which they had turned over to the FSB.

The appearance of the antiterror group is proof that unofficial hackers have become part of the Russian cyberwar front lines. By allowing militantly nationalist citizens to respond to Russia's enemies with cyberwarfare, the security services succeed in keeping distance between themselves and the perpetrating factions while accomplishing their greater goals.

CONCLUSION

I N THE EARLY years of the KGB's reorganization after the Soviet collapse, the Federal Counterintelligence Service (FSK) existed for only a short while. In 1995, the FSK was renamed the Federal Security Service, or FSB. The shift from "K" to "B" was more than symbolic; the renamed service was given a broad mandate to become the guardian of "security" for the new Russia. Fifteen years on, it is possible to draw some conclusions about Russia's security and how well it has been served by its security apparatus.

The largest single challenge facing the FSB and Russia in the decade of Vladimir Putin's rule was the tide of terrorist attacks from the North Caucasus. After the Nord-Ost siege, the FSB called the storming of the Dubrovka theater a victory, hoping to stave off the next calamity. But when the next attack occurred two years later at the Beslan school, the security service leadership utterly failed to take decisive action—indeed, failed to even arrive at the scene.

While the FSB insisted that the conflict in Chechnya was inflamed and supported by hostile foreign forces, in truth, the Chechens' most damaging tactics were conceived of by Chechen warlords. Russia's security services appear to have miscalculated the nature of the enemy in the battle against terrorism. Faced with guerrilla warfare, the security services responded in kind, carrying out operations to eliminate a generation of Chechen warlords and leaders, including Aslan Maskhadov, Shamil Basayev, and Zelim-khan Yandarbiyev. But when these leaders were wiped out, new ones took their place. To date, Russia's security services have failed to find an effective way to deal with terrorism.

This failure was underscored once again on Monday, March 29, 2010, when two female suicide bombers detonated explosives on Moscow's subway during rush hour. The first bomb exploded at 7:56 A.M. as a train rolled into the Lubyanka station, just a short walk from the FSB headquarters—a bombing that appeared to be aimed directly at the security service. Then, at 8:39 A.M., a second bomb was detonated on the platform at the Park Kultury station, near the famous Gorky Park. As a result, forty people were killed and eighty-four wounded.

The FSB claimed the bombings were revenge attacks for the insurgents killed by FSB squads in the North Caucasus earlier in the month. But the claim seemed to be dubious; such terrorist operations often take months to plan, and the insurgents had promised nearly two years earlier to inflict terror on Russia's cities and civilians. The bombings also raised anew an important question that had been asked following the Nord-Ost siege and Beslan massacre: If the secret services had been given so much support by the Kremlin in the name of providing security, why had they failed again to prevent such a deadly onslaught? The bombings clearly exposed the weakness of the FSB's shoot-to-kill policy in the North Caucasus, but neither the FSB nor the Kremlin showed any inclination to change direction. Putin declared that the "terrorists will be eliminated," while Medvedev called bombers animals and stated: "I have no doubt that we will find and destroy them all."[1]

When Putin was elected president in 2000, the security services, chiefly the FSB, rose to prominence with him, hoping for a resurrection from the long decade of the 1990s, when they had felt left out of the tumultuous new capitalism and uncertain politics. Putin, who had been an officer in the KGB for sixteen years, effectively invited the security services to take their place at the head table of power and prestige in Russia. But this invitation to join the New Nobility of Russia failed to bring the expected results, given the trust the Kremlin put in the security services.

The FSB invested energy in hunting down foreign spies, but the unseemly methods it used to do so raised questions about whether the threat was real or trumped-up. Likewise, the FSB targeted nongovernmental organizations out of fear that such groups might inspire a popular revolution against the Kremlin. This was a clear miscalculation; the organizations in question were too small to be significant threats, did not command widespread support in Russia, and did not advocate an uprising against the regime.

Putin opened the door to many dozens of security service agents to move up in the main institutions of the country, perhaps hoping they would prove a vanguard of stability and order. But once they had tasted the benefits, agents began to struggle amongst themselves for the spoils.

The FSB faced a profound challenge when Putin was accused of involvement in the 1999 Moscow apartment bombings as an effort to panic the population and successfully rise to power. While it is not known precisely who was behind the bombings, it is clear the FSB attempted to silence questions about the case in a way that only provoked further conspiracy theories.

Under Boris Yeltsin's presidency in the 1990s attempts to build civil society emerged along with the hope of an improved connection between the rulers and the ruled. But Putin deliberately attempted to roll back civil society, reducing the space for discussion in politics and public life. The security services meddled in politics to protect Putin, perhaps to demonstrate their power and loyalty to the Kremlin, or perhaps because they misjudged the threat of any opposition to the popular president.

The FSB was supposed to be a cog in the machinery of a state governed by the rule of law. But the rule of law remains a quite distant goal in today's Russia, where the security services appear to have concluded that their interests, and those of the state they are guarding, remain above the law. The mind-set of Russia's FSB has been undeniably shaped by Soviet and Tsarist history: It is suspicious, inward looking, and clannish.

Clearly, the times demand change. But the answers do not lie in the lessons of the past. Yuri Andropov's plaque may make the security services feel better about their identity, but it does not point to an efficient model in a modern democracy. Reaping lucrative property in the elite forests of the Rublyovka may comfort generals nearing the end of their careers but does not prepare a new generation to become fair arbiters and respected enforcers in a democratic society. While Putin awarded generals more privileges and benefits, they retreated from risk and responsibility and thus proved less than effective in their duties, leading to lasting questions about their role in Russia's future. If President Medvedev is serious about modernizing Russia and ending the "legal nihilism" that has run wild in recent years, he will need defenders of the state who are in tune with this goal, not a service deeply mired in the past.

APPENDIX 1
STRUCTURE OF THE FSB

SENIOR MANAGEMENT

Director, Chairman of the National Antiterrorist Committee
- First Deputy Director
- First Deputy Director, Chief of the Border Guards
- Deputy Director, Chief of Staff of the National Antiterrorist Committee
- Deputy Director, State Secretary of the FSB
- Deputy Director
- Deputy Director

DEPARTMENTS

1. Counterintelligence Service
- Department of Counterintelligence Operations
- Directorate of Coordination and Analysis of Counterintelligence Activity
- Directorate of Special Activities
- Directorate of Counterintelligence at Facilities
- Directorate of Information Support to Operational Detective Activity
- Information Security Center
- Department of Military Counterintelligence

This service is in charge of counterespionage, including supervision of the military-industrial complex, the Russian army and navy, and the pursuit of hackers who attack government resources on the Internet.

2. Service to Protect the Constitutional System and Combat Terrorism
- Directorate of the Operations Organization
- Operations Search Directorate
- Directorate to Combat Terrorism and Political Extremism

- Directorate to Combat International Terrorism
- Special Purpose Center

This service combats terrorism at home and abroad (including cooperation with the secret services of other countries) and conducts political surveillance and special operations.

3. Border Service

This service includes headquarters in Moscow, an intelligence department, regional directorates, and border troops along Russian frontiers.

4. Economic Security Service
- Directorate of Counterintelligence Support to Industrial Enterprises (Directorate P)
- Directorate of Counterintelligence Support to Transportation (Directorate T)
- Directorate of Counterintelligence Support to the Financial System (Directorate K)
- Directorate of Counterintelligence Support to the Interior Ministry, Ministry of Emergency, and Ministry of Justice (Directorate M)
- Organizational Analysis Directorate
- Directorate to Combat Contraband and Illegal Drug Trafficking (Directorate N)
- Administrative Service

This service supervises crucial industries and companies as well as the Interior Ministry and the ministries of emergency and justice.

5. Operative Information and International Relations Service
- Department of Operative Information (DOI)
- Analysis Directorate
- Strategic Planning Directorate
- Department of Unclassified Information
- Directorate of International Cooperation

Formerly the Department of Analysis and Prognosis, this service is responsible for providing assessments to the FSB leadership and the Kremlin and oversees intelligence operations and international activity.

6. Service of Organizational Personnel Activities (Human Resources)
- Directorate of Special Registrations
- Organizational Planning Directorate
- Personnel Directorate

7. Supply Service
- Finance and Economics Directorate
- Directorate of Material and Technical Support
- Directorate of Capital Construction

This service is responsible for maintaining FSB headquarters and for constructing military facilities for the FSB.

8. Scientific and Technical Service
- Directorate of Orders and Deliveries of Weapons and Military and Special Equipment
- Directorate of Operational Technical Measures (*eavesdropping and interception*)
- Research Institute of Information Technologies

This service offers technical support for operations.

9. Oversight Service
- Inspection Directorate
- Auditing Directorate
- Directorate of Internal Security

This service reviews personnel and investigates crimes committed by the FSB rank and file.

SUBDIVISIONS DIRECTLY SUBORDINATE TO DIRECTOR

- Investigative Directorate (*main investigative body of the FSB, supervises investigative sections in FSB regional departments*)
- Operation Search Directorate (*surveillance units*)
- Sixteenth Center for Radio-electronic Intelligence on Communications (*electronic intelligence*)
- Center for Special Equipment (*includes bomb squad units*)
- Communications Security Center (*software protection of government communications*)

- Center for Licensing, Certification, and Protection of State Secrets
- Administration Directorate
- Treaty and Legal Directorate
- FSB Reception Office
- Directorate of Assistance Programs (*disinformation operations; includes the Center for Public Communications*)
- Registry and Archives Directorate
- Directorate of Special Communications
- Directorate of Aviation
- Military Medical Directorate
- Watch Officer Service
- Military Mobilization

THE FSB IN REGIONS

According to the Regulation Concerning the Federal Security Service (Presidential Decree no. 960, August 11, 2003), the system is structured as follows:

- Directorates in regions (territorial security organizations)
- Directorates in the armed forces, in the field, and in other military formations
- Directorates in the Border Guards
- Aviation subunits, special training centers, special subunits, and all enterprises, educational institutions, scientific research, expert, forensic, military medical, and military construction subunits (among other institutions and subunits) designed to support the activity of the FSB
- Other directorates that exercise separate authority of the FSB

By 2010 the structure of the central apparatus of the FSB defined by Presidential Decree no. 960 was improved as a result of reforms in 2005–2006 when two Presidential Decrees were signed: no. 1383 (December 1, 2005) and no. 1476 (December 26, 2006). The details are derived from open sources and information gathered by Agentura.ru.

APPENDIX 2
THE EVOLUTION OF THE FSB

December 3, 1991. Mikhail Gorbachev, the Soviet president, disbands the Committee of State Security (KGB) of the Soviet Union.

January 24, 1992. Boris Yeltsin, the Russian president, creates the Ministry of Security of the Russian Federation.

December 21, 1993. The Ministry of Security is renamed the Federal Counterintelligence Service (FSK). In his decree, Boris Yeltsin notes, "The system of the Cheka-OGPU-NKVD-MGB-NGKB-KGB-MB turned out to be incapable of being reformed. Reorganization efforts in recent years were external and cosmetic in nature. . . . The system of political investigation is preserved and may easily be restored."[1]

January 5, 1994. The investigative directorate of the FSK is transferred to the Public Prosecutor's Office. FSB prisons, including the Lefortovo, are handed over to the Interior Ministry. The border troops are made an independent agency.

November 22, 1994. Yeltsin restores the investigative directorate of the FSK. Lefortovo prison is returned to the secret service.

November 26, 1994. The FSK-orchestrated attack on the Chechen capital, Grozny, is disastrous.

April 3, 1995. The FSK is renamed the FSB, or Federal Security Service.

June 14, 1995. A hospital in the southern Russian town of Budennovsk is captured by Chechen rebels led by Shamil Basayev. On June 19, after a failed storming, the Russian authorities are forced to allow Basayev (with some hostages) to return to Chechnya. In the end, 129 people are killed.

January 9–18, 1996. Salman Raduev attacks Kyzlyar in Dagestan, a republic contiguous to Chechnya. Chechen rebels are surrounded and stormed by the Russian army, special operations forces, and FSB special troops but manage to flee to Chechnya.

August 31, 1996. A ceasefire agreement is signed in Khasavyurt. The Khasavyurt accords mark the end of the first Chechen war and stipulate the withdrawal of Russian troops from Chechnya by December 31, 1996.

September 1997. The special unit to combat organized crime, the URPO (Directorate of Analysis and Suppression of the Activity of Criminal Organizations), is created.

July 6, 1998. The Directorate to Protect the Constitutional System is created. URPO is disbanded. The Directorate of Economic Counterintelligence is turned into the Department of Economic Security.

July 25, 1998. Vladimir Putin is named director of the FSB.

October 8, 1998. The Special Purpose Center of the FSB is formed. The center included two FSB special operations units: Alpha and Vympel. In July 1999 two special units that had belonged to the Moscow department of the FSB and to the Directorate of Economic Counterintelligence are also transferred to the center.

April 3, 1999. The Department of Economic Security is reorganized, creating the directorates of Counterintelligence Support to Industrial Enterprises (Directorate P), Transportation (Directorate T), the Financial System (Directorate K), and to Combat Contraband and Illegal Drug Trafficking (Directorate N).

August 16, 1999. Nikolai Patrushev replaces Putin as FSB director.

August 28, 1999. The Department to Protect the Constitutional System and Combat Terrorism is established on the base of the Counterterrorism Department and the Directorate to Protect the Constitutional System. This marks the first time in Russian history that counterterrorism and political surveillance are merged in one department of state security.

September 9, 1999. In an apartment building explosion in southeast Moscow, 94 people are killed. Four days later, on September 13, a large bomb explodes in a basement of an apartment block on Kashirskoye Highway in southern Moscow, killing 118 people.

November 16, 1999. The Assistance Programs Directorate is created. The new directorate includes the Center of Public Communications (press office).

February 7, 2000. Putin, then prime minister and acting president, signs the "Regulations for FSB Directorates in the Armed Forces," in which the functions of military counterintelligence are expanded to detect possible threats to the regime in the rank and file.

March 26, 2000. Putin is elected Russia's president.

January 22, 2001. The FSB is put in charge of the counterterrorist operation in Chechnya.

April 24, 2001. Nikolai Patrushev expands the rules for FSB officers attached to state structures, organizations, and companies.

October 23, 2002. A theater on Dubrovka Street in Moscow is captured by Chechens. The tragedy, known as the Nord-Ost hostage crisis, lasts for three days. On October 26 the theater is stormed by FSB special troops and 130 people are killed, most poisoned by fentanyl, the gas used by the special forces.

March 11, 2003. President Putin abolishes the Electronic Intelligence (FAPSI) and Border Service as independent agencies. The border troops are absorbed by the FSB; FAPSI is divided between the FSB and the Federal Protective Service. On the same day, the Aviation Directorate of the FSB is created.

June 30, 2003. An amendment to the "Law on the Organs of the Federal Security Service" is signed, stipulating that the FSB will have a special body for foreign intelligence.

July 4, 2003. The leadership of the Regional Operations staff to conduct counterterrorist operations in Chechnya is handed over from the FSB to the Interior Ministry.

July 11, 2004. Putin makes structural changes to the FSB. The number of deputy directors is reduced, and the departments are renamed as services.

September 1–3, 2004. A school in Beslan, North Ossetia, is captured by Chechens; 334 people are killed.

July 12, 2005. By presidential decree, all FSB prisons, including Lefortovo, are ordered to be transferred to the Ministry of Justice. The move is completed in January 2006.

March 6, 2006. The "Law on Counteraction of Terrorism" is signed by Putin. According to the law, the FSB is named as the chief body to combat terrorism and the National Antiterrorist Committee (NAK) is established. A high-level interdepartmental agency headed by the FSB director, the NAK is tasked with coordinating the security services' antiterrorist activities.

July 5 and 7, 2006. The FSB is given the right to eliminate terrorists abroad.

August 28, 2006. Putin changes the color of the uniforms of the FSB, the Federal Protective Service, the Service of Special Facilities, and Foreign Intelligence from army green to black.

January 31, 2007. Putin announces a significant increase in financing for the FSB, but no figures are presented.

May 12, 2008. Alexander Bortnikov is named director of the FSB. Nikolai Patrushev is appointed a secretary of the Security Council of Russia.

March 29, 2010. Terrorism returns to Moscow: Two female suicide bombers almost simultaneously detonate explosives on packed metro trains in Moscow. Forty people are killed.

ACKNOWLEDGMENTS

THIS BOOK WAS written in several months, but it is based on ten years' experience covering the Russian secret services. Every year sources disappear, and people inside have become increasingly unwilling to talk.

We began gathering information when we launched our Web site, Agentura.ru, in September 2000. During those years many friends encouraged us to keep up our coverage. This book could not have been written without their support.

We will never forget the rainy night in November 2002 we spent at the tiny cafe on Stariy Arbat Street near the *Versiya* office, while our offices there were being raided by FSB agents because of our reportage of the Nord-Ost siege. At the time, nobody knew what the FSB planned to do, so our editor, Rustam Arifdjanov, fearing our arrest, had asked us to stay out of the office. As we sat waiting at the cafe, suddenly a gaggle of journalists we had worked with at the investigative section of *Segodnya* newspaper arrived, headed by Fedor Gladkih, who turned the cafe into a sort of a temporary press office. It is hardly a coincidence that we had stood alongside Fedor in the apartment building facing the Dubrovka theater during the siege in 2002, and again in 2004 found ourselves alongside him in an abandoned hotel during the Beslan crisis, and had shared a car with him in Beirut in July 2006.

Marina Latysheva, our best friend for many years and a member of the Agentura.ru team, has always supported us across the board.

Alexei Shvachkin, a Moscow lawyer, accompanied Soldatov to interrogations at the FSB's Lefortovo prison and has offered his support and friendship in the subsequent years. Lena Bereznitskaya-Bruni, an editor of Newsru.com, helped to organize constant public pressure, reporting every interrogation of the authors and finally succeeding in forcing the FSB to drop its charges.

We are also indebted to Michael Shevelev, our deputy editor at *Moskovskie Novosti*, who continued to encourage us even when the publication was closed down. Oleg Panfilov, the director of the Center for Journalism in Extreme Situations, supported us when we found ourselves in an uncertain transition period—when *Moskovskie Novosti* had closed and before we joined *Novaya Gazeta*.

Our special thanks goes to Valery Shiryaev, a man with a peculiar fate—a KGB officer in the 1980s who became director of *Novaya Gazeta* in the 2000s and was involved in the decision to hire us. We stayed on at *Noyava Gazeta* for three years.

We are grateful to Olga Pashkova, the courageous and flamboyant director of *Ezhednevny Journal,* who invited us to write for the journal—the last media willing to accept our ideas. And we thank Yevgenia Albats, who proposed the idea of a series of stories about the KGB's resurrection for the *Ezhednevny Journal,* which laid the groundwork for this book.

We are also indebted to Yuri Gervis, FSB officer turned lawyer, who represented Valentin Moiseev, a diplomat accused of spying for South Korea, and his friend Andrei (whose surname cannot be revealed for reasons of privacy).

Thanks goes to the prominent Soviet dissident Sergei Grigoriants—head of the Glasnost organization and spearhead of a series of conferences, "KGB Yesterday, Today, Tomorrow," in the 1990s—for providing his insights on Soviet state security's legacy to the authors.

We would like to thank the officers of the FSB, Foreign Intelligence, Military Intelligence, and the Interior Ministry, who shared their knowledge and opinions with us, but who, for obvious reasons, cannot be named here.

A very special thanks goes to Nick Fielding, a brilliant investigative British journalist. From our first meeting in 2000 he was very supportive of the Agentura .ru idea. His book *Defending the Realm: Inside MI5 and the War on Terrorism* in many ways guided our approach to covering the Russian secret services. Nick was always ready to offer insights and provide practical help, no matter where he was, and he was the first person we consulted on our most controversial investigations. When he learned we were going to write a book, he immediately offered his help, which has proved invaluable to the project.

John Kampfner, chief executive at the Index on Censorship, was enthusiastic about this project from the beginning, and we are very grateful for his thoughts on the final stage of the writing. Stephen Aftergood, head of the Secrecy Project at the Federation of American Scientists, the source of inspiration for creation of Agentura.ru, encouraged our work. Mark Urban, a BBC journalist and author of *Big Boys' Rules,* a book about SAS operations in Northern Ireland, shared his thoughts for the chapter about the tactics of the secret services in the North Caucasus. Peter Gill, professor of politics and security at Liverpool John Moores University, provided the important research perspective for some chapters.

Our friend Sian Glaessner, a producer for the BBC, polished our English and was always ready to help with her gentle advice.

To Mark Franchetti at the *Sunday Times,* the most experienced Moscow foreign correspondent, we owe enormous thanks. His support after we were fired from the *Novaya Gazeta* was invaluable, and our meeting at a cafe on Pokrovka Street was the first in the long chain of events that led to this book. Ilana Ozernoy offered crucial encouragement, having proposed the very idea of writing the book in English for an American audience. But this book would not have been possible without Mort Rosenblum, who convinced Clive Priddle at PublicAffairs to take an interest in the project. We are deeply indebted to Clive for his trust in the idea. Our thanks go to all people at PublicAffairs who were involved in the project.

Special appreciation is also due to David Hoffman, a contributing editor at the *Washington Post*, who spent two very hard weeks with us in Moscow's cold winter helping to frame and edit the manuscript. We are greatly indebted to our editor, Morgen Van Vorst.

And we are deeply grateful to Robert Guinsler, our agent at Sterling Lord Literistic, Inc.

NOTES

INTRODUCTION

1. The estimates about the size of the FSB are drawn from our research over many years contained at the Web site agentura.ru and updated regularly.

2. *Komsomolskaya Pravda,* "Direktor Federalnoi sluzhbi bezopasnosti Rossii Nikolai Patrushev: Esli mi slomaemsya i uydem s Kavkaza–nachnetsya razval strain" [FSB director Nikolai Patrushev: If we break ourselves now and leave the Caucasus, the collapse of the country is imminent], December 20, 2000.

3. On the black uniforms, see Decree of the President, Russian Federation, no. 921, August 28, 2006.

4. Our findings for *Ezhednevny Zhurnal* are posted on the Web site agentura .ru.

CHAPTER 1

1. For further reading, see Yevgenia Albats, *The State Within a State: The KGB and Its Hold on Russia: Past, Present, and Future* (New York: Farrar, Straus, and Giroux, 1994).

2. A. I. Kokurin and I. V. Petrov, *Lubyanka. Organi VchK-OGPU-NKVD-NKGB-MGB-MVD-KGB 1917–1991* [Lubyanka organs: VChK-OGPU-NKVD-NKGB-MGB-MVD-KGB 1917–1991] (Moscow: Fond Demokratia, 2003).

3. Author interviews with former KGB officers. Also see Timothy Colton, *Yeltsin: A Life* (New York: Basic Books, 2008), pp. 258–259.

4. In 1993 Sergei Grigoriants, a famous Soviet dissident, organized a series of conferences titled "KGB: Yesterday, Today, Tomorrow." The conferences were attended by officials from the secret services, who had to answer questions in public. As Alexei Kandaurov, chief of the FSK Center for Public Communications in 1993–1994, acknowledged to Andrei Soldatov in December 2006, the only reason he took part in these meetings was the fear that the dismantling of the secret service was a real possibility, given the example of what had been done to the Stasi, the East German secret police.

5. Author interview, November 2009.

6. Author interview, July 2008.

7. In Russian, the *Federalnaya Sluzhba Bezopasnosti.* To be referred to as the FSB throughout this book. It was not a coincidence that at first the agency was named the FSK, in which K meant *Kontrrazvedka*—counterintelligence. Only in 1995 was the FSK renamed the FSB, replacing *Kontrrazvedka* with the much wider term *Bezopasnost*—security.

8. The Foreign Intelligence Service is the *Sluzhba Vneshney Razvedki*, or SVR, in the remainder of this work.

9. Federal Agency for Government Communications and Information, *Federalnoye Agentstvo Pravitelstvennoy Svyazi I Informacii*, or FAPSI.

10. Author interviews with FAPSI officers, 1997–1999.

11. See the dossier on General Georgi Rogozin at agentura.ru, based on reports in *Moscow News* issues of April 23 and April 29, 1995.

12. Human Rights Watch, "Russia: The Ingush-Ossetian Conflict in the Prigorodnyi Region," May 1996, New York, p. 86.

13. See "The War in Chechnya: Necessity of Holding the International Tribunal," VI roundtable, Fund Glasnost, July 15, 1995, Moscow. See also Memorial, *Rossia-Chechnya: Cep oshibok I prestupleniy* [Russia-Chechnya: Chain of mistakes and crimes] (Moscow: Zvenia, 1998).

14. Author interview, July 2007.

15. The unit was named Analysis and Suppression of the Activity of Criminal Organizations, or URPO by its Russian acronym.

16. Yuri Shekochikhin, "Bratva placha I kinjala-3" [Criminal group of cloak and dagger, Part 3], *Novaya Gazeta*, May 25, 1998.

17. www.agentura.ru.

18. Igor Korotchenko, "Svidetelstva polkovnika FSB Mikhaila Astakhova" [The evidence of FSB colonel Michail Astakhov], *Nezavisimaya Gazeta*, April 28, 1997.

19. Monastyretsky was arrested on April 12, 1996, and was released on September 30, 1997, on his own recognizance. In 2001, he was cleared of all charges. For an example of how the press was used in the struggle, see Alexander Khinshtein, "Bomba iz Shveicarskogo banka, marshalskaya zvezda ili konec svyazi-4" [Bomb from Swiss bank, the epaulet of the marshal, or the end of connections, Part 4], *Moskovsky Komsomolets*, April 14, 1998.

20. Andrei Soldatov, "FBR Rossiyskogo razliva" [Russian version of the FBI], *Sevodnya*, January 12, 2000.

21. For details, see agentura.ru.

22. Decrees of the President, Russian Federation, no. 367, March 24, 2003; no. 774, March 14, 2003; and no. 324, March 11, 2003.

23. Irina Borogan, "Zagovor bivshih. Kak delyaut karieru goniteli dissidentov" [Plot of the formers: How the oppressors of dissidents build their careers in Russia], *Versiya*, June 17, 2002.

24. Andrei Stenin, "Veterinaram otpustili grehi" [Veterinarians are forgiven], *Rossikaya Gazeta*, September 25, 2004.

25. Aleksander Birman, "Rossia lidiruet po chislu chlenov SWIFT" [Russia is leading on the number of SWIFT members], *Sevodnya*, September 18, 1996.

26. Andrei Soldatov, "Fapsi—obshestvennosti: 'menche znaesh—krepche spish'" [FAPSI—to the public: The less you know, the sounder you sleep], *Sevodnya*, December 12, 1999.

27. "Nachalas reforma v FSO" [Reform begins at the Federal Protective Service], agentura.ru, August 7, 2004.

28. Decree of the President, Russian Federation, no. 318, February 7, 2000.

29. Andrei Soldatov and Irina Borogan, "Nashi specluzhbi–na territorii bivshego Sovetskogo Soyuza" [Our secret services: On the soil of the former Soviet Union], *Novaya Gazeta*, March 27, 2006.

30. Vladimir Vasiliev, the chairman of the Duma's State Security Committee, confirmed in an interview with the authors in May 2008 that the FSB had no parliamentary oversight. Irina Borogan, "Zakon o gostaine ustarel" [Law on state secrets is outdated], *Novaya Gazeta*, May 5, 2008.

CHAPTER 2

1. Olga Kravets, "Proshanie Lubyanki" [Goodbye of the Lubyanka], *Kompania*, December 1, 2007.

2. For example, on July 18, 2002, Aleksander Mezhov, an FSB lieutenant colonel, was sentenced to three years and a month in jail for passing secret information to the security service of the group Most (controlled by oligarch Vladimir Gusinsky). "Sotrudnik FSB pohitil I prodal bolee 10 tic. Sekretnikh documentov" [FSB official has stolen and sold more than 10,000 secret documents], newsru.com, February 28, 2003.

3. Authors' interview with an officer of the Moscow department of the FSB, Summer 2003.

4. Andrei Soldatov and Irina Borogan, "Spionov stanet bolche" [There will be more spies], *Moskovskie Novosti* no. 43, November 12–18, 2004.

5. Roman Shleynov, "Slavyanski shkaf zamdirectora FSB" [A secret of the deputy director of the FSB], *Novaya Gazeta*, June 23, 2001.

6. Based on authors' interviews with officers of the Moscow department of the FSB, Summer 2008.

7. Soldatov's interview with General M., a head of the directorate in the counterterrorism department, August 2000.

8. Official site of the Russian Orthodox Church, "Svyateshi Patriarch sovershil osveshenie rospisi khrama Svyatoi Sofii na Lubyanke" [Patriarch opened the cathedral of Saint Sophia on Lubyanka], Patriarchia.ru, December 18, 2006.

9. Kirill Vasilenko, "Catholicism—non grata," *Vremya Novostei*, April 22, 2002. See also www.agentura.ru.

10. In an interview with *Izvestia*, Zdanovich did not deny he was placed at VGTRK as the officer of the active reserve. "Alexander Zdanovich: bivshikh

chekistov ne byvaet" [Zdanovich: There are no former Chekists], *Izvestia*, June 3, 2002.

11. Ibid.

12. Maksim Varyvdin, "Vlasti ne znayut, kuda Nord-Ost duyet" [The authorities do not know where the Nord-Ost is going], *Kommersant*, November 1, 2002.

13. Decree of the President, Russian Federation, no. 587, December 11, 2004.

14. Natalia Gevorkyan, Natalia Timakova, and Andrei Kolesnikov, *First Person: An Astonishingly Frank Self-Portrait by Russia's President* (New York: Public Affairs, 2000).

15. "Moscow to Retaliate for Latvia Visa Refusal," *Interfax*, August 16, 2001.

16. Andrei Soldatov, "Lubyanka lux" [Lubyanka lux], *Delovaya Khronika*, September 19, 2002.

17. "Russian Trio Caught; IBU Boss Speaks of Systematic Doping," *The Earth Times*, February 13, 2009.

18. "Victor Cherkesov: Nelzya dopustit, chtobi voini prevratilis v torgovtsev" [Viktor Cherkesov: We can't let warriors turn into traders], *Kommersant*, October 9. When in 2007 Putin questioned the FSB's loyalty, he turned to the anti-drug agency headed by his friend Victor Cherkesov to conduct a secret investigation into allegations of corruption in the FSB leadership. Alexander Bulbov, Cherkesov's deputy, who had been put in charge of the investigation, was in turn accused by the FSB of illegal phone tapping and sent to jail. He was released on November 13, 2009.

CHAPTER 3

1. *Komsomolskaya Pravda*, "Vladimir Putin: Gosudarstvenny perevorot Rossii ne grozit" [Vladimir Putin: A state coup is not a threat for Russia], July 8, 1999.

2. Reuters, "UK Charity Teaching Chechens to Make Bombs, Say Russians," August 10, 2000.

3. From an FSB official report of its activities in 2002, published December 16, 2002, on the Web site of the FSB, www.fsb.ru.

4. Simon Saradzhyan and Kevin O'Flynn, "FSB: 4 British Spies Uncovered," *Moscow Times*, January 24, 2006.

5. See Russian president's official Web site, kremlin.ru. The speech was at an FSB conference on February 7, 2006.

6. BBC Russian Service, "Putin sravnil opponentov s shakalami" [Putin compared his opponents to jackals], November 21, 2007.

7. Alexander Konovalov, "Valentin Danilov zaprosil pomilovanie" [Valentin Danilov asked for a pardon], *Kommersant*, December 1, 2006.

8. Viktor Tereshkin, "Delo Aleksandra Nikitina. Opravdanni Spion" [The case of Alexander Nikitin: Spy acquitted], *Sekretnie Materiali*, October 2, 2000.

9. "Baikalskaya Volna: mi bili spokoini s samogo nachala, tak tak nikakikh zakonov ne narushali" [Baikal wave: We were calm from the beginning, because we never broke the law], anti-atom.ru, November 24, 2002.

10. See VimpelCom's Web site, http://www.vimpelcom.com.

11. "FSB spasla Bilain ot nashestvia varyagov" [FSB saved Beeline from Viking invasion], www.cnews.ru, September 19, 2005.

12. Andrei Soldatov and Irina Borogan, "Spiono-money" [Spy-money], *Novaya Gazeta*, April 14, 2008.

13. Irina Borogan, "Generali spionskikh karierov" [Generals with spy careers], *Versiya*, February 11, 2002.

14. Irina Borogan, "Sutyagin: Ya ochen khochu vernutsa domoi" [Sutyagin: I want to be back home], *Versiya*, October 13, 2003.

15. The story of Yakimishen's controversy was reported by the authors in "Prevrashenia rezidentov" [Transfigurations of the spies], *Moskovskie Novosti*, August 22, 2004. No actions were taken by the authorities. The information about Yakimishen was included in the text of Application no. 30024/02 by Igor Vyacheslavovich Sutyagin against Russia at the European Court of Human Rights (application was proved admissible on July 8, 2008).

16. *RIA Novosti*, "FSB presekla deyatelnost bolee sta inostrannih agentov v 2008 godu" [FSB pre-empted the activities of more than 100 foreign spies in 2008], January 2, 2009.

17. *Stringer*, "German Ugryumov zastrelilsa, a komanduyushi OGV d Chechnye daet pokazania?' [German Ugryumov shot himself, and a commanding officer in Chechna is questioned], June 29, 2001.

18. Irina Borogan, "Generaly shpionskih karierov" [Generals with spy careers], *Versiya*, February 11, 2002.

19. Yuri Snegirev, "Shpion iz 11-A" [Spy from the class 11-A], *Komsomolskaya Pravda*, February 2, 2002.

20. Authors' interview with Yuri Gervis.

21. Irina Borogan, "Generali spionskikh karierov" [Generals with spy careers], *Versiya*, February 11, 2002.

22. In July 2008 Soldatov was called for interrogation to Lefortovo because he had interviewed the famous double agent Sergei Tretyakov, a colonel in the Russian foreign intelligence service who defected to the United States in 2000. His interrogator turned out to be Pavel Plotnikov, Yuri Plotnikov's younger brother, who a few years before had worked at the same "spy" section of the FSB Investigative Directorate.

23. Borogan's interview with Kaybyshev's lawyer, Yuri Gervis, published at agentura.ru, "Zateyat spionskoe delo Im ne udalos" [They've failed to launch a spy case], October 12, 2005.

24. Anastasia Kirilenko, "O Pisme akademika Reshetina" [About the letter of academician Reshetin], izbrannoe.ru, December 10, 2007.

CHAPTER 4

1. The details in this chapter are largely drawn from our reporting for *Novaya Gazeta*, which can be found at agentura.ru and the website of *Novaya Gazeta*, novayagazeta.ru.

2. A. I. Kokurin and I. V. Petrov, *Lubyanka. Organi VchK-OGPU-NKVD-NKGB-MGB-MVD-KGB 1917–1991* [Lubyanka organs: VChK-OGPU-NKVD-NKGB-MGB-MVD-KGB 1917–1991] (Moscow: Fond Demokratia, 2003).

3. Oleg Khlobustov, *Gosbesopasnost Rossii ot Aleksandra I do Putina* [State security of Russia: From Alexander I to Putin] (Moscow: Eksmo, 2005).

4. Sergei Sokut, "Zashita lichnisti, obshestva, gosudsrstva" [Defense of person, society, state], *Nezavisimaya Gazeta*, November 20, 1998.

5. In the 1990s the Service to Combat Terrorism and Protect the Constitutional System was created within the Moscow Department of the FSB. In 2002 this service was divided into two: the so-called Sluzhba BT (Antiterror Service) and a completely new structure with the unpronounceable name of SZOKS i BPEh (Service to Protect the Foundations of the Constitutional System and Combat Political Extremism). It was the first time in the history of the Russian security services that fighting political extremism was separated from counterterrorism; the first was now equal in importance to the second. It was staffed by officials who had previously worked in antiterrorism, and therefore there were frequently cases where a specialist in Islamic extremists was transferred to oversee Moscow higher educational institutions. Authors' interviews with FSB officials.

6. Andrei Soldatov, "Podvid razvedchika" [A sort of spy], *Novaya Gazeta*, February 21, 2008.

7. Andrei Soldatov, "Kto na Novikova" [Who's after Novikov], *Novaya Gazeta*, March 20, 2008.

8. Agence France-Presse, "Russian Who Says He Spied on Opposition Denied Asylum in Finland," March 2, 2009.

CHAPTER 5

1. Irina Borogan, "Anticrisisni paket Kremlya: Kak I dlya chego sostavlyaut 'chernie' spiski" [Anticrisis packet of the Kremlin: How and why the blacklists are formed], *Ezhednevny Journal* and agentura.ru, June 2, 2009.

2. Petr Tverdov, "Rashid Nurgaliev: 'Mi ne dopustim razgula prestupnosti'" [Rashid Nurgaliev: "We do not let crimes happen"], *Nezavisimaya Gazeta*, February 10, 2009.

3. BBC Russian Service, "MVD RF sozdalo sluzhbu po borbe s extremismom" [The Interior Ministry established the counterextremism service], April 23, 2009.

4. *Rossiyskaya Gazeta*, "FSB is afraid of possible cyber attacks by terrorists on the communications of state bodies," April 15, 2009.

5. "MVD: Yesterday, today, tomorrow," Rashid Nurgaliev, *Rossiyskaya*, July 15, 2009.

6. Petr Tverdov, "Rashid Nurgaliev: 'Mi ne dopustim razgula prestupnosti' [Rashid Nurgaliev: "We do not let crimes happen"], *Nezavisimaya Gazeta*, February 10, 2009.

7. Joint Decision of the General Prosecutor's Office, the FSB, and the Interior Ministry, no. 270/27, 1/9789, 38, December 16, 2008.

8. Details are derived from the series of articles published by Irina Borogan in 2009 as a joint project of agentura.ru and *Ezhednevny Journal* for monitoring the government's campaign against extremism.

9. Irina Borogan, "Anticrisisni paket Kremlya: Kak I dlya chego sostavlyaut 'chernie' spiski" [Anticrisis packet of the Kremlin: How and why the blacklists are formed], *Ezhednevny Journal* and agentura.ru, June 2, 2009.

10. *Nezavisimaya Gazeta*, "Rashid Nurgaliev: 'Glavnim kriteriem ocenki nashei raboti yavlayetsa doverie grazhdan'" [Rashid Nurgaliev: "The main criteria for our job's assessment is the trust of citizens"], February 2, 2008.

11. "Yevgeny Martynov: Uroven technicheskogo osnachenia territorialnikh podrazdeleniy segodnya eshe ne pozvolyaet ikh avtomatizirovat v polnom obieme" [Yevgeny Martynov: The level of technical supply of regional departments does not let us automate the whole system], interview with the head of the program for installing the database, in the issue "Technologies in State Bodies," cnews.ru, 2007.

12. The official site of the Department of the Interior Ministry in Ryazan, press release of the statement of First Deputy Minister Mikhail Sukhodolsky, February 12, 2009.

13. Aleksander Rodionov, "V Rossii obyavlen novy etap borbi s ekstremismom–Internetu I blogosphere pridetsya tugo" [A new stage in the struggle against extremism is announced], Novy Region news agency, April 29, 2009.

14. The details of the contract can be found at the state Web site, www .zakupki.gov.ru, where are all state contracts are listed.

15. Irina Borogan, "Antikrisizni paket Kremlya: Dlya chego nuzhna baza dannikh extremist" [Anticrisis measures of the Kremlin: Why they need the database on extremists], *Ezhednevny Journal* and agentura.ru, July 1, 2009.

16. The Constitution of the Russian Federation in English, www.constitution .ru/en/10003000–01.htm.

17. Nina Ognyanova, "Attack on the Press 2007: Europe Analysis; Rewriting the Law to Make Journalism a Crime," Committee to Protect Journalists, February 2, 2008.

18. Committee to Protect Journalists, "President Signs Law Labeling Criticism of State Officials 'Extremism,'" July 28, 2006.

19. Yulia Galyamina and Anastasia Aksenova, "Deja vu in dissident view," kasparov.ru, June 16, 2009.

CHAPTER 6

1. Government Decision no. 482, September 17, 2005. (These cars are not intended to be used for urgent actions. For these purposes, the FSB purchased in December 2008 a fleet of vehicles specially painted and equipped with the insignia FSB OF RUSSIA or BORDER GUARD SERVICE and an emblem of the FSB [axisglobe.com, "Vehicles of Russian Federal Security Service to Have New Signs of Distinction," January 18, 2009].)

2. According to advertisements published at the Web sites www.rublevka-online.ru and www.rublevka.osan.ru.

3. Irina Borogan, "Chekisti pashut kak loshadi" [Chekists work like horses], *Novaya Gazeta*, March 23, 2006. The full list of the landowners is available at the Web site www.novayagazeta.ru.

4. Sergei Minenko and Dmitri Simakin, "Rublyovku zaminirovali" [Rublevka is mined], *Nezavisimaya Gazeta*, March 31, 2006; RIA Novosti, "Property of Oleg Deripaska: Profile," December 22, 2008.

5. See Web site www.kraya.ru, the section on real estate.

6. Irina Borogan, "Chekisti pashut kak loshadi" [Chekists work like horses], *Novaya Gazeta*, March 23, 2006.

7. Federal Agency for State Property Management letter, no. CE-08/16064, June 13, 2006.

8. Andrei Soldatov, "Polkovnik pishet v Evropeisky Sud" [The colonel writes to the European Court], *Novaya Gazeta*, October 23, 2008.

9. On January 14, 2010, the European Court ruled in a related case on the petition of one group of military and FSB servicemen who had complained that their pensions were too low. Among the petitioners was Innokenty Osipov, a retired FSB officer who sought a higher pension for his years of service. The court decided that the Russian authorities should pay Osipov 418,244 rubles, or 11,370 euros. European Court, First Section, "Case of Kazakevich and 9 other army pensioners' cases v. Russia," Judgment, Strasbourg, January 14, 2010.

10. Ugryumov died in May 2001.

11. On April 26, 2007, Vladimir Putin signed decree no. 545, conferring on Patrushev the Order of Honor for his professional successes and "his many years of service in the economic sphere."

12. Dmitry Butrin and Boris Gorlin, "Nagrada nashla rodnyu geroya" [The award found the family of the hero], *Kommersant*, May 3, 2007.

13. Darya Pylnova and Dmitry Shkrylev, "Kto prinyal na grud" [Who was awarded], *Novaya Gazeta*, December 25, 2006.

CHAPTER 7

1. FSB press release, "V FSB Rossii podvodilis itogi vystuplenia voleibolnogo cluba Dynamo-Moskva" [Russia's FSB analyzes the results of the volleyball club Dynamo-Moscow], October 23, 2002, available at www.fsb.ru.

2. I. Trisvyatsky, "Posle specoperacii director FSB prishel bolet za Dinamo" [After the special operation, FSB director came to support the Dynamo team], *Sovetsky Sport*, October 28, 2002.

3. Dynamo official Web site: www.dynamo.ru.

4. Ibid.

5. Decree of the President, Russian Federation, no. 241, February 21, 1996.

6. Order of the Director of the Border Service, no. 713, December 27, 1999.

7. Dynamo press release, April 22, 2009. See www.dynamo.ru.

8. See the national volleyball federation Web site: www.volley.ru.

9. In January 1991 Golovatov commanded the Alpha group sent to Lithuania to storm a television station in Vilnius that had been captured by adherents of independence. A total of fourteen people died, including one Alpha officer. Golovatov resigned a year later, because, as he conceded later, "the president of Lithuania required Yeltsin to deliver a list of 'enemies of the Lithuanian people,' and I was no. 5 on this list. . . . On these grounds I made the decision to resign." *Veterani,* "Istoria v licah: Interview Michaila Vasilievicha Golovatova," nos. 6–7, June 13, 2008.

10. Allsport Web site, "Glavnim trenerom Sbornoi Rossii po svinbolu stal nachalnik Centralnogo pogranichnogo cluba FSB" ["The main trainer of the Russian pig-racing team became a chief of FSB Central Border Club"], October 30, 2006.

CHAPTER 8

1. *Vechernyaa Moskva,* "Na zdanii FSB snova poyavilsa profil Andropova" [On FSB building, the profile of Andropov is resurrected], December 21, 1999.

2. Christopher Andrew and Vasili Mitrokhin, *The Mitrokhin Archive: The KGB in Europe and the West* (London: Gardners Books, 1999).

3. In 1968 Andropov issued a KGB chairman's order, "On the tasks of state security agencies in combatting the ideological sabotage by the adversary," calling for struggle against dissidents and their imperialist masters. See also A.I. Kokurin and I.V. Petrov, *Lubyanka. Organi VchK-NKVD-NKGB-MGB-MVD-KGB 1917–1991* [Lubyanka organs: VchK-NKVD-NKGB- MGB-MVD-KGB 1917–1991] (Moscow: Fond Demokratia, 2003).

4. Vladimir Solovyov and Elena Klepikova, *Yuri Andropov: A Secret Passage into the Kremlin,* translated by Guy Daniels (New York: Macmillan, 1983), pp. 131–132.

5. The start of campaign to present Dzerzhinsky as a great economist coincided with the election of Yuri Andropov as general secretary. In 1982 the Znamya literary journal published an article devoted to Dzerzhinsky's work in the Economic Council. In 1987 the second rash of mythmaking occurred on the 110th anniversary of the birth of Dzerzhinsky. A major article by prominent Soviet journalist and propagandist Otto Latsis entitled "In the Stream of Revolutionary Building" was published in *Izvestia.* Now Felix Dzerzhinsky was served up as an ideologue of the New Economic Policy (NEP). It merely stated that "It is difficult to overestimate the role of Dzerzhinsky in the revival of the country's economy, in the development in practice of the Leninist ideas of economic responsibility, self-financing, and socialist planning." The popularity of Dzerzhinsky was further promoted when in the early 1980s three film blockbusters devoted to Dzerzhinsky were produced by the KGB and aired on Soviet TV.

6. Nikolai Patrushev, "Taina Andropova" [The mystery of Andropov], *Rossiyskaya Gazeta*, June 15, 2004.

7. "Luzhkov podtverdil svoe jelanie vernut Felixa na Lubyanku" [Luzhkov confirmed his will to get Felix back to Lubyanka Square], grani.ru, September 14, 2002.

8. Radio Free Europe, "Andropov's Ghost," February 9, 2009.

9. "Vladimir Shults: Our task, as it was early—to prevent a crime," *Nasha Vlast': Dela i Litsa* no. 4 (2001).

10. There were also personal reasons for promoting Andropov's image. Karelia was the key region in Andropov's career; he was a party official there before he went to Hungary, and the respectful KGB/FSB department created a cult over Andropov and his activity in the region guaranteeing the region special status in the eyes of Moscow. It is generally thought that Putin mostly recruited his colleagues from the FSB department in St. Petersburg to fill posts in Moscow. In fact it was a bit more complicated than this. The district of St. Petersburg is close to Karelia, considered to be important as it shares a border with Finland. FSB officers who served in Karelia kept close ties with their colleagues in St. Petersburg; some of them, like Nikolai Patrushev, director of the FSB in 1999–2008, served in both Karelia and St. Petersburg. Many colonels and generals in high positions in the FSB had previous experience in Karelia. Among them were Rashid Nurgaliev, who was appointed in 2000 as deputy director of the FSB and in 2004 headed the Ministry of Internal Affairs; Vyacheslav Ushakov, in 2003 appointed as deputy director of the FSB; Vladimir Anisimov, deputy director in 2004–2005; and Vladimir Pronichev, who in 2003 headed the border service of the FSB with the rank of first deputy director.

11. A. Yu Andropov, *Izbrannie rechi i statii* [The selected speeches and articles] (Moscow, 1979), p. 275.

12. Bukovsky's archives are available at the Web site http://bukovsky-archives.net/.

13. Radio Free Europe, "Rossiyskie archive zarkivayutca" [Russian archives are closing], March 7, 2008.

14. National Security Archive, "The Moscow Helsinki Group 30th Anniversary: From the Secret Files," May 12, 2006.

15. Agence France-Presse, "Russia Rejects Probe into Katyn Massacre," January 30, 2009.

16. Memorial, "Preporirovannaya istoria ili PR po-chekistsky" [Fixed history or PR in the CheKa way], March 16, 2009. See also Wojciech Materski, Anna M. Cienciala, and Natalia S. Lebedeva, *Katyn: A Crime Without Punishment* (New Haven, CT: Yale University Press, 2008).

CHAPTER 9

1. For details of the FSB's support in producing *Lichny Nomer*, see Elena Egereva, "Igri Patriotov" [Patriots' games], *Afisha*, December 6, 2004.

2. A cassette was passed to the *Independent*, which published it. See Helen Womack, "Russian Agents 'Blew Up Moscow Flats,'" *The Independent*, January 6, 2000.

3. Andrei Soldatov and Irina Borogan, "Chekistsky Zakas na Mifi" [Che-Ka's demand for myths], *Ezhednevny Journal*, May 3, 2006, available at agentura.ru.

4. Yuri Gladilshikov, "Mejdu Dogvillem I Manderlaem" [Between Dogville and Manderlay], *Russky Journal*, December 30, 2004.

5. The first press office in the KGB was created on Andropov's order in November 1969 (Oleg Khlobustov, "KGB bez prikras 1954–1991 godi" [The KGB without embellishment], proza.ru, May 23, 2007). According to Oleg Nechiporenko, then an officer in the KGB's First Chief Directorate (foreign intelligence), the main task of the bureau was not to answer journalists' requests, but to work with them: "The press bureau carried out much more diverse tasks than communications with the media. In particular, it worked with the creative people, wishing to create product—film or book—on a subject of secret services. Authors sent their works (stories, scripts, etc.) or asked the bureau to help with documents. . . . In their works they mostly created a positive image of the secret services" ("Oleg Nechiporenko: Bitva s golovoi kak glavny front" [Oleg Nechiporenko: The battle with the head as a main front], *Soobshenie* no. 4 [2005]).

6. Liza Novikova and Maya Stravinskaya, "Polozhitlny opyt KGB" [The positive experience of the KGB], *Kommersant*, February 7, 2006.

For the FSB version of the resurrection of the KCB competition, see also Sergei Ignatchenko, a chief at the FSB Center for Communications, "Premia FSB" [Competition of the FSB], *Argumenti I Facti* no. 14, April 6, 2006. Also available at the FSB Web site www.fsb.ru.

7. "Podvedeni itogi konkursa FSB Rossii na luchee proizvedenie literaturi I iskusstva o deyatelnosti organov Federalnoy Sluzhbi Bezopasnosti" [The results of the competition of the FSB are anounced], www.fsb.ru, December 8, 2006.

8. Andrei Soldatov, "Britanci ne ostavili kamnya na kamni" [The British did not lose a rock], *Novaya Gazeta*, January 26, 2006.

9. For details of the spy rock scandal, see also Jeremy Page and Richard Beeston, "The 'British' Spy Operation Found Lurking under a Rock," *Sunday Times*, January 24, 2006.

10. "V FSB chtitayut, chto popavchee v ruki Rossiyskoi Spetscluzhbi ustroistvo, kotoroe ispolzovalos britanskoi razvedkoi v Moskve, yavlyaetca plodom supersovremennikh tekhnologiy" [The FSB believes the device taken by Russian secret service that was used by British Intelligence is a product of supermodern technologies], *Interfax*, January 26, 2006. Also available at the FSB Web site: www.fsb.ru.

11. That the different rock was taken by the FSB was confirmed by Sergei Ignatchenko, a chief of the FSB Center for Public Communications, at a press conference on January 23, 2006. Available at the FSB Web site: www.fsb.ru.

12. On Putin's position toward spy rock scandal see Steven Lee Myers, "Putin Says Foreigners Use Private Groups to Meddle in Russia," *The New York Times*, January 26, 2006.

13. For details of the documentary *Caucasus Plan*, see Radio Liberty, "Russia: Documentary Alleges West Sought Chechen Secession," April 23, 2008; *RIA Novosti*, "Film Plan Kavkaz osnovan na svidetelstvakh uchastnikov sobitiy" [The documentary is based on testimony from participants in the events], April 25, 2008.

14. A special commission was formed to these ends within the framework of the FSB Consultative Council. This council consisted of former and current officers of the secret services. Yury Levitsky, a former foreign intelligence officer, was elected chief of the commission in charge of media. It had a relatively short life, however, and was later disbanded. See details at agentura.ru.

15. Full text is published in Vasily Stavistky, *Taini Dushi* [The mysteries of soul] (Moscow: AST, 1999).

16. Evgeny Krutikov, "Begushi chelovek" ["Running man"], *Izvestia*, January 29, 2001; Yuri Snegirev, "Kak khoteli vzorvat Volzhkskuyu TEC" ["How they wanted to explode the Volgzhkaya energy station"], *Komsomolskaya Pravda*, January 30, 2001.

17. Yuri Borodin, "Vasily K," *Ogonyok* no. 52 (January 2001).

18. Author interview with Tretyakov, March 19, 2009.

19. Alexander Mikhaylov, a FSB spokesman in 1994–1996, admitted to Soldatov in March 2002, "Disinformation involves having a direct impact on the enemy, not on society as a whole. And if we're talking about enemies— well, yes, assistance operations are operations which have an impact on the enemy." The interview was published as Andrei Soldatov, "Ispoved dezinsormatora s Lubyanki" [The confession of the disinformator from the Lubyanka], *Versiya*, March 2002.

20. TV broadcast, *Vesti*, RTR (Channel 2), September 24, 1999.

21. Rustam Arifdjanov, "A gorod ne znal, chto uchenia idut" [The town does not know that a training is taking place], *Sovershenno Sekretno* no. 6, June 2002.

22. Marina Latysheva, "Recidivist spezsluzhb" [The criminal of the secret services], *Versiya*, September 29, 2003.

23. Marina Latysheva, "Bezzashitny advocat" [Unprotected lawyer], *Versiya*, October 29, 2003. Trepashkin spent three years in jail; in August 2005 he was released on parole, but under protest from the Prosecutor's Office he was sent back to prison. He was eventually released on November 30, 2007. See details at agentura.ru.

24. Ekaterina Blinova, "Gostaina propavshego tiraja" [The state secret of disappeared copies], *Nezavisimaya Gazeta*, January 29, 2004.

25. The main point of the allegations against the FSB was that Achemez Gochiyaev, the main suspect according to FSB's version, was an innocent busi-

nessman made a scapegoat by the FSB and falsely accused in carrying out a terrorist attack. In fact, Gochiyaev was well known in his native Karachaevo-Cherkassia, a tiny republic in the North Caucasus, since the mid-1990s as a leader of local Islamist group. Since the early 1990s Karachaevo-Cherkassia has witnessed the growth of local Islamist movements: The Jamaat of the Republic established close ties with Chechen rebels, and the Karachaev Battalion was sent to Chechnya in the late 1990s. Gochiyaev, Adam Dekkushev, and Yusuf Krymshamkhalov were members of the so-called Muslim Society No. 3, founded in 1995. According to the Russian secret services, by 2001 Muslim Society No. 3 counted more than 500 members and began a campaign of terror in nearby regions. In the spring of 2001 a series of terrorist attacks took place in the towns Mineralnie Vodi, Essentuki, and Cherkessk. One of the bombers was soon arrested and turned out to be a member of the society Arasul Hubiev. Then more than twenty members of the society were captured, and some tried to flee to Georgia. But the detentions did not disrupt the society's activities. It managed to carry out two spectacular terrorist attacks in Moscow: the suicide bombing in the Paveletskaya metro station on February 6, 2004, and the female suicide attack near the Rizhskaya metro station on August 31, 2004.

By then Adam Dekkushev and Yusuf Krymshamkhalov had been captured in Georgia's Pankisi valley by Georgian secret services and handed over to Russia. On the first day of the trial in November 2003, Yusuf Krymshamkhalov partially admitted his guilt, acknowledging that he had accompanied a shipment of the explosives. He also admitted he had received training at a rebel camp. For his part, Adam Dekkushev confirmed that together with Krymshamkhalov he had accompanied a shipment of hexogen, packed in sugar bags, without having any idea as to what was inside. In January 2004 both were sentenced to life imprisonment. For further details, see agentura.ru and http://studies.agentura.ru.

26. As the Soviet Union was a country with very limited access to many areas, everything depended on the relationship between the journalist and his or her "handler" from the KGB. Sergey Pismensky, in the early 2000s the deputy head of the FSB section in charge of the Interior Ministry (Section M), and in 1980s the KGB "handler" for the German media, told Irina Borogan in 2000 that it was relatively easy to persuade foreign journalists to be loyal in Soviet times: The very first critical report would ruin any hopes for subsequent trips or interviews with high-ranking officials.

27. Alexander Igorev, "Nasha rabota interesney shpionskih romanov" [Our work is more interesting than spy novels], *Gazeta*, May 6, 2002.

28. Committee to Protect Journalists, "Russian Authorities Deny British Journalist Entry Visa," June 5, 2006.

29. Luke Harding, "To Be a Journalist in Russia Is Suicide," *The Guardian*, November 24, 2008.

30. "Russia Refuses Journalist Entry," BBC Web site, February 27, 2008.

31. FSB Director's Order, no. 343, "O vnesenii izmeneniy v perechen, utverzhdenny prikazom FSB Rossii ot 14 Sentyabrya 2007 No. 465" [About

the changes in the list, established by FSB order no. 465, signed September 14, 2007], July 15, 2009.

32. Andrei Soldatov, "FSB stavit journalistov na control" [FSB puts journalists under control], *Ezhednevny Journal*, February 16, 2010.

CHAPTER 10

1. For details and maps, see the official Web site of Metro 2, www.metro .ru/metro2.

2. See the official GUSP Web site section on history at http://gusp.gov.ru.

3. Decree of the President, Russian Federation, no. 349, March 9, 1996.

4. Victor Baranets, "U supersecretnoy sluzhbi Rossii poyavilas svoya emblema" [Super secret service obtains insignia], *Komsomolskaya Pravda*, April 12, 2000.

5. Decision of the Moscow Mayor, no. 681, July 6, 1998.

6. Yuri Zaicev, Metro 2 section, http://www.metro.ru/metro2/.

7. Vadim Mikhailov answers the questions of Internet customers of the newspaper *Izvestia*, October 29, 2002, available at http://online.izvestia.ru.

8. Oleg Filin, "Diggeri planeti Undeground" [Diggers of the underground planet], *Noviy Akropol*, January 2002, available at www.newacropolis.ru.

9. Andrei Soldatov, "Maskirovka" [Camouflage], *Versiya*, May 27, 2002. The story and the map are available at agentura.ru.

10. agentura.ru.

11. Georgy Aleksandrov, "Sekretnoe metro. Speclinii I segodnyaprodolz hayut stroit" [Secret underground: The lines are still being built], *Argumenti I Facti*, October 15, 2008.

12. www.rzhd.ru.

13. Sergei Mironov, "Spezcluzchbi" [Secret services], *Kommersant*, April 19, 2006.

14. Zhizn, "Stolknulas s generalom" [Meeting with the general], September 29, 2008.

CHAPTER 11

1. At Lefortovo, the main prison of Stalin's secret services, peculiar detention methods were employed. In the early 1930s Chekists believed that prison could reeducate, and they even arranged boat trips on the Moscow River for Lefortovo's inmates. But such ideas were soon abandoned. Writer Yevgenia Ginsburg, who was kept at Lefortovo during Stalin's Great Terror in the late 1930s, wrote in her book *Into the Whirlwind* that loud tractor engines were often kept running in the prison's courtyard to deaden the screams of prisoners being shot in the basement. Nobel Prize laureate Alexander Solzhenitsyn, in his groundbreaking work *The Gulag Archipelago*, wrote that in the 1940s

there were "psychological" cells at Lefortovo—painted black, with an electric light that was never turned off. Inmates were also tortured with the roar of a wind tunnel built at the nearby Central Air and Hydrodynamics Institute.

2. Yeltsin's opponents, who staged a violent revolt in October 1993, were sent to Lefortovo. Later prisoners at Lefortovo included diplomat Valentin Moiseev, suspected of spying for South Korea; metals magnate Anatoly Bykov, accused of ordering the murder of a former business partner; Alexander Litvinenko, the FSB officer who later fled to Britain; Platon Lebedev and Alexei Pichugin, senior Yukos managers and partners of the oil oligarch Mikhail Khodorkovsky, who fell afoul of the Kremlin by seeking to influence politics; and the scientist Igor Sutyagin, who was convicted of spying for the United States.

3. Irina Borogan, "Lefortovsky labirint" [Lefortovo labyrinth], *Versiya*, December 2, 2002.

4. According to Parliamentary Assembly Doc. 10568, "Honoring of Obligations and Commitments by the Russian Federation," "Investigative authority was fully restored by the law, although the FSK, one of its predecessors, had already been conducting criminal investigations on the basis of a presidential decree. Russia's fourteen investigative detention prisons and several special troop detachments also returned to the control of the security service. Contrary to what was written in the Assembly's 2002 report, Lefortovo pretrial detention center is not the only one that is in use: indeed, since the FSB is a centralized institution with regional departments, it has at its disposal also SIZOs [detention centers] in the regions." Parliamentary Assembly of the Council of Europe, June 3, 2005.

5. Assembly debate on January 25, 1996 (6th and 7th Sittings). See Doc. 7443, report of the Political Affairs Committee, rapporteur: Mr. Muehlemann; and Doc. 7463, opinion of the Committee on Legal Affairs and Human Rights, rapporteur: Mr. Bindig. Text adopted by the assembly on January 25, 1996 (7th Sitting).

6. Parliamentary Assembly Doc. 10568: "We were told in November 2004, during our meeting in Moscow with the Deputy Director of the FSB, Mr. Ushakov, that the Parliamentary Assembly's recommendations were not binding and that, given the investigative powers afforded to the FSB by the relevant legislation, they absolutely needed a high security detention centre to hold and interrogate suspects."

7. Decree of the President, Russian Federation, no. 796, December 7, 2005.

8. Andrei Soldatov and Irina Borogan, "Kak FSB sdelala vid chto vernula turmi Minustu" [How the FSB pretended to return the prisons to the Ministry of Justice], *Ezhednevny Journal*, January 12, 2006.

9. Natalya Matveeva and Pyotr Orlov, "Vzyatka pod grifom sekretno" [Bribe under the secret stamp], *Rossiskaya Gazeta*, March 25, 2008.

10. Decree of the President, Russian Federation, no. 602, June 12, 2006.

11. It is impossible to establish how many special detention centers are now at the disposition of the Lubyanka, as the strength and composition of FSB units are a state secret.

CHAPTER 12

1. This account of the activities of the terrorists is drawn from materials of Criminal Case no. 229133 and "Decision on Ceasing the Criminal Investigation," October 16, 2003, and appendix no. 133.

2. On November 1, 2002, Shamil Basayev published on the rebels' Web site, Kavkazcenter, his letter "Abdullah Shamil vzyal otvetstvennost na sebya" [Abdullah Shamil takes responsibility], claiming responsibility for the hostage taking in Nord-Ost.

3. See details on Budennovsk's hostage crisis in Andrew Higgins, "Chechens 'Release Human Shields,'" *The Independent*, June 21, 1995.

4. See details about Kobzon's and Khakamada's visits to the theater in Michael Wines, "Hostage Drama in Moscow: The Moscow Front—Chechens Kill Hostages in Siege at Russian Hall," *New York Times*, October 25, 2002.

5. See the obituary of Shamil Basayev published in *The Times of London*, July 11, 2006.

6. Andrei Soldatov, "Ot Pobedi do Beslana" [From victory to Beslan], *Moscovskie Novosti*, October 2004.

7. See dossier on Department V at agentura.ru.

8. Andrei Soldatov, "Ot Pobedi do Beslana" [From victory to Beslan], *Moscovskie Novosti*, October 2004.

9. Irina Borogan and Andrei Soldatov, "Mertvie budut za zhivikh" [The dead will replace the living], *Versiya*, October 27, 2002.

10. Andrei Soldatov, "Ot Pobedi do Beslana" [From victory to Beslan], *Moscovskie Novosti*, October 2004.

11. Testimony of Boris M. Blokhin, *Nord-Ost: Unfinished investigation, a collection of documents published by victims and their families* (Moscow: Organization of Victims of Nord-Ost, 2006), p. 178.

12. The number of victims derived from the Web site nord-ost.org, supported by relatives of victims. The Web site referred to the decision of the Moscow prosecutor's office on October 16, 2003.

13. Irina Borogan, "Vragi gosudarstva" [The enemies of the state], *Versiya*, June 14, 2003.

14. *Odnako*, Leontiev's program on Channel One, October 24, 2002.

15. Telechannel Rossia Vesti, "Interview s Alexandrom Zdanovichem" [Interview with Zdanovich], October 26, 2002.

16. Andrei Soldatov, Irina Borogan, Marina Latysheva, and Anna Stavitskaya, *Journalisti i terrorism* [Journalists and terrorism] (Moscow: Center for Journalism in Extreme Situations, 2008).

17. Giulietto Chiesa, "Da Mosca due giornalisti testimoni dell'attcco 'La versione ufficiale non corrisponde ai fatti'"Il gas e' immeso alle 6,15 gli Alfa sono entrati 15 minuti dopo. L'attaco deciso prima dell'esecuzione degli ostaggi,"*La Stampa*, October 28, 2002.

18. See also the OSCE press release "OSCE Media Watchdog Concerned over Increased Pressure on Media in Russia," November 3, 2002.

19. Andrei Soldatov, "Geroy Rossii. Sistema Nikolaya Patrusheva: posle teraktov chekistov ne otpravlayut v otstavku, a nagrazdayut i povichayut" [The heroes of Russia: System of Nikolai Patrushev: After the terrorist attacks, the officers of the FSB are not fired, but awarded and promoted], *Moskovskie Novosti*, September 2, 2004.

CHAPTER 13

1. Interview with General Prosecutor Vladimir Ustinov, *Echo Moskvy*, July 6, 2004.

2. For details see agentura.ru.

3. The list of victims was published by the opposition Web site ingushetia .ru on July 26, 2004.

4. In March 2004, Putin launched an overhaul of Russia's state machinery. All federal bodies were ordered to conform to a standard hierarchy: At the top was a ministry, then a service, and lastly an agency. The state bodies were to change their internal structure as well, with departments being renamed services. The FSB, as a federal service, fell into the middle spot in the order, and Putin duly signed the decree on July 11, 2004. Putin had given the FSB's leadership three months to make the changes. Those three months were filled with violence, including the attack on Ingushetia on June 21–22, two planes blown out of the air near Moscow by female suicide bombers on August 24, a suicide bomb attack in Moscow on August 31, and finally the capture of the Beslan School on September 1–3, 2004. According to a 1998 statute, the FSB, Interior Ministry, foreign intelligence (SVR), Federal Protective Service, and Ministry of Defense were all tasked with fighting terrorism. However, the FSB, which has a counterterrorism department inherited from the KGB, had the primary role in counterterrorism until 2003, when the MVD became more heavily involved, taking over management of the Regional Operations Staff responsible for counterterrorist operations in the North Caucasus. In August 2003, the Interior Ministry further strengthened its anti-terrorism capabilities with the creation of "Center T," which was integrated into the organized crime division. The situation was further confused, however, when following the Interior Ministry's takeover of the Regional Operations Staff for the North Caucasus, it also took control of the Combined Group of Forces in the North Caucasus, responsible for military actions in the region. See also the *PSI Handbook of Global Security and Intelligence: National Approaches* (Santa Barbara, CA: Praeger Security International, 2008).

5. Decision of the President, Russian Federation, no. 352-rps, August 2, 2004.

6. In Budennovsk (June 1995), when terrorists captured the hospital, the operational staff was headed by Sergei Stepashin, director of the FSB, and Victor Erin, Minister of Internal Affairs. The dual leadership is explained by the policy that when hostage takers have asked, or might ask, for money, they should be dealt with as common criminals. Under these circumstances the FSB steps back and is replaced by the ministry of internal affairs. See details in *PSI Handbook of Global Security and Intelligence: National Approaches* (Santa Barbara, CA: Praeger Security International, 2008).

7. *RIA Novosti,* "U boevikov v Beslane bylo oruzhie, pokhishennoe so sklada v Ingusehetii" [The fighters in Beslan had weapons seized in Ingushetia], September 10, 2004.

8. Anna Politkovskaya, "Poisoned by Putin," *The Guardian,* September 9, 2004.

9. "According to the report of the head of the Special Purpose Center of the FSB, there were enough forces. Eight assault groups were formed. It was enough," Valery Andreev stated at the trial. *Pravda Beslana,* December 15, 2005. There were forty-seven hearings in the Supreme Court of North Ossetia on the case of Kudaev, December 15, 2005; transcripts are available at the Web site www.pravdabeslana.ru.

10. Report of the Parliamentary Commission on the Beslan events, 2006, available at agentura.ru and pravdabeslana.ru.

11. Ibid.

12. *Peterburg Novosti,* Television Channel TRK, September 1, 2004.

13. Pravda Beslana. Forty-seven hearings in the Supreme Court of North Ossetia on the case of Kudaev, December 15, 2005, www.pravdabeslana.ru.

14. *Pravda Beslana,* Account of the meeting of Vladimir Putin and members of the committee "Mothers of Beslan," September 2, 2005.

15. Andrei Soldatov and Irina Borogan, "Beslan: den shturma" [Beslan, the day of the storming], *Moscow News,* September 6, 2004.

CHAPTER 14

1. Yelena Tregubova, "Prioritet Kremlya zhizn zalazhnikov" [The priority of the Kremlin—the life of the hostages], *Kommersant,* October 25, 2002.

2. *Itar-Tass,* "Dumskie centristi chtitayut nesvoevremennoi sosdanie parlamentskoy komissii po rassledovaniyu obstoyatelstv terakta v Moskve" [Duma centrists consider "untimely" the creation of a parliamentary commission on investigation of circumstances of the terrorist attack in Moscow], October 29, 2002.

3. Ibid.

4. Sergei Yuriev, "Putin vstretilsa s Yavlinskim" [Putin met Yavlinsky], *Komsomolskaya Pravda,* October 30, 2002.

5. E. A. Vorobyev et al., "Otchet Komissii SPS" [Findings of the Public Commission of SPS], November 21, 2002.

6. Irina Borogan, "Vragi gosudarstva" [Enemies of the State], *Versiya,* July 14, 2003. In July 2008, the court in Strasbourg made a decision to limit access to the case at the request of Russia, newsru.com, July 3, 2008. The official criminal investigation from Nord-Ost was suspended on June 1, 2007.

7. Conclusions of the report by the Organization of Victims of Nord-Ost, December 29, 2006. See www.nord-ost.org.

8. Larissa Kaftan and Alexander Gamov, "Putin rasskazal zapadnim journalistam o terakte" [Putin told foreign journalists about a terrorist attack], *Komsomolskaya Pravda*, September 7, 2004.

9. BBC, "'No Mistakes,' Beslan Report Says," December 26, 2005.

10. *Novaya Gazeta*, "Sud amnistiroval beslanskih milicionerov" [Court amnesties policemen of Beslan], May 29, 2007.

11. Yulia Petrovskaya, Yevgeni Grigoriev, and Dmitry Suslov, "Zakaev vzyal reiskthag" [Zakaev won the German parliament], *Nezavisemaya Gazeta*, January 30, 2004.

12. NTV interview with Nikolai Patrushev, October 6, 2004. Transcript available on the Web site www.ntv.ru and on the FSB Web site, www.fsb.ru.

13. Marina Lepina, "Ramzan Kadyrov pobedil Abu Al-Walida" [Ramzan Kadyrov has won over Abu al-Walid], *Kommersant*, August 21, 2003.

14. "Po dannnim specluzb za terakt v moskovskom metro na lichniy chet Al-Valida postupilo USD 4.5 mln" [According to the secret services' data, Al-Walid was paid USD 4.5 million for the terrorist attack in Moscow metro], fsb.ru, September 25, 2004.

15. "Terroristicheskie organizacii Al Qaeda I Bratia Musilmane yavlyautsa osnovnoi prichinoi napryazhennosti v Chechnhe" [Terrorist organizations Al Qaeda and Muslim Brotherhood are the main reason for tensions in Chechnya], fsb.ru, December 21, 2004.

16. "On the fight against terrorism, Russian Federation Federal Law no. 130-FZ," signed by Russian Federation President B. Yeltsin, fas.ru, July 25, 1998.

17. Federal law "O protivodestvii terrorismu" ["On countering terrorism"], March 6, 2006.

18. Andrei Soldatov, "Hero Rossii" [Hero of Russia], *Moscovskie Novosti*, September 2, 2004.

19. Svetlana Olifirova, Zinaida Lobanova, and Tatiana Putilova, "35 neizvestnih geroya Nord-Osta" [35 unknown heroes of Nord-Ost], *Komsomolskaya Pravda*, February 27, 2002.

20. Decree of the President, Russian Federation, no. 913, August 19, 2004: "O Yezhkove A. P." [About Yezhkov], and no. 914, August 19, 2004: "O Labuntse M. I." [About Labunets]. Also see Yuri Gavrilov, "Vladimir Putin podpisal neskolko ukazov, seriozno izmenivshih rasstanovku sil v "silovih" vedomstvah" [Vladimir Putin signs a number of decrees, significantly altering posts in the secret services], *Rossiyskaya Gazeta*, June 20, 2004.

21. Andrei Soldatov, "Te zhe, tam zhe" [The same people, in the same positions], *Moskovskie Novosti*, October 1, 2004.

22. Zvezda TV Channel, "President Putin vstretilsa v Kremle s vishimi oficerami" [President Putin met in the Kremlin with highly placed officers], March 9, 2007.

23. Yevgeny Krutikov, "Sergei Smirnov: S lichnim sostavom vsegda chto-to proishodit" [Sergei Smirnov: These are routine changes in personnel], *Izvestia*, May 31, 2000.

24. Sergei Shishin, the chief of the Internal Security Directorate of the FSB in 2002, said: "The Directorate of Internal Security at the FSB took an active role in the investigation of illegal activities of the so-called Department of Security of the Group MOST, in which former KGB and FSB officers conducted illegal phone-tapping of Gusinsky's competitors attempting to recruit FSB officials. Because these activities were carried out by our former colleagues, our Directorate was involved when the General Prosecutor's Office conducted the operation." "Sergei Shishin: nam udalos viyavit predatelya v sobstvennikh ryadakh" [We managed to identify a traitor in our own ranks], *Gazeta*, December 17, 2002.

25. FAS.org, On Organs of the Federal Security Service in the Russian Federation, Article 24.

26. Joint Decree of General Prosecutor's Office and the FSB no. 20–27/10, May 18, 2002.

27. Andrei Soldatov and Irina Borogan, "Neprikasaemie" [Untouchable], *Novaya Gazeta*, May 7, 2007.

28. Vladimir Putin, speech to Parliament, July 8, 2000.

29. Dmitry Medvedev inaugural speech, May 7, 2008. RIA Novosti, "Rossia dolzhna preodolet pravovoi nigilism" [Russia should win legal nihilism], May 7.

CHAPTER 15

1. Philip Taubman, "Soviet Reports 9 Died in Hijacking of Jet by Family," *New York Times*, March 11, 1988.

2. Irina Borogan, "Opasnie Igri. Neizvestnie Podrobnosti vzrivov FSB" [Dangerous games: Details of the explosions of the FSB], *Versiya*, May 13, 2002.

3. Irina Borogan and Andrei Soldatov, "Speci po terroru. FSB prevrashaetsa v armiy" [Specialists on terror: FSB is turning into an army], *Versiya*, December 22, 2003.

4. Yuri Shekochikhin, "Bratva plasha i kinjala" [The criminal group of the cloak and dagger], *Novaya Gazeta*, May 25, 1998; the member of Parliament's request to the prime minister, November 2, 1998 (signed by S. Mitrokhin, Yu. Shekochikhin, and A. Kuznetsov) is available at the Web site of the Yabloko Party, www.yabloko.ru.

5. The names and details of activities of the special units were derived by authors from official accounts, recollections of the officers involved, and sources in the Interior Ministry and the FSB. The authors published an account in *Moscovskiye Novosti*, "Tyzheli Feis i drugie" ["Heavy FSB squads and others"], September 2004; a shorter version appeared in *RUSI/Jane's Homeland Security & Resilience Monitor* 4, no. 19 (December 2005–January 2006). On January 19, 2006, the authors published in *Novaya Gazeta* the expanded version, with comments of the members of the State Duma (Committee of Security), experts, and a former officer of the Special Purpose Center of the FSB.

6. Vladimir Poletayev, "Tre Stepen Gotovnosti" [Three levels of readiness], *Rossiyskaya Gazeta*, August 19, 2004; and *Kommersant*, "Chem Proslavilies bat-

aloni Vostok i Zapad" [How the battalions East and West became known], April 15, 2006.

7. Authors' interview of a colonel in the Interior Ministry, October 2005.

8. Andrei Soldatov and Irina Borogan, "Borba s terrorismom: likvidatori" [The battle with terrorism: Liquidators], *Novaya Gazeta*, January 19, 2006.

9. Vyacheslav Izmailov, "Gruppa SS-12," *Novaya Gazeta*, August 12, 2004; International Helsinki Federation for Human Rights, "Chechnya: Disappearances and Extrajudicial Killings in Sernovodsk and Other Villages of the Sunzha District of Chechnya," July–August 2004.

10. Mark Franchetti, "Russian Death Squads 'Pulverise' Chechens," *Sunday Times*, April 26, 2009.

11. Andrei Soldatov, "Ot pobedi to Beslana" [From victory to Beslan], *Moskovskie Novosti*, October 4, 2004.

12. Boris Andreev, "Ego hoteli vzyat zhiviem?" [He was wanted caught alive], *Komsomolskaya Pravda*, March 9, 2005; Speznas Rossii, "Udarnaya Sila FSB" (interview with Sergei Polyakov, vice president of the Association of Veterans of the Alpha Group), August 2006.

13. Memorial Web site "Death squads on the North Caucasus: Summer 2009," available at www.memo.ru.

14. Mark Franchetti, "Dirty War Rages on Russia's Doorstep," *The Times*, September 20, 2009.

15. Human Rights Watch, "Letter to Yuri Chaika, Prosecutor General of the Russian Federation Regarding Recent Disappearances in Dagestan," October 23, 2009.

16. Author's interview with Valery Dyatlenko, December 2005, published at *Novaya Gazeta*, January 19, 2006.

17. Andrei Soldatov and Irina Borogan, "Boryba s terrorismom: likvidatori" [Struggling with terrorism: Liquidators], *Novaya Gazeta*, January 19, 2006.

18. Agentura.ru, Studies and Research Center, "Terrorism prevention in Russia: One year after Beslan," September 2005, available at http://studies.agentura.ru.

19. Memorial, "Sdacha v plen Magomeda Hambieva–resultat specoperatsii, soprovozhdavsheisya zakhvatom zalozhnikov" [Surrender of Magomet Hambiev is the result of a special operation that included capture of hostages], March 10, 2004.

20. The Memorial's report "Chechnya, 2004: Kidnappings and disappearing of people" (available on the Memorial Web site: www.memo.ru). See also Andrew Kramer, "Chechnya Is Gripped by Political Kidnappings," *New York Times*, July 18, 2009.

21. Memorial Bulletin of Human Rights Center, "Chechnya, 2004: 'New' methods of anti-terror. Hostage taking and repressive actions against relatives of alleged combatants and terrorists." The text in English is available at Memorial's Web site www.memo.ru/hr/hotpoints/caucas1/msg/2005/03/m33236.htm.

22. "Amir Magas: 'This is war between Islam and kufr [infidel],'" kavkaz center.com, November 4, 2006.

23. Natalya Krainova, "Suicide bomber kills 2 police in Chechnya," *Moscow Times*, May 15, 2009.

24. ABC News, "Chechen War Over: Russia," April 16, 2009.

CHAPTER 16

1. Mark N. Katz, "Russia and Qatar," *MERIA* 2, no. 4 (December 2007).

2. Musa Muradov, "Zelimkhan Yandarbiyev popal v cherny spisok OON" [Zelimkhan Yandarbiyev lands on UN's blacklist], *Kommersant*, June 27, 2004.

3. Vladimir Baranov, "Borba s terrorom po shariatu" [The battle against terrorism in the Sharia way], *Rossiyskaya Gazeta*, February 27, 2004.

4. On the confessions and allegation of torture, see Mikhail Zigar, "Sergeya Ivanova podshili k delu" [Sergei Ivanov was attached to the case], *Kommersant*, April 13, 2004. On use of the confessions at trial, see Agence France-Press, "Qatar opens trial in Yandarbiyev murder," April 12, 2004. The Qatari police claims are also reported in Tom Parfitt, "Russian Agents Face Conviction for Chechen Assassination," *Daily Telegraph*, May 16, 2004.

5. The details of activities of the agents are derived from the publication of the Web site KavkazCenter, June 1, 2004, "Order to kill Yandarbiyev issued by Sergei Ivanov." The Web site is supported by Chechen rebels, and the details could not be independently verified by the authors. The trial of the Russians in Doha was closed at the request of Russian representatives. In this case the authors believe the information is generally correct. Also, the authors relied on Jamestown Foundation, "The Assassination of Zelimkhan Yandarbiyev: Implications for the War on Terrorism," May 17, 2005; and on the reporting of *Kommersant* in Moscow.

6. Mikhail Zigar, "Sergeya Ivanova podshili k delu" [Sergei Ivanov was attached to the case], *Kommersant*, April 13, 2004.

7. Andrei Zlobin, "Washington rasskajet Mosckve o postsovetskom prostranstve" [Washington will tell Moscow about post-Soviet area], *Vremya Novosti*, March 22, 2004.

8. Jamestown Foundation, "Yandarbiev Assassination: Still More Questions Than Answers," March 23, 2004.

9. Radio Free Europe, "Analysis: The End of 'Namedni,'" June 7, 2004.

10. UPI, "Commentary: Russia's Media Loss," June 2, 2004.

11. Itar-Tass, "Obmen arestovannimi v Dokhe I Moskve nevozmozhen: diplomatichesky istochnik v rossiyskoy stolice" [Exchange of the arrested in Doha and Moscow is impossible: Diplomatic source in Russian capital], March 2, 2004.

12. According to AFP, "In what escalated into a diplomatic row between the Gulf state and Russia, Qatar expelled the first secretary of the Russian Embassy late last month after detaining him and the agents in connection with the murder of Yandarbiyev in a car bomb. Qatar's expulsion announcement was made just hours after the return to Doha of two Qatari nationals who were released by Moscow." "Russia to respect Qatari court verdict," April 20, 2004.

13. Mikhail Zigar and Musa Muradov, "V tishine dva mesyatsa" [Two months in silence], *Kommersant*, April 27, 2004.

14. Jaber Al Harmi, "Two Russian Intelligence Officers Sentenced to Life in Prison in Assassination of Chechen Rebel Leader," AP, June 30, 2006.

15. Mikhail Zigar, "Katarskikh uznikov vozvrashayut na rodinu" [Qatar's prisoners are returned to homeland], *Kommersant*, November 11, 2004.

16. Tom Parfitt, "Qatar Hands Back Moscow Agents Jailed for Murder," *Daily Telegraph*, January 16, 2005.

17. Bahrain News Agency, "Qatar Meets Russia's Request to Hand Over Two Citizens," December 24, 2004.

18. *Kommersant*, "Pryamaya rech: Geroev dadut?" [Direct speech: Are they about to be awarded?], December 24, 2004.

19. Tom Parfitt, "Qatar Hands Back Moscow Agents Jailed for Murder," *Daily Telegraph*, January 16, 2005.

20. Jamestown Foundation, "Whereabouts of Yandarbiev's Accused Killers Unknown," February 22, 2005.

21. Pavel Yevdokimov, "Breid Vympel KGB" (based on memories of general Yuri Drozdov, a head of Directorate S [Illegal Operations] of the founder of Vympel), *Spetsnaz Rossii*, August 1, 2009, available at www.fsb.ru.

22. Itar-Tass, "Putin postavil spetsluzhbam zadachu naiti I unichtozhit vsekh ubiyts sotrudnikov Rossiyskogo posolstva v Irake" [Putin gave the secret services the task to find and eliminate all assassins of the employees of the Russian embassy in Iraq], June 28, 2006.

23. "Patrushev: specsluzhbi sdelayut vse, chtobi poimat ubiyc diplomatov" [Patrushev: The secret services did all to catch the diplomats' assassins], vesti.ru, June 28, 2006.

24. Andrei Soldatov, "U FSB prosto ne ostalos sil" [FSB has no resources], *Novaya Gazeta*, July 10, 2006.

25. "FSB budet lovit terroristov za granitsei" [FSB will catch terrorists abroad], www.edinros.ru, June 6, 2006.

26. Federal Law no. 153, July 27, 2006, "About the changes in separate bills of the Russian Federation due to approval of the Federal law concerning the ratification of the Convention of the Council of Europe on terrorism prevention and the Federal Law on terrorism prevention." Federation Council decision no. 219-SF, July 7, 2006, "On use of formations of the Armed Forces of Russia and Special Purpose forces beyond the borders of the Russian Federation for suppression of international terrorist activity."

27. Kavkazsky Uzel (news agency established by the human rights group Memorial), "Hamzat Gizba bil shurinom Shamila Basayeva" [Hamzat Gizba was married to the sister of Basayev], August 18, 2007.

28. Prague Watchdog, "Ego ubili prishlie" [He was killed by strangers], August 1, 2008; Jamestown Foundation "North Caucasus Rebels Seek to Expand into Abkhazia, South Ossetia, and Azerbaijan," September 26, 2008.

29. Author's interview with the Abkazian official, September 2007.

30. Sean O'Neill, "Baikal: The Gangsters' Gun," *The Times*, July 21, 2008.

31. Jamestown Foundation, "Chechen Refugees in Azerbaijan Ask for Help," January 11, 2007.

32. Summary of Amnesty International's Concerns in Europe and Central Asia, July–December 2006; Kavkasky Uzel news agency, "Pravozashitniki trebuyut nakazat ubic bejenca iz Chechni" [Human rights activists pledge to punish the assassins of a refugee from Chechnya], April 14, 2007.

33. The details of killings in Azerbaijan and Abkhazia are derived from the authors' research for "Likvidatori. Pravila provedeniya likvidaciy za rubezhom" [Liquidators: The rules for liquidations abroad], *Novaya Gazeta*, December 13, 2007.

34. Authors' interview with officer of the Ministry of Internal Affairs who preferred to remain anonymous, October 2008. Also, "Likvidatori. Pravila provedeniya likvidaciy za rubezhom" [Liquidators: The rules for liquidations abroad], *Novaya Gazeta*, December 13, 2007.

35. Fedor Bramin, "'Groza' v Stambule" [The pistol Groza in Istanbul], *Spetsnaz Rossii*, no. 12, December 2008.

36. *RIA Novosti*, "Dubai police chief says criminal group behind Yamadayev's murder," February 31, 2009.

37. *Sabah*, "İstanbul'da gizli Çeçen zirvesi" [Secret summit in Istanbul concerned the Chechen problem], March 21, 2009.

38. The English translation is available at the Web site axisglobe.com "French intelligence to help Turkish secret services to investigate Russian hitmen murders," March 23, 2009.

39. Authors' interview with Litvinenko, November 2003. Andrei Soldatov and Irina Borogan, "Tri tovaricha iz FSB" [The three friends from the FSB], December 15, 2003.

40. Mark Urban, "Litvinenko Killing 'Had State Involvement,'" BBC Newsnight, July 7, 2008.

41. House of Commons, Foreign Affairs Committee, "Global Security: Russia," second report of session 2007–2008, printed November 7, 2007.

CHAPTER 17

1. In October 1993 at the conference, "KGB: Yesterday, Today, Tomorrow," SVR (Russian foreign intelligence service) spokesman Yuri Kobaladze said: "If some people used to argue about whether it was correct to separate intelligence, now there are no such discussions. My own opinion, shared by most in the SVR—it was the correct decision. First of all, because the SVR is not a law enforcement agency: It's not engaged in political surveillance inside the country, does not hunt for spies. If intelligence breaks the law, it does it in other countries." Glasnost Foundation, October 1–3, 1993.

2. Federation of American Scientists, "Russian Intelligence-Related Legal Documents: On Organs of the Federal Security Service in the Russian Federation, Federal Law no. 40-FZ," fas.org.

3. Andrei Soldatov, "Skolko u nas razvedok" [How many intelligence agencies we have got], *Versiya*, June 10, 2002.

4. Nikolai Poroskov, "U razvedchikov mirnoi zhizni ne bivaet" [Intelligence officer has no calm days], *Vremya Novostei*, December 19, 2003.

5. According to the Conflict Studies Research Center report: "The intelligence vacuum left in all former Soviet republics was far greater than the weaknesses in their security structures. The intelligence apparatus in the Soviet Union needed only a small number of operatives in the republics. . . . All the operations were planned, run and monitored from Moscow. The fragments of the locally collected 'puzzle' were then sent to Moscow where appropriate analyses were run and decisions taken. In the post-Soviet period the intelligence bodies of the individual republics were sometimes able to look at their non FSU neighbors but had no means to operate either in more distant countries, if only as liaison offices, or to follow many world events." Gordon Bennett, *The SVR: Russia's Intelligence Service* (Sandhurst, UK: Conflict Studies Research Center, 2000).

6. Law no. 86-FZ, June 30, 2003.

7. Andrei Soldatov, "Voiska prevrashayutsa v organi" [The troops are turned into organs], *Moskovskie Novosti*, October 2004; Andrei Soldatov, "Skolko u nas razvedok" [How many intelligence agencies we have got], *Versiya*, June 10, 2002; Andrei Soldatov and Irina Borogan, "Nashi specsluzhbi–na territorii byvshego Soyuza" [Our secret services—on the soil of the former Soviet Union], *Novaya Gazeta*, March 27, 2006.

8. Roman Yakovlevsky, "General Ushakov vykhodit na svyaz" [General Ushakov is connected], *Belorusskaya Delovaya Gazeta*, April 2, 2003.

9. Artur Sitov, "X-files: Yrie Roshka-1. Portret odnogo politicheskogo trupa" [X-files: Yuri Roshka: portrait of the political body], *Moldavskie Vedomosti*, April 3, 2009.

10. Orkhan Djemal, "Vybor Kalashnikova" [The choice of Kalashnikov], *Novaya Gazeta*, November 4, 2004.

11. *RIA Novosti*, "Patrushev: Novie 'barkhatnie revolutsii' finansiruyutsa zapadom" [Patrushev: New color revolutions are financed by the West], May 12, 2005; IPS News, "Belarus: NGOs Deny Plot to Overthrow Government," May 14, 2005.

12. Dmitry Mineev, "U nijegorodskih chekistov–noviy nachalnik" [The Chekists of Nizhny Novgorod get a new chief], *Komsomolskaya Pravda*, June 10, 2009.

13. For details and insignia, see the dossier on the department at agentura.ru.

14. The Commonwealth of Independent States (CIS) is a regional organization founded by participating countries on December 8, 1991, to unite former Soviet Republics, but Latvia, Lithuania, and Estonia did not join.

15. The council is known as the SORB: Soviet Rukovoditelei Organov Bezopasnosti I Specialnikh Sluzhb.

16. See Institute for Advanced Strategic and Political Studies, "CIS Antiterrorism Center: Marking Time in Moscow, Refocusing on Bishkek," November 3, 2002. According to the group, an Israeli think tank based in Washington, "This supervision arrangement implicitly treats CIS member countries as a field of action for Russia's internal security agency."

17. See agentura.ru profile of the CIS Antiterrorism Center. Armen Zakharyan, the Armenian representative in the ATC, told the authors in the

summer of 2007 that he had been sent to Moscow after a falling-out with the chief of the Armenian Service of National Security.

18. Itar-Tass, "Naibolee serioznaya terroristicheskaya ugroza dlya stran SNG iskhodit s territorii Afghanistana–glava Antiterroristicheskogo Centra SNG" [The most serious terrorist threat is from Afghanistan], October 18, 2005.

19. Stephen Grey, *Ghost Plane: The True Story of the CIA Torture Program* (New York: St. Martin's Press, 2006), p. 174. Also see Frank A. Clements, *Conflict in Afghanistan: A Historical Encyclopedia* (Santa Barbara, CA: ABC-CLIO, 2003), pp. 260–261.

20. The United States also helped, adding the Islamic Movement of Uzbekistan to its list of international terrorist organizations in October 2001. In May 2002 the new U.S.-backed Afghan authorities handed over eight IMU members to Uzbekistan. eurasianet.org, "Uzbekistan: There's No Place Like Home," September 18, 2002.

21. *RIA Novosti*, "Alisher Usmanov etapirovan iz Kazani v Uzbekistan" [Usmanov handed over from Kazan to Uzbekistan], October 24, 2005.

22. Further details of the abductions were derived from the investigation conducted by the authors and published in *Novaya Gazeta*. Andrei Soldatov and Irina Borogan, "Specsluzhbi byvshego Soyuza–na territorii Rossii" [The secret services of the former Soviet Union—on Russian soil], *Novaya Gazeta*, February 27, 2006. The Turkmenistan secret services were the first to show the way. According to information from Russian human rights activists, in the mid-1990s there was a special section in the Turkmen embassy in Moscow in charge of abductions of Turkmen dissidents, headed by first secretary Rakhman Allakov. Memorial Human Rights Center, "Turkmenistan/Russia: kto stoit za napadeniem na Avdy Kulieva?" [Turkmenistan/Russia: Who is behind the attack on Avdy Kuliev?], August 16, 2003. In 2002 Ramin Nagiev, a lieutenant colonel at the Ministry of National Security of Azerbaijan and a whistleblower who had fled to Russia in 1998, was all but kidnapped in Moscow. He was met near his house by two people calling themselves FSB agents. They drove him to the suburbs of Moscow, where they met with a vehicle bearing Azerbaijani diplomatic plates. As Nagiev was being handed over from one car to the other he managed to escape. The next day he left Moscow for France, where he was granted political asylum.

23. These details were furnished by Karinna Moskalenko and Anna Stavitskaya, Iskandarov's lawyers.

24. Irina Borogan, "S takimi druziami vragov ne nado" [With such friends we do not need enemies], *Ezhednevny Journal*, November 27, 2008.

25. In CIS countries the extradition procedure is complex, requiring consent from the General Prosecutor's Office. It is long, held in open court, and subject to appeal. The main problem is that the General Prosecutor's Office often refuses extraditions to Uzbekistan and Tajikistan, as they cannot always submit evidence of the crime committed, and the charge made is not always covered by Russian legislation. The European Union considers that torture is used in Central Asian prisons, and it is willing to allow appeals in the Euro-

pean Court for Human Rights, where Russia finds itself constantly blamed for human rights violations.

26. Irina Borogan, "GB bez Granits" [State security without borders], *Novaya Gazeta*, August 21, 2008.

27. RATS official site, "Normative Documents: Shanghai Convention on Combatting Terrorism, Separatism, and Extremism," www.ecrats.com.

28. Irina Borogan, "GB bez Granits" [State security without orders], *Novaya Gazeta*, August 21, 2008.

29. BBC, "Canada Angry at Uighur Sentence," April 20, 2007.

30. Xinhua News Agency, "China bans Falun Gong," June 22, 1999.

31. Timeline of illegal expulsions of refugees from Russia to the countries of their origin, August 2008. Report by Elena Ryabinina, Program of Assistance to Political Exiles from Central Asia of the Civic Assistance Committee.

32. uzreport.com, "Hizb ut-Tahrir, IMU try to spread their activity to Russia," April 2, 2008.

CHAPTER 18

1. The National Anti-Terrorism Committee (Nacionalny Antiterroristichesky Komitet, or NAK) was established with 300 FSB officers (the committee is headed by an FSB director) in spring 2006 to be in charge of coordinating all federal-level antiterrorism policies and operations.

2. Andrei Soldatov, "Cyber-surprise," *Novaya Gazeta*, May 31, 2007. The authors confirmed that the phone number and name Stanislav gave were correct. Stanislav confirmed his name in a phone conversation but refused to explain the nature of his interest in patriotic hackers.

3. Kavkaz.org was registered on March 2, 1999, in Pompano Beach City, Florida, in the United States. See whois.publicinterestregistry.net.

4. Voice of America, correspondent report, December 16, 1999.

5. Masha Eismont was detained and searched in Vnukovo airport in Moscow on her way back from Chechnya on December 25, 1999, and accused of drug smuggling, although she was released after five hours. Author's interview with Eismont, 2008. Babitsky disappeared on January 15, 2000, in Chechnya. Russian authorities at first denied knowing his whereabouts, but on January 28 they admitted to having him in custody. The FSB claimed to have charged him with "taking part in an illegal armed group." Then Russian authorities exchanged Babitsky for two Russian soldiers, supposedly captured by the Chechens, thus placing the responsibility for Babitsky's fate on rebels. The Russian and foreign media, as well as media organizations around the world, did not buy this version and kept pressuring the authorities. Babitsky was eventually released and was found in the neighboring republic of Dagestan on February 25. See details about the kidnapping of Babitsky in Aleksander Pronin, "Obmen s predoplatoi" [Prepaid exchange], *Kommersant-Vlast*, February 15, 2000; and Federal News Service, press conference of Andrei Babitsky, March 7, 2000, transcript available at agentura.ru.

6. Radio Liberty, "Chechnya: Rebels Use Internet in Propaganda War with Russians," May 5, 2000.

7. Azer Mursaliev, "S Lermontovim napereves" [With Lermontov], *Kommersant-Vlast*, September 7, 1999.

8. "Tomskie hackeri tri goda vedut informacionnuyu voinu protiv chechenskih exstremistov" [Tomsk's hackers have been waging information war for three years against Chechen extremists], newsru.com, January 30, 2002.

9. Interfax, "FSB ne chitaet hackerov hackerami" [FSB does not consider hackers as hackers], February 2, 2002; newsru.com, "FSB ne vidit narushenia zakona v deistviyah tomskih hackerov protiv saita Kavkaz-Tsentr" [FSB does not see the crime in activities of Tomsk's hackers aimed against Kavkaz-Tsentr], February 4, 2002.

10. For details on FAPSI, see agentura.ru.

11. The bases in Cam Rahn Bay, Vietnam, and in Lourdes, Cuba, were closed in 2002.

12. The official name was the Glavnoye Upravlenie Radioelectronnoi Razvedki Na Setyah Svyazi (GURRSS), Main Directorate of Electronic Intelligence in Communications.

13. Federation of American Scientists, Secrecy Project, FAPSI profile, www .fas.org.

14. Andrei Soldatov, "Fapsi–obshestvennosti: 'menche znaesh–krepche spish'" [FAPSI to public: "It's better to know nothing"], *Segodnya*, December 2, 1999.

15. Vladislav Sherstyuk, a former chief of the Third Directorate, was placed in the Kremlin Security Council in December 1999 to preside over the information security section. Hostile intrusion as the main Internet threat for Russia became an essential part of the Russian concept of information warfare. In 1997 Vladimir Markomenko, then the deputy director of FAPSI and the only official voice to define Russian information warfare, asserted that the "information war" concept comprises four components:

1. The suppression of components of the infrastructure of state and military administration (destruction of command and control centers); electromagnetic pressure on components of the information and telecommunications system (electronic warfare);

2. Acquisition of intelligence through intercepting and deciphering information flows transmitted via communications channels, and also though spurious distribution and electronic information-intercepting devices especially planted on premises and within technical systems (electronic intelligence);

3. Unauthorized access to information resources (by the use of software and hardware for penetrating systems that protect enemy information and telecommunications systems) with subsequent distortion, destruction, or theft, or a disruption of the normal operations of these systems (hacker warfare);

4. Formation and mass dissemination by enemy information channels or global data interaction networks of disinformation or tendentious in-

formation for influencing the opinions, intentions, and orientation of society and decisionmakers (psychological warfare).

See the section on the FAPSI at agentura.ru.

16. Nathan Hodge, "Kremlin Launches 'School of Bloggers,'" Wired.com, May 27, 2009.

17. Yelena Chernenko and Darya Guseva, "Napryazhenie v Seti" [Tensions on the Net], Russian edition of *Newsweek*, August 17, 2009.

18. kavkazcenter.org was hosted in Sweden starting in 2004, after moving from Lithuania, where the Web site had been shut down by Lithuanian authorities on hate speech charges after it published a letter from Shamil Basayev claiming responsibility for the Beslan school hostage crisis.

19. Center for Journalism in Extreme Situations, "Monitoring of violations of journalists' rights, coverage of events in Chechnya," October 2005, www.cjes.ru.

20. Andrei Soldatov, "Terror: otsenka ugrozi" ["Terror: Assessment of threat"], *Bolshaya Politika*, April 2006, available at agentura.ru.

21. Arthur Bright, "Estonia Accuses Russia of 'Cyberattack,'" *Christian Science Monitor*, May 17, 2007.

22. *RIA Novosti*, "Estonia has no evidence of Kremlin involvement in cyber attacks," September 6, 2007.

23. Andy Greenberg, "When Cyber Terrorism Becomes State Censorship," *Forbes*, May 14, 2008.

24. Agence France-Presse, "Pro-Russian cyber attack hits Lithuania: Regulator," June 30, 2008.

25. Project Grey Goose: Phase I, Report 17, October 2008, "Russia/Georgia cyber war: findings and analysis," provided to the authors by Rafal Rohozhinsky.

26. Dancho Danchev, "Coordinated Russia vs Georgia cyber attack in progress," ZDnet, August 11, 2008.

27. Anna Maplas, "British Diplomat Quits Amid Sex Tape Scandal," *Moscow Times*, July 10, 2008.

28. ABC News, "U.S. Protest Russian 'Sex Tape' Used to Smear American Diplomat," September 23, 2009; Kyle Hatcher, "U.S. Complains to Russia About 'Sex Tape' Smear Campaign Against American Diplomat," *Huffington Post*, October 23, 2009.

CONCLUSION

1. UPI, "Medvedev: Terrorist Bombers 'Are Animals,'" March 30, 2010.

APPENDIX 2

1. Decrees of the President, Russian Federation, no. 2233, December 21, 1993, "Ob uprazdnenii Ministerstva Rossiyskoi Federacii I sozdanii Federalnoi sluzhbi kontrrazvedki Rossiyskoy Federacii" [Concerning the abolition of the Ministry of Security and the creation of the Federal Counterintelligence Service].

INDEX

Aaviksoo, Jaak, 235
Abkhazia, 8, 202–203, 213, 214–215
Act on Operational-Investigative
    Activity (1995), 56
"Active measures," 108–109
Afghanistan, 102, 107, 172, 214,
    216–217
Agentura.ru, 7, 151, 246
Aidarov, Miroslav, 170
Akhmadov brothers, 138
Akhmedov, Ibat, 198
Al Qaeda, 171, 172, 207
Al-Walid, Abu, 171
Albats, Yevgenia, 7
Aleksandrov, Dmitry, 231
Aleksey II, Patriarch, 26
Alksnis, Viktor, 77–78, 80
Almazov, Sergei, 19
Alpha unit (A department)
    about, 85f, 140–141, 248
    KGB and, 24, 85f
    Nord-Ost and, 122, 140, 141
    Ryazan exercise, 111–112
Alternative Futures, 39–40
Andreev, Valery, 161, 162, 169–170
Andrew, Christopher, 92
Andropov, Yuri
    about, 92–93
    celebrations for, 93–94
    FSB, 7, 85f
    image-making, 91–96, 100
    KGB, 3, 7, 11, 55, 91, 92–93, 103,
        175
    plaque/statues of, 91, 93–94, 242
Anisimov, Vladimir, 103, 162
Apartment building bombings
    about, 109–110, 120, 171, 248
    fictionalized movie account, 102
    Putin's response, 18, 109

Putin's rise to power and, 109,
    111, 241
question on perpetrators,
    109–110, 111, 112, 241
Ryazan training exercise and,
    110–112
Arabs in Chechnya, 171, 172
Archives on state security
    Bukovsky and, 97–98
    claims on openness, 99
    declassifying attempts, 97
    Interagency Commission to
        Protect State Secrets, 98
    KGB, 12–13, 97, 98, 100
    National Security Archive,
        George Washington University
        and, 98–99
    opening, 12–13
Argumenti I Fakti (newspaper), 119
Armenia, 214, 215
Army
    Central Army Sports Club and,
        84–85
    FSB and, 21
    rank hierarchy, 175
Assassinations abroad
    in Abkhazia, 202–203
    Azerbaijan and, 203–205
    Chechens in France and, 206
    federal antiterrorism bills and,
        201–202
    Gitsba, 202–203
    holding Qatar athletes and, 198
    Iraqi insurgents kidnappings and,
        200–202
    Israeli example and, 200
    Litvinenko poisoning,
        206–208
    Putin and, 197, 198, 199, 207

ANDREI SOLDATOV and **IRINA BOROGAN** are co-founders of the Web site Agentura.ru. Soldatov and Borogan worked for *Novaya Gazeta* from January 2006 to November 2008. Agentura.ru has been reported on and featured in the *New York Times*, the *Moscow Times*, the *Washington Post*, Online Journalism Review, *Le Monde*, the *Christian Science Monitor*, CNN, the Federation of American Scientists, and the BBC. The *New York Times* called it "A Web Site That Came in from the Cold to Unveil Russian Secrets."